A Geography of Consciousness

Also by William Arkle

The Great Gift

Letters From A Father: Selected Writings

WILLIAM ARKLE

A GEOGRAPHY OF CONSCIOUSNESS

Introductions by
Colin Wilson
and
Bruce G Charlton

Sun Wise
Books

First edition published in Great Britain by
Neville Spearman Limited
© William Arkle 1974

Second enlarged edition published by
Sunwise Books
© Nick Arkle 2019

ISBN: 978-1-69530-866-4

sunwisebooks.com

Cover painting: *Thy Will Be Done* by William Arkle

CONTENTS

The executive vector. The sympathetic vector. Separating events from consciousness. The ideal vector. Development and balance. Analogy of the manager and the factory. Filters of consciousness. Definition of matter consciousness. Volume of experience related to a level of attitude. Bodies of communication.

Ratio of number of bodies to time and space perception. The idea of solidity. 'Matter is communication'. Evolution cycles. The ignition experience. Relationship of evolutionary cycles to astronomical cycles.

The analogy of the harp. The cause of pain. The value of individuality. Consciousness not subject to physical death. Return to physical birth. Natural groupings and their qualities. The concept of original sin. The importance of initiative. The wheel of birth and death. The saviour.

Transformation of signals in the human ear. Distortions in the channels of communication. Short circuits. False circuit complexes. Simultaneous development of several bodies. The false personality. Separation of false personality from true consciousness. Psychological illness and therapy.

The living cell. Cell groupings and organisations. Group consciousness. The entity. The function of monitors. Co-operation with the entity evolution. Relation of monitor to computer. Disturbing the work of entities. The cure of false circuits. Present day treatment. The value of high tone therapy.

The relationship of entities to the Self. The type of help available. Group work. Bringing the whole nature into unity of purpose. The sense of balance.

William Arkle

Introduction to the New Edition
by Bruce G Charlton

William Arkle is not well known, indeed he could justifiably be called obscure; yet I regard him as the most recent representative of a lineage of Romantic authors and artists that could include Blake, Coleridge, Owen Barfield, CS Lewis and Tolkien in England; Goethe, Novalis and Rudolf Steiner in Germany; and Emerson, Thoreau and Whitman in the United States.

I believe that, as a spiritual philosopher, Arkle is fully worthy to stand with these illustrious names – because he brings something original, different and vital to the conversation. He provides something that we would not want to be without.

But although a writer of memorable paragraphs, an unique and elating painter, and an innovative composer, Arkle is not the match of his great predecessors in *artistic* achievement. He reaches his highest attainment in the abstract realms of metaphysical philosophy, which is always challenging to read. If you persevere with this book you will discover much that will stay in your recollection and enhance your life – but to gain this you must be prepared to work hard.

My part in the matter...

A Geography of Consciousness by William Arkle is a book of concentrated wisdom and enlightenment, which can make a very positive difference to life; it would perhaps be my first choice as a 'desert island' book – but it is also a difficult book that requires slow and focused study. My task here is to persuade you to make the sustained effort required to obtain the great rewards that this text offers!

Perhaps an account of my own experience with the work of William Arkle might serve as a bridge? At the age of eighteen I discovered Arkle, from a local BBC TV documentary; I learned that he was a painter and spiritual philosopher, a religious thinker, and something of a 'guru' who had attracted disciples from abroad. I was amazed to find that he lived only about a mile from me, through the woods and on top of the hill in Backwell, Somerset, England.

At that time I was a young atheist, training in science, aiming at medicine; and so, while I felt a fascination drawing me, I made no attempt to contact Arkle. I asked a few questions about the family (my sister knew them, slightly); and tried, but failed, to find his writings in the Bristol bookshops or library system.

A year later my family had moved to Scotland, and I was pleased and surprised to find a copy of *A Geography of Consciousness* in the Edinburgh City Library; which I borrowed and read for the summer of 1978; but eventually it had to be returned. Yet there were parts of the book that made a permanent impact, lodging in memory – especially the image of awakening on a sunny morning, from the Foreword; which must have come to mind hundreds of times through my later life.

I was also fascinated by Colin Wilson's assertion (from his introduction) that Arkle did not just write *about* the world of higher consciousness: he really *lived* it (confirming my impression from the TV programme). As the years went by I began to recognise how rare this was; and how most writers and artists, including the best, utterly fail to live-up-to their works. This made Arkle special, in the way that William Blake was special (and the comparison between Blake and Arkle was one that Colin Wilson had made).

However, I found myself put-off by Arkle's use of geometry and physics as a metaphorical description – I just could not battle through these abstractions; because of my suspicion that on the other side was something that I would not accept from my atheist-scientist perspective. I was also averse to Arkle's confident discussions of God and divinity (which, at that time, I could not even entertain as a possibility). In the end, *A Geography of Consciousness* instead made me attracted to the work of Colin Wilson. I began reading Wilson (starting with *The Outsider*) and have never stopped since! Yet I now regard Arkle as the greater man; a deeper and more important thinker, who went beyond Wilson.

I happened to be good friends with Arkle's nearest neighbours up on Backwell Hill, and after leaving Backwell I began to revisit and stay with them. One memorable evening I visited William Arkle's son, Nick, to see his music studio and hear some of his compositions; and during this visit I briefly said hello to William, or 'Bill' as everyone called him. If Bill had been alone and had had free time, perhaps this might have led to something (despite my continued suspicion of spiritual and religious matters); but he was walking from one place to another with a small group of people, clearly busy; so the entirety of my personal contact with William Arkle amounted to a brief introduction, an exchange of pleasantries! This non-event has long been a source of regret to me; although in my more realistic moods I acknowledge that I was not then ready for more.

But I do recall being very impressed by the house, and its vast ex-chapel covered with Arkle's strange and evocative paintings; with evidence of all manner of creative work afoot. The place was buzzing, even in the evening; yet buzzing in a pleasant and meditative way, like a bumble bee... Arkle's seemed like some sort of ideal life; secluded study, meditation and convivial living with family, friends and pupils. My brief experience confirmed Colin Wilson's statement that Arkle lived in accordance with his ideals.

My life then entered the early adult phase of focusing on work; in my case as a psychiatry researcher, lab scientist, literary scholar, and then a university academic. I lived at the other end of Britain and pretty much stopped visiting Backwell; and my interests became mainstream, and materialistic. Although I still failed to engage; Arkle did not go away. Whenever I was in a second-hand bookshop, I would take a look to see if I could get my own copy of *A Geography of Consciousness*. And eventually, some considerable time later, I was walking through Bloomsbury, London and saw a strange 'mystical'-looking shop that I thought might possibly be carrying a copy. I walked in – and there it was, right in front of me! So I bought it, and began to feel (at the back of my mind, almost unwanted) that there might be some synchronicity drawing me to Arkle.

Even so, things did not really get-going until 2008, some thirty years after that first encounter; when I discovered extensive web pages (created and hosted by Michael Perry) containing most of Arkle's writings and paintings. This led, by stages, to a more and more intense engagement with Arkle's writings; until some five years ago when they took a place at the centre of my spiritual life.

Arkle is a Christian. He is, however, a very unusual Christian – as are several of the other Romantics I listed above – such as Novalis, Blake, Steiner and Barfield. One certainly does not *need* to be a Christian to get a great deal from Arkle - but I would say that Christians could potentially get the most from him; if they can get past the fact that he is non-denominational, unorthodox and heretical. But, if you are not a Christian, you do need to be someone who is prepared to entertain the *possibility* that we live in a creation, not a universe of merely accidental causal forces. You also should be someone who regards it as at least *conceivable* that this ongoing creation originated in a loving personal God; such that each individual's life has a purpose and a meaning.

In sum; if you are prepared to accept – at least hypothetically - the assumption that our reality was created by a loving God – then you are ready to start reading *A Geography of Consciousness*.

So, what can a reader expect to find in this book? In what follows I will draw-upon my understanding of Arkle's philosophy, integrating information

I have derived from the full range of his available prose works, as well as conversations with some of those who knew him.

The assumptions of *A Geography of Consciousness*

William Arkle lived by the belief that he had direct and personal knowledge both of the nature of reality of God the creator and of his own true and divine self. Knowledge of, on the one hand, God; and, on the other hand, the 'real-self', was the basis upon-which his entire 'system' was built, and which guided his life.

Where does our real-self come from; and why is it valid? Arkle's answer is that it originates as a fragment of the divine, a droplet of the ocean that is God, or a little flame from the cosmic fire that is God. This is the basis of the real self, and it is why we are literally children of God, since we inherit a part of God. However, the real self is also the product of our own, unique personal choices and experiences, and how we have learned from them.

For Arkle, this uniqueness is vital. God wants each of his children to be different, an expression and development of his or her own nature. In sum; for Arkle the real self is both universal, because it includes a part of God; and individual, because it is the product of unique experience.

Our destiny, our purpose – should we choose to follow it – is therefore also both universal and unique. Universal because we may all work together on creation and create for each-other in a spirit of love; unique because each person (God, human, angel) brings something absolutely distinctive and irreplaceable. Each 'player' has his own part in the symphony of the universe and adds a specific new voice to manifestation.

Most spiritual writers will, at this point, recommend some method or technique of disciplined meditation or special prayer in order to achieve such intuition; but not Arkle. Arkle insists that there is no single method, but to the contrary each individual must 'quarry-out' his own path for himself, by trial and error, by doing his best and learning from experience. Since the self we aim at is meant to be unique, the method for attaining it is likewise unique. Arkle emphasises that the difficulty of learning for oneself is not an accident, but part of the process, built-into God's plan; because this is the best way to learn.

What we learn 'the hard way' is learned better – indeed, it is often the case that tough lessons are the only ones that are effective. And, for Arkle, this is the basic nature of this created world. This is a world where we get the lessons, some pleasant, some tough (whatever works), individually-tailored for each person (as much as possible), that are needed for us to learn and grow toward higher levels of consciousness, higher levels of divinity.

For Arkle, this is a well-designed world; a world that is trying to teach us what we most need to know. But what is the purpose of this world – what is it trying to help us grow towards?

Ultimate purpose: God's yearning for grown-up friends

Arkle believed that God's reason for creation was to manifest a universe in which his children (humankind and also angels) could develop towards higher levels of divinity, and eventually grow-up into what might be termed mini-gods – at the same level of development as God the creator.

For Arkle the 'master metaphor' – and indeed a literal reality at the spiritual level – is The Family. The ideal, loving and creatively-active human Family (which we can all imagine, even if we have no personal experience) is the model for the universe; and provides an understanding of the goal of the universe.

At this point we need to recognise that, for Arkle, God is both Father and Mother. God is a 'dyad' of primal Heavenly Parents, whose children include all of humankind. (And, indeed, all the angels; whom Arkle regards as God's children who begin in Heaven as helpers of God, and who work 'down' through incarnations away from divine influence and towards greater materiality; developing *in the opposite direction* from Men, but getting the same various life experiences in the end.) Because we are all members of a single Family; ultimately God, humans and angels are all of the same *kind*, all related, and have the same ultimate possibility. We can all become creators, eventually – perhaps working with our Heavenly Parents and within our Heavenly Parents' creation; perhaps manifesting other new creations. And we can also (albeit limited by personal capacity and perspective) potentially understand each other's motivations.

So the Big Problem for God is how to create a universe in which spiritual children can grow-up to become mini-gods, on a level with our Heavenly Parents, choosing to work in harmony with our Heavenly Parents in continuing the work of creation. Behind all this is the very 'human' motivation of God to have others of his and her kind *at God's level*, with whom to be *friends*. Thus, God wants children, and hopes that at least some of these children will develop to spiritual adulthood, and choose to become God's grown-up companions and collaborators.

For Arkle, the word *friend* is loaded with significance – he sees the loving friendship of divine people as the highest goal of reality, and the highest form of relationship; because it is chosen voluntarily, and because it happens between those of equal stature. As an ideal, it is something at best glimpsed during this earthly, mortal life; but we can get an analogy from imagining the best possible outcome of a child growing-up in a loving family.

A child born into an 'ideal' family will be immersed in love and automatically responsive to the environment; mostly passive and not fully conscious. As a child matures through adolescence into adulthood; he may achieve complete spiritual independence from the parents – a state of agency, of being an independent agent. At this point he becomes potentially 'free', and able to live consciously from his own inner knowledge and motivations; that is, from his real self, which is divine. Arkle's concept of a 'friend' is when such a grown-up, free, conscious child voluntarily chooses to return to a fully loving relationship with his parents; but now on a level (but complementary) footing, as one adult with another.

Both the young-child and the adult-child love the parents; but only the adult love is the freely chosen love between different-equals. Further, as with mortal humans, the parent-child relationship will always be maintained. God is creator of this reality; we grew inside this creation; so even if or when a human rises to the status of a mini-god or divine friend, and works with the Heavenly Parents on the continuing development and creation of this reality; it will be in the context of God's already-existing primary creation.

It is in this sense that God has set-up creation, and hopes that at least some of us humans will have experiences, make choices, learn and develop; and ultimately choose to become divine friends with the creator – still God's children, but now grown up to share the same stature as our divine parents. In a nutshell; for God's purposes to be attained, God's yearning needs to meet-with our personal desires. We must each decide (from a personal kind of love; not merely abstract love) to 'meet God halfway' and join with God in the everlasting 'project' of creation.

Arkle envisages this process has being, typically, a long and slow one; involving multiple smaller steps (which are described in some detail) and multiple incarnations (perhaps in several or many different 'universes'). So, Arkle is a proponent of reincarnation, the need for this arising from the very large gulf that initially exists between Men and God; and the extreme difficulty, thus slowness, of our learning all the many things we need to learn to ascend this ladder. But Arkle's understanding is that nobody is forced to incarnate, and nobody is compelled to live a particular life without consent. In contrast, our spiritual selves have chosen, and agreed-with, the nature and circumstances of each incarnation.

For Arkle, this process of learning is something that happens best when we are incarnated, that is when we have bodies and are living in a dense, 'viscous' material world removed from deity; rather than being pure spirits in a deity-permeated celestial environment. The reason seems to be that the incarnated life, in the solid, reluctant often-adverse environment of earth, best provides the *resistance* (and indeed opposition) that we each need to push-against and overcome in order to develop.

It seems that Arkle also very likely had a direct apprehension of his own multiple incarnations, although he does not mention this in his writings. At any rate, reincarnation is a significant element in his scheme; which he explains by the analogy of multiple 'universes' or 'universities', in ascending layers, in each of which the reincarnated spirit may learn different types of lessons.

But why does God *want* us to go through this prolonged process?

God wants colleagues and friends; not servants or worshippers

Traditional religions have usually asserted that God/ the gods want humans to be obedient servants and glorifying worshippers. Arkle, by contrast, regards such attitudes to God as man-made, somewhat immature, and (unintentionally) wounding to God.

He asks us to consider that an ideal and loving human parent does not want his grown-up children to adopt a servile and worshipping attitude to his parents; no more does God – although as younger children obedience is necessary and some level of hero-worshipping almost inevitable. Arkle then makes the point that neither human beings, nor this world we live in, seem to be *designed* to encourage servile obedience and worship – indeed, there would not be much point to having mortal embodied life if these were the ideals; since it would surely be better for us to remain in Heaven, as angelic spirits, surrounded-by and immersed-in the love of God; taking it all for granted; and with no reason to disobey or assert ourselves.

However, since this world is actually full of temptations, challenges and suffering; and since we ourselves are so varied and prone to mistakes and sins; and since we already know that this world was made for us by a loving God; by a kind of 'reverse engineering' (of inferring purpose from design) all this implies that temptations, challenges, suffering, variety, error and (even) sin are 'part of the plan' for our own learning and development towards that ultimate aim of becoming God's divine friends.

In other words, if God had merely wanted Men to be obedient 'puppets', this could easily have been achieved by designing everybody to be perfectly obedient and consistent by nature; and then putting such creatures into a tidy and wholly-Good environment that ensured they would do what was wanted of them. If God had desired servants and worshippers, he could have stamped-out great populations of 'clones'; each identically programmed with the requisite motivations and behaviours... The fact that we are, instead, distinctive individuals, intermittently rebellious, inconsistent, and live in a world of temptations and suffering means that God must *want* us to experience, learn and develop; and by a messy 'trial and error' process. It seems the mess and errors are part of God's plan!

Distinct from automata; friends are each unique – each friend is a one-off, and valued as such. We know this from our own aspirations. We want a friend to be an independent person, who can surprise us. We want each friend to be himself or herself – and the more *individual* a friend becomes, the better. In the real world, friendship is being continually energised, developed, self-renewed by learning from our experience of personal interactions.

Therefore, to understand the nature of this world, we need to recognise that it is ultimately a world of unique individuals, who are intended to become even more individual as they move to higher levels of spiritual evolution. The great hope is that such individuals will choose to become allied by love, will choose to become real, deep, divine *friends*; and harmonised by this love (as an ideal family is harmonised by love in its aims and activities) will work *together* in the work of *creation*.

Our attitude to God

From this, Arkle argues for a very different attitude to God from that of traditional religion.

In particular, we ought not to behave as if God were malicious; for example by assuming that God requires propitiation and sacrifices to satisfy his demand for justice; or by assuming that we must engage in submissive rituals of obedience and worship to prevent God becoming angry at our presumption.

Instead, Arkle would like us always to bear in mind that God is our loving parents, who want the best for us - both as a whole (*all* the children of God), as well as each and individually; and who are working 'behind the scenes' to help us learn and grow spiritually. But for this to happen, we must acknowledge that this world is indeed a place of learning; which is to say that this is a meaningful world – a world made of communications telling us things we need to know.

This world, and indeed our-selves, are not meant to be 'perfect' – because perfectly-designed people in a perfectly-designed world – who were perfectly happy; could not learn and develop. People start-out and would end-up all the same, and stuck in the state of contented but un-free, unconscious puppets. Therefore, God's task was the difficult one of making a world in which there could be learning and development; and our task is the difficult one of learning and growing, step by step, towards spiritual adulthood. As we may recall from adolescence; such development is intrinsically difficult, indeed painful; and is not a smooth, uninterrupted upward ascent but more of a roller-coaster – indeed somewhat like a game of snakes and ladders. Arkle repeatedly reminds us that it is vital to recognise that the hardships of life we personally suffer are never from God's malice, but always from God's love (if we could but understand the Big Picture and Eternal Timescale behind our own specific and immediate situation); working towards our attaining the highest possible level of deity. There is no 'easy way' to do this – just as there is no easy way to get through adolescence, learn mathematics, or how to play a musical instrument.

Ultimately, all real learning is active; it is a self-learning; and Arkle says that God will always try to let us work-out our lessons for ourselves – only intervening when our situation is hopeless or we become 'stuck' – and as soon as possible handing responsibility back to us. If we are to become fully-developed individuals, this is how things must be.

Our attitude to God, Arkle says, is therefore to approach God as a growing child ideally regards his loving parents, having absolute trust that our parents always want the best for us, and know far more than we do. The parents have a long-term view, with the aim of nurturing grown-up, independent, and loving children. Such parents (whether human or divine) do not seek to maximise the immediate pleasure of their children, nor to alleviate all instances of hardship, pain and misery; nor to give their children whatever they want or ask-for, here-and-now. The ideal parents' main loving-concern is to ensure that their children learn and grow; to give their children what they *need*. Therefore children are (by stages) given the greatest possible freedom, including freedom to make mistakes and do wrongs, and take the consequences of attitudes and actions; in hope that they will become responsible agents; will learn from their mistakes and the bad outcomes of wrong-thinking and wrong-doing.

For similar reasons, a life of development cannot be a life of continual pleasure or bliss; since this would stultify learning. The ideal life of learning is varied, and contains a mixture of novelty (new challenges) and cycles of repeated challenges that we have not yet learned-from. And such is, indeed, the nature of our actual lives, as we observe them.

A world of communications

Arkle regards the whole world as meaningful, therefore potentially telling us important things. He rejects such concepts as randomness or luck; and instead sees all of life as a conversation between 'Beings' who are in relationships.

Behind this lies his core belief that nothing is absolutely 'dead', *everything* is a Being (or part of a Being) that is alive and conscious – but with widely varying degrees of life and consciousness. So that humans and dogs are more conscious than trees, and trees more conscious than mountains – but everything shares in a vast web of inter-relationships and communications. This means that, in reality, we are never alone; nor do we ever lack the potential to understand and learn-from our situation.

However, most people, for most of the time (and, apparently, some people for all of the time) have decided that everything except humans are unconscious and most are not-alive. That is, we assume that we are 'alone' in a materialist universe rather than a creation, and inhabit a world mostly of 'things' rather than Beings. We assume that – ultimately – things 'just happen', life means nothing and is going nowhere.

In *A Geography of Consciousness*, Arkle shows us that these are no more than assumptions – and mostly they are unconsciously adopted. If, instead, we become conscious about the fact that these are assumptions, we can examine them and may decide to reject them in favour of an understanding of a living, conscious reality – and, what is more, a living conscious reality made 'for us' such that we can potentially know and learn-from it.

So, for Arkle we are never isolated, never cut-off from meaning, purpose or love (except when we do this to ourselves). He urges that we recognise that we are immersed in a 'sea' of communications; of information and guidance; and that, behind everything, our Heavenly Parents are doing their best to enable us to learn what we most need. They are not trying to make our lives always easy and pleasant; but worthwhile and educative.

When we suffer – as so often happens – this is because (in an ultimate and long-term sense) sometimes suffering is the only thing we will respond to. For instance the alcoholic who sometimes *must* reach rock-bottom, and acknowledge that fact, before he can overcome his addiction. We might suppose 'in theory' that we should be able to learn important lessons without need for suffering – but experience suggests otherwise. For *that specific individual*, the addiction experience, and overcoming it, may contain vital lessons he personally *needed* to learn, but which he *would not* learn by any easier or more pleasant way.

And that individual might learn the true interpretation of his life directly from God, and learn what God intended by it – but we, as detached outsiders, cannot know more than there was *some* important reason of *some* sort relating to *someone*.

But why are such insights not more common, and what stands in our way when we try to live in accordance with them?

The problem of false selves

If our true self is divine in origin (developed from a fragment of the living God) then one major theme of *A Geography of Consciousness* is to explain the various other more superficial and less fundamental selves that tend to dominate our lives; sometimes to the point of almost completely imprisoning and neutralising the true self.

Arkle terms these selves 'entities' and explains that they often serve useful purposes – for example in performing procedures and functions automatically – so (once the function has been learned) we do not need to think about walking, catching a ball, or driving a car. There are many such processes, with varying degrees of dominance – and many will clash, and point in opposite directions; so that people are very inconsistent and self-contradicting in their behaviour, according to the functioning of one, then another, 'self'.

Another false self is what we term our 'personality'. We tend to think that this combination of the inborn and the learned is the bottom-line reality – but it is just a surface; changeable by disease, degeneration, and situation – furthermore, subject to fakery and self-deception. Indeed, we all have – to some degree – 'multiple personalities'; which we switch-between according to circumstances.

So, a basic problem is that most people, most of the time, do not know their true self, and are not living from their true self; but instead are simply doing and thinking... well, pretty much whatever the processing activity of these superficial selves happens currently to be churning-out. As often or not, even this is automatic and unconscious.

By contrast, the true self is the source of unity – it is what makes us a person, a Being, unique and existing through time and eternity; it is what relates us to God and to all other Men. We all have a single true self; but it may be buried deep; it may have near-zero influence, we may even be unaware of it.

So, to make spiritual progress, we each need to find, liberate, become conscious-of, and live-our-lives-from the true self. For Arkle, to be free is first to become conscious: consciousness is the pre-requisite of freedom, and freedom is an attribute of deity and creation.

We start by *knowing* (both from our divine self within, and by divine guidance from without) what is *the right thing* to do, in the exactly specific situation that is developing; taking into sufficient account all the other relevant Beings and the purposes of creation; and continue by choosing to do *that* – aware that we could choose otherwise. Only then are we fully responsible for what we do; only then are we personally creative.

The problem of suffering and evil in the world

The importance of Arkle for a modern reader is that he provides answers to the major problem for modern Man when confronted by traditional Christianity: the existence of suffering and evil in the world.

Pain, failure, sin... all these are aspects of reality that the spiritually-developing Man *needs* to know – and to know from personal experience – *if* he is to become able to participate in the work of creation. These are aspects of reality, because they always will be present to some extent. And that is so, because *not* everybody (not all Men and angels) will choose to favour and participate-in the work of creating. Some Men will (from their genuine freedom) opt-out into (for example) abstract and impersonal bliss. Some angelic spirits (i.e. those that become 'demons') will oppose and try to destroy ongoing creation. At any rate; in an eternally-creating reality, of always-developing spirits, there will eternally be opposition and conflict.

So un-creative and anti-creative aspects of living are real and inevitable, and we need to learn to recognise and deal with them; both in our-selves and in others. It is not enough to know *about* them; if we are to participate in loving-creation we must also know *from the inside*, from personal experience. It is insufficient to know only the positives (love, hope, faith...); we need also to know the negatives (fear, despair, resentment...). Which is why this world is such a mixed-bag, and why each human life is so challenging.

For Arkle; God is wholly-Good and wholly-Loving, but limited in power; and the work of creation is continuous and never complete, because eternal. We men and women are ultimately divine in our innermost selves, but we also have multiple other conflicting selves – including false selves subject to temptation, errors, evils etc. Our task is to navigate and learn-from this difficult but highly 'educational' environment, which is designed to teach each of us (from experience) those specific lessons he or she most needs to learn.

Thus regarded, there is no genuine 'problem' of pain. My suffering is *in some way* a part of God's loving long-term plan for me, and for my spiritual siblings: God's other children. Understanding of his own suffering is open to anybody and everybody, by means of direct knowledge from God on the one hand, and the intuitions of a Man's true (and divine) self on the other. I am assuming here that he is indeed asking the question from the true self (and not from the superficial level of personality, nor from the one or other of the merely-expedient 'automatic' or false selves). The question must also be asked from correct assumptions regarding the nature of reality. Finally, the 'asker' must be prepared to hear and accept the answer given.

Given such a context, we each *can* know the meaning of our own suffering.

What we *cannot* know, is the meaning of *every* individual person's suffering, or the suffering of groups or classes of people – elsewhere in the world or in history, and in term of whatever vague, shallow and false assumptions we bring to the question. Yet this is *exactly* what so many modern people demand! They ask something about some suffering happening to someone somewhere; and they demand a short, snappy, wholly-satisfying response to be fired-back at them! For example they demand why some hundreds/ thousands/ millions of people were subject to genocide and expect an answer that covers all cases; or precisely why some specified remote person (read-about in the mass media or a history book) had to suffer in precisely the way they (reportedly) did...

Indeed, typically this is not an honest question; because the person asking has already decided that there is not, and cannot be, any 'good reason' for suffering – because they already have assumed that *everything that happens* is random or mechanically-determined, and therefore has no 'reason'. And in a world without ultimate meaning, nothing less than permanent continuous happiness, or blissful unconsciousness, will suffice.

Arkle is an antidote to such false expectations. He gives pain and suffering their full place in life, but does not despair in the face of it because he knows *why*; and he knows that behind the Everything of all-creation, there are our loving Heavenly Parents. Arkle does not despair because he does not expect mortal life to be easy; because it is meant to be about learning, which is difficult. And he refuses to be distracted by vague demands and generalisations, in a situation when each person and situation is unique - and in which the intention is that we should each become more unique.

The graphs and geometrical diagrams... the physics metaphors

As I have already emphasised: *A Geography of Consciousness* is not an easy book. One of the strangest and most difficult aspects is that Arkle presents his ideas via a series of elaborate metaphors that are illustrated by graphs and geometry diagrams. This is a considerable obstacle, a stumbling block, for readers who have come to the book because of interest in the spiritual content. These mathematical and scientific analogies presumably arise from Arkle having been trained as an engineer in the Royal Navy and continuing this scientific interest in later life. This was an unusual background for a spiritual philosopher and painter – although Rudolf Steiner shared a similar root in science, and also used geometrical diagrams to illustrate his lectures.

Surveying his writings, it seems to me that Arkle quite naturally thought using abstract models and comparisons – he apparently found this an effective way of clarifying his established understanding, and creatively pushing it into new understandings. In other words, Arkle's mathematical and scientific abilities were a source of strength, and a basis for his major insights, as well as making life more difficult for his readers! What Arkle is doing in *A Geography of Consciousness* is to show the arguments, the trains of thought, leading up to his spiritual conclusions. That is, Arkle is 'showing his workings'; rather than simply stating conclusions (as he does in some other of his writings).

I think this reflects the two ways Arkle worked: he reasoned like a scientist from premises and assumptions that he had reached by direct intuitive apprehension; and he also sought direct intuitive confirmation of the products of his logical reasoning. When these two methods agreed, he could be more confident in the truth he had reached.

My advice to those readers who are put-off by the graphs and diagrams is: just continue reading as best you can, skimming to get the 'gist' of the points. It is often easier to come back to the graphs *after* you understand where they are leading; the pictures then may help to make the key points more memorable.

Furthermore it is important to remember that Arkle's *core* metaphor is much simpler and more accessible than science or geometry; it is The Family. Arkle repeatedly points-out that *The Family is a microcosm of the whole of creation*. That is, the ideal family is a group of Beings in a loving and creative, open-ended relationship; and so is The Universe.

Almost everyone has an innate understanding of The Family – what it could be, and what it should ideally be – and this can serve as a Master Key to unlock a true understanding of God's creation and our place in it.

How to live life

Arkle regards it as a huge and harmful error that modern Man has come to regard 'matter' as the only *real* reality. For modern man, only that is real which can be perceived, detected, measured... everything else (including, ultimately, truth, beauty, virtue; the spiritual and the divine) is purely subjective, imaginary, an illusion, an epiphenomenon of material processes. This set of (often unconscious, often denied) metaphysical assumptions is sometimes termed positivism, materialism, reductionism or scientism – but it is the normal, mainstream, public and official world view in the developed world (and has been for several generations). It is also how almost everybody now regards their lives and the world.

We (nowadays) therefore live in a world that is both privately and 'officially' made from *dead matter*. From our-selves; we look-out upon dead matter that is passively acted-upon by other dead matter, in processes of passive causality or random occurrence. A world of dead matter is a world without real meaning, a world going nowhere in particular; a world in which the small and brief human self feels overwhelmed and crushed by the vast mass of meaninglessness and death that is the cosmos...

No wonder that so many people are so bored and despairing; and recurrently seek to forget their situation by plugging into stimulation or obliterating consciousness with intoxication. If whirling matter is the only reality; since we have only ultimate disease, degeneration and death to look-forward to; *not*-thinking and un-consciousness seem the only rational responses.

Yet, if Arkle is correct, we are dwelling in a meaning-saturated universe: a creation whose existence and purpose exists for the development of our own unique selves, in a context of all other persons and Beings.

Our task, then, is *first* to recognise this reality. We need to reject the 'model' of a futile, material 'reality', utterly *indifferent* to ourselves and our concerns. We need to realise that we actually dwell inside a vast and complex multitude of communications that have been created for us by loving divine parents; and that we are surrounded by 'messages' that we could be reading and learning from – instead of denying and ignoring.

Arkle's second hope is that we may allow such a recognition to permeate our lives; overcoming the false selves that smother us and the nihilistic ideas that impinge upon us. Then we shall personally *experience* this living, conscious, communicating reality – at first seldom and weakly, later more often and with greater strength. We will know that we belong in the universe, have a personal destiny, and the chance to choose a wonderful destination.

Cosmic Perspective and Common Sense

A common response to such ideas is that it all sounds very *nice*, if only it was real; but this kind of stuff is merely wishful-thinking... dreamed-up out of nothing and in defiance of 'the evidence'. Hence the need for the difficulties and rigours of *A Geography of Consciousness*. If we make the effort to follow Arkle's arguments and explanations, our reward is the knowledge that his vision is hard-won and reality-based.

It is vital to recognise that for all his idealism and positivity, Arkle is indeed a 'hard-nosed' thinker. His understanding of God's nature and purposes – God's hopes, wishes, feelings and yearnings - are common-sensical and perfectly straightforward. He certainly regards our Heavenly Parents as far higher and vastly more powerful than us; but they are at the same time real, living, feeling persons; with whom we can have the kind of affectionate relationship that we might hope to enjoy with our parents, siblings, spouse, children or best friends.

Arkle's description of our world and our lives, their joys and miseries, is matter-of-fact – confirmable by anybody. He knows that most of us will experience lives that include struggle, hardship and adventure; seldom a life of continuous bliss or ecstasy – and he explains that (overall) what kind of life we have is the kind of life that each of us requires. A life of gentle, non-stop euphoria would be useless for learning: adverse circumstances are sometimes necessary.

Since we are here by choice; here to learn; and learning is work: we must expect that we shall experience whatever most helps our own learning. It is up to each of us to read the communications of the world; to interpret, understand and *respond correctly*. We shall experience *whatever we **need** in order to learn* – and we may be one of those people who resist learning what we most need. And if so, extreme situations may be required.

Yet all human lives have moments of joy, periods of hope, imaginations and actualities of love; and we need to understand and learn from these, just as much as from adversity. Our highest, most elated and ecstatic, moments have *vital* lessons. Indeed, if we *fail* to learn from our happiness, from the good-times of 'sweetness and light', then affliction may become the only teaching option.

Arkle therefore envisages a very 'human' life – with all its best and most glorious times; and including all the usual errors, weakness, inconsistency, wickedness and other genuine flaws to which we are all inevitably prone – since we are only very-partially-developed divine Beings, with a *long* way still to go, much to learn. When properly understood, and properly responded to, all such lapses from our ideal behaviour will become learning experiences: sources of exactly that spiritual development which is our purpose here on earth and in these mortal lives.

So, even the toughest and most miserable life can, if we do indeed learn its lessons, yield significant - *eternally* significant - fruits for our-selves. And this is the basis of Arkle's most obvious and distinctive attribute: his optimism. He is tremendously positive about life; and he lived in accordance with his ideas to a much greater extent than most people achieve.

Arkle's cosmic optimism shines-through his writings; and also his paintings, poems, music and his other creative works. Most importantly, we can also see that it is a common-sense optimism, which anyone who makes the effort may share. And that is why *A Geography of Consciousness* is such an important book.

Bruce G Charlton graduated with honours from the Newcastle Medical School, took a doctorate at the Medical Research Council Neuroendocrinology Unit, and has a Masters degree in English Literature from Durham. He has held *university lectureships in physiology, anatomy and epidemiology; and was until 2019 the Reader in Evolutionary Psychiatry at Newcastle University and Visiting Professor of Theoretical Medicine at the University of Buckingham. From 2003-10 Bruce edited the international journal* Medical Hypotheses *(Elsevier). He has published considerably more than two hundred scientific papers and academic essays, and contributed journalism to UK national broadsheets and weekly magazines. Bruce Charlton is author of* Psychiatry and the Human Condition (2000); Thought Prison: The Fundamental Nature of Political Correctness (2011); Not Even Trying: The Corruption of Real Science (2012); Addicted to Distraction: Psychological Consequences of the Modern Mass Media (2014); *and (with Edward Dutton)* The Genius Famine (2016). *He is the creator of* williamarkle.blogspot.com, *and also blogs at* charltonteaching.blogspot.com.

Introduction to the First Edition
by Colin Wilson

I would place the author of this book among the half dozen most remarkable men I have ever met—and I suppose this would include some of the most eminent writers and thinkers of our time. This book which I am introducing is not an easy one; I suppose I may as well be frank and say that in parts it is extremely tough going. But I think it is an important book, and my aim in this introduction is to clear away some of the difficulties.

Let me speak first of the author, William Arkle.

Like most writers, I receive a fair amount of correspondence from strangers. And since I write about questions of human evolution and the nature of human consciousness, many of these are from occultists and people with theories about how man can become a god overnight. Very often, the writers send me manuscripts and explain indignantly that publishers are too materialistic to understand the importance of their work. But it is usually pretty easy to see why publishers are not interested. The manuscripts are often full of important ideas; but they are never properly thought-out, with consideration for the reader. And I always find myself reflecting that it is a pity that the intelligent people are so often egocentric and lacking in self-criticism, while the sane, decent, healthy people are so often mediocrities. There are very seldom exceptions to this rule.

In 1960, William Arkle sent me a reproduction of one of his paintings, and it was certainly a striking painting; it was an abstract, geometrical sort of landscape with abstract human figures, a little like Wyndham Lewis's. The colours were all very light, yellows and greens and reds. But although it was striking, it was not, in the last analysis, a good picture. It is hard to explain this except to say that in spite of its abstract nature, it lacked real complexity. The letter that accompanied it talked about spiritual values and so on, and it was clear that this is what the picture intended to express. Arkle lived in Bristol, and he invited me to call and see him if I ever came through.

I seem to remember that I assumed he was probably a man in his fifties. My guess was that he had probably started life in the Church of England, tried a few evangelical sects, and ended up by producing some occult religion of his own.

In 1961, my wife and I were driving to Blackpool to the Long Playing Record Festival, and it seemed a good opportunity to call on the Arkles. So we found our way—after some difficulty—to a large house in Royal York Crescent, with a fine view over the valley. And we were met by a tall, good-looking man in his early thirties, with a clean cut face of the Charlton Heston type and a lock of hair on his forehead that made him resemble that Sargeant drawing of Yeats that can be found in the Collected Plays. I was introduced to his wife Elizabeth, who did not look in the least dreamy or mystical; in fact, she looked one of those cheerful, healthy girls that Shaw put into early plays. I was not surprised to learn she loved horses.

The enormous house belonged to them, and I discovered that they made a living by buying houses, re-decorating them themselves, and then letting them as flats. It seemed fairly strenuous work for a visionary, but apparently it solved the basic problem of making a living. And neither was I surprised to learn that he had been an engineer and served in the navy towards the end of the war. There was something about him that suggested that he was not one of these subjective, egocentric people who find the practical work unbearable.

I asked him some years ago for a biographical sketch, and I may as well quote what he sent me:

'Born 1924. After school, trained in engineering for the navy. After demobilisation, I had a strong urge to go to Art school which I did for two years. But I did not finish the course as I felt strongly that the attitudes to painting that I was being taught were not right for me.

'My first marriage broke up as I left Art school. I was reading a lot of mysticism and esotericism generally and developing meditation and the ability to tune my nature, as it were . . .'

Later in the same letter, he says: 'I married Elizabeth about 1952 (it is typical of him not to be sure of the date—he wrote 1953 and then changed it) and this helped me to integrate properly with ordinary life and widened my interests (and responsibilities).'

Certainly, the remarkable thing about him is that he is so integrated with ordinary life—considering the completely otherworldly nature of his basic vision.

Arkle is a true mystic and visionary. I have met a great many people who have been obsessed by religion, spiritual values and so on. And a large percentage of them struck me as being 'religious' for negative reasons—frustration, maladjustment, boredom. 'She lost everything she had and gave the rest to God'—as Saki remarks about a girl who became a nun. But very occasionally, one meets people who are mystics for the same reasons that Newton and Einstein were scientists—because they are balanced and healthy, and their minds move naturally beyond the personal. Einstein once remarked to Leopold Infeld: 'A finely tempered nature longs to escape from personal life into the world of objective perception and thought; This desire may be compared with the townsman's irresistible longing to escape from his noisy, cramped surroundings into the silence of mountains. . . .' And it was quite plain to me that this explains Arkle's mysticism; it is almost a natural evolution of his interest in engineering.

There were dozens of his paintings on the walls at Royal York Crescent —it was clear that he was a prolific painter—and I found these extremely interesting, although perhaps not for the reasons he intended. They all revealed the kind of mysticism that Blake communicates in the first part of the *Book of Thel*—the feeling that the world is basically a beautiful and good place, full of forces of benevolence, and that man only fails to see this because he shuts his eyes to it. Many of the paintings were landscapes, with a great, dreamy, angelic face hovering over them. The landscapes themselves were not minutely realistic, but looked rather as if some Swedenborgian visionary—perhaps Balzac's Seraphita—had attempted to communicate his vision of the 'other world': green, misty distances, golden bars of cloud, great rolling hills.

Now these paintings could easily have slipped into mere sentimentality, like Peter Scott's sunsets and ducks winging home ward. In fact, they avoided this. But I still found them unconvincing. I hesitate to use the word naive, but that is certainly one of the impressions they conveyed. And this was not necessarily the artist's fault. The trouble is that we live in a complex age, and affirmation, whether in music, painting or poetry, has to take account of the discords as well as the harmonies. It is no longer possible for a poet to 'pipe his woodnotes wild' as if he was sitting on a hilltop all alone. The major writers, artists and musicians of the past hundred years have tended towards pessimism, and their pessimism has seemed more convincing than the optimism of the eighteenth-century rationalists. Voltaire fought that battle with Leibnitz a long time ago. And yet here was a man who could paint a picture of a bank clerk with his rolled umbrella and brief case, leaving the front door of his suburban home, and the strange angelic figure hovering above him and reaching down protectively.

This, I should add, was one of Arkle's earliest paintings. The latter ones had lost this plangent touch of naivety; a Cezanne-like quality had crept into some of them, and this feeling of rigour and discipline made them far more satisfying to me. I liked one of them so much that he gave it to me, and it is still hanging in our hall, over the telephone. I looked at it before I began writing this piece. It is a tall, castle-like building in a landscape, and the treatment is distinctly Cezanne-ish. But the colours are all too light and glowing, pinks and pale-blues and apple greens. It is all sweetness and light. It reminded me that my first comment on the geometrical picture he sent me was that it reminded me of a Sun light Soap advertisement with a whole rainbow-range of colours.

Perhaps I make it sound as if Arkle is simply an odd sort of wild-man, something out of Rousseau. This would be completely false. What is so impressive about him is that he obviously possesses real spiritual strength; he is not merely an artistic counter part of Dale Carnegie. He is fairly constantly in touch with the 'realities' of life—meaning problems relating to bank managers, old cars, impossible tenants. He has two very attractive and boisterous children, and since he has moved to another house, a whole menagerie of animals—ponies, dogs, guinea pigs, rabbits, chickens, hamsters, fish. . . . He makes a living, but is a long way from being rich. And his wife has developed an enthusiasm for antiques and old paintings, as one of her hobbies, so that he spends a lot of time driving to old junk shops to pick up her purchases. And in the midst of this busy and complex life, he remains undividedly absorbed in his vision of a higher human consciousness, and continues to paint, compose music, write books and gather together a small group of friends with whom he discusses questions of human evolution. There is a Shelleyan purity about his idealism, and it seems to give him a considerable degree of freedom from the usual worries and depressing trivialities that tax the optimism of most of us. His head may be in the clouds, but it is emphatically not in the sand.

What puzzles and interests me so much about him is: How is it possible to see the modern world so affirmatively? If, that is, you are involved in it, and not privileged to look at it from a distance? Because the lesson of the past century and a half is that visionary idealism tends to come into sharp conflict with the unpleasant reality. Sweetness and light doesn't stand a chance against darkness and dirt. Wordsworth fled to the Lake District, and still protested 'The world is too much with us'. And Blake makes his little boy ask:

'Father, O Father, what do we here
In this land of unbelief and fear?

One of Arkle's favourite composers is Delius; but the music of Delius is full of an immense nostalgia for lost beauty, for the briefness of summer days. It is significant that his most beautiful paintings are settings of the poems of Ernest Dowson.

Now to some extent, the answer to these questions is to be found in this book. Arkle is *not* a naive, unreasoning optimist. His ideas about man and his potentialities are carefully thought out, and they continue to deepen and develop. He has a very clear idea of what man is, and what he is capable of. Since that first night in 1961, I have stayed with Bill Arkle many times—in fact, every time I could find an excuse to go through Bristol—and I have had ample opportunity to observe the way his mind works, and his method of attacking these problems of human consciousness.

Perhaps the simplest way of explaining what he is doing is to say that, without actually being influenced by other writers or philosophers, he stands squarely in the midstream of evolutionary philosophy. But this in itself needs further qualification.

Aldous Huxley coined the term 'perennial philosophy'—or borrowed it from Leibnitz—to describe the basic mystical philosophy that regards man— in his fundamental nature as identical with God. Not only is the Kingdom of God within you; God is within you. According to the *Bhagavad Gita*, man is born and reborn endlessly, until he frees himself from the delusions of Maya—the world— and recognises his own god-like nature. As soon as this happens, this self-realisation as God, man will naturally cease to do the merely human things he has always done, and will enter into contemplation of his god-like nature. And whether he chooses to resist it or not, there is no alternative; he will keep being reborn until he consents to follow the upward path to godhead.

This philosophy has been expressed, in different forms, by the great mystics of every race and religion. Obviously, it expresses some deep intuition that comes to man in moments of heightened consciousness. It was the driving force behind the so-called 'romantic philosophy' of the nineteenth century. It is not a 'belief'; it is something that *happens to consciousness.* Man normally feels imprisoned in his everyday routine, his everyday personality; he comes to accept this feeling of limitation. And then, for no reason at all, there occur these moments of absurd, delightful wellbeing. Now, wellbeing in itself may mean nothing; it may be nothing more than sudden freedom from pain, or the pleasure due to a good meal or a bottle of wine. But these moments always carry a very definite sense of being *real* insights or glimpses of something that is true. At this point, someone always comes up with the old chestnut about the man who thought he saw the answer to the universe whenever he was drunk, and one day, wrote it down on a piece of paper; the next morning he looked at the paper and read: 'There's a strong smell of petrol around here.' (Russell tells it in *Mysticism and Logic*.) This may or may not invalidate certain experiences of mystical insight—I say 'may not' because in the visionary state produced by psychedelic drugs, there *is* a sense of seeing 'a world in a grain of sand'—or a smell of petrol. Anyway, no one denies that many so-called mystical experiences are merely a reflection of the belly. And equally, the mystics would argue, there are certain mystical experiences which carry a stamp of complete authenticity, a glimpse of something that is objectively true. These are the kinds the 'perennial philosophy' is concerned with.

Now apart from the 'perennial philosophy', there is also an important current that may be called evolutionary philosophy. The mystics, for the most part, tended to see the aim of their disciplines as a more-or-less static union with God—perhaps what Buddha meant by Nirvana. I am not using the words 'static union' in a critical sense; I am only saying that its focus is upon the idea of achieving one-ness with the divine principle. The evolutionist is much more interested in the process of becoming; he is aware of evolution as a process of *activity*.

Although the *Bhagavad Gita* expresses a kind of mystical evolutionism, it would, on the whole, be true to say that true evolutionism has appeared only in the past two centuries; the great religions of the past all emphasise that final goal in which man blends with the godhead. (This is true even of Plato.) Gurdjieff and his pupil Ouspensky may be cited as a good example of modern evolutionism. Ouspensky states (in *The Psychology of Man's Possible Evolution*): '. . . if we take historical mankind, that is, humanity for ten or fifteen thousand years, we may find unmistakeable signs of a higher type of man'. And 'Our fundamental idea shall be that man as we know him *is not a completed being;* that nature develops him to a certain point only and then leaves him, either to develop further *by his own efforts* . . . or to live and die . . . as he was born'. 'Evolution of man in this case will mean the development of certain *inner* qualities and features which usually remain undeveloped, *and cannot develop by themselves.*' And elsewhere, Ouspensky has this excellent simile: 'We have in us, so to speak, a large house full of beautiful furniture, with a library and many other rooms, but we live in the basement and the kitchen and cannot get out of them.' And in one of my own books I compare man to an aeroplane with four engines, who only uses one of them, and so flies lop-sided; then one day, by accident, the other three engines roar into life and he suddenly knows what it is to possess tremendous power *and to fly straight.* (This lop-sidedness the Catholics call original sin.) The obvious question is: How do we get the other engines to work *all the time?*

Gurdjieff stated the basic principle in three words: 'Understand the machine.' What machine? Your own being. Man takes his inner being for granted, as a motorist takes the engine of his car for granted. If it goes wrong, he relies on a garage mechanic. But there are no garage mechanics for the human mind, except the crude witch doctors who call themselves psychologists—and who tire no more psychologists than Cornelius Aggrippa was an atomic physicist.

But to return for a moment to evolutionism. I would say that most evolutionists deny the statement that human nature doesn't change much, that there is nothing new under the sun, etc. On the contrary, there may be feeling that a new type of man has been emerging in the past two hundred years and that the human race is now ready for an evolutionary leap. I know two brilliant Americans, Earl and Barbara Hubbard, who are devoting their lives to this proposition, and who are bringing together an incredible number of serious thinkers—not cranks, but biologists, psychologists, physicists, philosophers, all men of intellectual standing— who subscribe to it.

I think it would be true to say that there is a common agreement among these scientists and philosophers that the question of evolution must be approached as rationally and scientifically as possible. Professor Abraham Maslow alone—the head of the American Psychological Association—has created a new psychology based upon the proposition that man's 'instinctoid' drives are not his purely animal nature; that he has equally 'instinctoid' drives that are directed *at higher values,* and that these are as fundamental as his 'lower instincts'. And it can be seen that this proposition— that man has a 'higher nature' that is just as instinctoid as his lower nature—is a flat contradiction of much of what has passed for psychology since Freud.

I am trying to emphasise that a revolution is really taking place, at this moment, and that this may be the beginning of the most exciting epoch in human history. And it is not a crank revolution; neither is it confined to pseudo-scientists like Teilhard de Chardin (who, for all his importance, must be regarded as a visionary rather than as a scientist). An anthology of this new evolutionism would contain pieces by Julian Huxley, Michael Polanyi, Sir Karl Popper, Hadley Cantril, Karl Jaspers, as well as Teilhard and Bergson and Shaw and Ouspensky and Nietzsche.

Now there are a great many different starting points for evolutionism. In Bergson and Shaw, it remains purely a philosophy, a dogmatic belief, so to speak. Bergson ties in his belief in an 'élan vital' with his belief that the world is not accessible to logic, that thought is a kind of cheat, a mis-representation, like taking photographs of a flowing river. Shaw expressed his evolutionism in drama and parable, and made no attempt to relate it to the major European tradition of science and philosophy.

But a philosopher who was not primarily an evolutionist provided the basic method for this new philosophy—Edmund Husserl. There is no room here to dilate upon Husserl's phenomenology, but I must try to indicate its fundamental nature. One might say that Husserl proceeded from the same basic insight as Freud— although there was no direct influence—that the human mind is a far larger thing than the Victorian rationalists had realised—that there is a vast, turbulent undersea area of which normal consciousness is unaware. Then how can 'everyday consciousness' learn about this hidden realm? Freud was a practising doctor; he worked by rule of thumb, and left the theory to take care of itself, making sure only that it was in accord with his observations. Husserl was a philosopher and a mathematician; he tried to devise techniques by which one could, so to speak, take radar soundings of these unknown depths. It is basically a descriptive method, that aims at grasping what happens in the subconscious by sheer scientific hard work. A simple analogy might help. Suppose you wanted to know what drives a car, but you had no idea of how to raise the bonnet. Does this mean that you are doomed to remain ignorant forever? Not if you have the painstaking temperament of a true scientist. You can observe minutely what happens when you press the starter, touch the accelerator, apply the brake, pull out the choke, and so on. You can listen carefully to where various noises proceed from. You can observe where the various wires under the dashboard disappear to. And you can peep in through the radiator grid to get glimpses of what goes on. It will never be quite as satisfactory as raising the bonnet; but if you are really persistent, it is amazing how much you can learn. In the same way, if you stop accepting your conscious life, with its feeling, perceptions, responses, as something that just 'happens', and attempt to analyse and classify, it is amazing how quickly you begin to learn things that were 'hidden', taken for granted as part of the subconscious processes.

As far as the actual 'geography of consciousness' goes, Gurdjieff produced one of the most complex and complete systems, all based upon self-observation. He declared, for example that man has five centres, the intellectual, the emotional, the 'moving' centre, the instinctive and the sexual centre, and that these work with different kinds of energy. He also declared that there are four distinct levels of consciousness: sleeping consciousness, the so-called waking consciousness, self-remembering (which is what happens when you get that sudden delightful sense of yourself in a place: 'What *me, here?*) and 'objective consciousness', which human beings never experience. I say 'so-called waking consciousness because according to Gurdjieff, our everyday consciousness is a form of sleep, little better than actual sleep in bed. And Gurdjieff's system aims basically at the development of 'alarm clocks', methods of awakening from the one-engined state to the four-engined state.

I have said all this to try to provide the reader with some kind of background to Arkle's book. For the disconcerting thing about him is that he does not take any great interest in other people's systems, and is so concerned with trying to capture his visions of man's higher nature in paint —the paintings, incidentally, becoming steadily more impressive as the years go on—that he really can't be bothered to relate what he is trying to do to Maslow, Cantril, Polanyi, Popper and the rest. He has simply thought very hard about these states of higher consciousness, tried to grasp how they come about, and then tried to find a terminology that makes all this clear. In some ways, he reminds me of the mystic Jacob Boehme, who attempted exactly the same sort of thing, and who tried to use analogies from alchemy. Arkle is an engineer with a wide knowledge of physical science, and he tries to use this to clarify his arguments.

Some of the difficulty of the book arises from his scientific training. He notices, for example, that man has an ordinary will, which he uses for everyday purposes, and a 'true will' which awakens in moments of intensity or insight, when he 'completes his partial mind'. If I were writing this book, I would take that as my starting point, and offer examples of the awakening of the 'true will' from literature and my own experience; then, having brought this to the reader's attention—so that he is 'with me'—I would go on to try to piece together the insights that arise from these moments in which we operate on our 'true will'. In other words, I would proceed in a fumbling and thoroughly empirical way—for my own benefit as much as the reader's. Arkle is concerned with getting the whole thing laid out clearly, like a text book, and it is obvious that an immense amount of planning went into the book before the actual writing began. The consequence is that the chapter on the will occurs towards the end, and the book begins with a much more ambitious and difficult section on Fields of Consciousness, classifying them and using the analogy of vectors.

Nevertheless, he states his aim with great clarity and simplicity: 'Intense experiences come to many people and the record of them gives an indication of an order of consciousness quite different from that which we are used to. Between the two extremes of these orders of consciousness can be found a graded series of states which will be set into a structure and related to a theory of existence.' Nothing could be clearer, and everything he has to say, whether on the Self, Types of Consciousness, Religion, Education, or even Astrology, is dove-tailed into the 'system' which is laid down in the opening chapters. It is a difficult book, and for my taste, is lacking in examples and illustrations; but it is not a long-winded book, and it can be extremely rewarding. For the range of subjects it covers, it is a short book; and if you find one section difficult, it does no harm to skip to another one. Little by little it will be seen that the whole thing fits together.

One of Arkle's chief preoccupations in this book is man's mechanical aspects—what I call 'the robot'. When you learn anything at all difficult—typing, speaking French, driving a car—you learn it slowly and consciously, and then pass on the knowledge to a robot in the subconscious, who now takes over the driving, and does it far more efficiently than you could do it consciously. But then, if I am learning something interesting or difficult, it has the effect of waking me up, raising my consciousness to a level of intensity that I would find difficult to achieve without this stimulus. This 'awakening' is also what we feel setting out on a holiday or engaged in some competitive sport, or in something with an element of danger, like water skiing. The more the robot takes over, the less we experience these awakened states. Obviously, the robot is the chief villain as far as 'sleep' is concerned. Arkle has a great deal to say about these mechanical states; in fact, he goes into the whole question of different 'circuits'—that is to say, the robotic activities of each of Gurdjieff's 'centres'. And it is this careful analysis that constitutes the chief value of his book, for his approach is in many ways more illuminating than Gurdjieff's.

The reader will soon observe that Arkle differs from Gurdjieff, and from some of the mystics I have mentioned, in his specifically social concern. He never ceases to be concerned about education, the forces in society that shape our minds, and to ponder on how the whole system could be improved. He is intensely concerned with people—far more so than I have ever been. Perhaps this explains the unworldliness of his paintings, and the rigorous, abstract nature of this book. I live in isolation and simply write and think; there is little direct communication. Arkle teaches painting, and tries to communicate his ideas directly to his students. If he feels that someone has intelligence and sensitivity, there are no limits to his patience and sympathy.

I should also add that he is concerned with direct *experience* of man's higher nature, as much as with attempting to describe it. I myself had a rather amusing experience of this some years ago, at a time when he was living out in the country, at Alveston. He had apparently been having considerable success in inducing semi- mystical states in his students, and wanted to try it on me. I wasn't too happy about the idea, for my scientific preoccupation has meant that I try to run my 'peak experiences' in double harness with my categorising intellect; I am a born phenomenologist. I don't much like peak experiences on their own. I am like a surveyor who cannot enjoy a country walk unless he has brought his instruments with him. Still, I agreed to try. Arkle made me lie down on a sort of psychologist's couch and close my eyes, then tried to instruct me in losing my consciousness of my body, to carry the mind into outer space, so to speak. Obviously, it was a method that could work very well for someone who was already in sympathy with his aims and ideals. It would be like listening to certain familiar music and soon being carried away on its wings, feeling one's personal worries and preoccupations dropping away and that tremendous feeling of relief flowing through one's whole body. In such a state, his suggestions would certainly have had the effect of intensifying the experience to the level of mystical consciousness. But at eleven o'clock in the morning, my mind didn't feel in the least like relaxing into mystical consciousness; it would have derived more pleasure from a stiff half hour of phenomenological analysis. So after a period that seemed rather long, but may only have been ten minutes or so, he gave up, with the comment: 'I'm afraid you're probably too rationalistic.' It struck me as funny because he was obviously unaware of why it hadn't been successful: that to try to persuade my mind to float into mystical experience was like trying to teach an elephant to tap-dance. He is very much the visionary, without that analytical interest in what actually makes people tick—the kind of interest Balzac possessed in such abundance. He would have fascinated Balzac; but I am sure Balzac holds no interest whatever for him.

In the early part of 1973, after this volume had been accepted for publication, Arkle produced one of his most concentrated expressions of belief, a ten thousand word 'Letter from a Father', and there was some discussion about whether to include it in this book as an appendix.[1] The idea was finally dropped: not only because of its length, but because its approach has so little in common with the rest of the volume. On the other hand, this introduction would certainly be incomplete without some comment on it. I have read this 'Letter' several times, and each time its importance seems to grow.

----

[1] It is included as an appendix in this new edition.

The 'Father' is, of course, God, and the letter is intended to 'justify the ways of God to man', an ambition that most modem philosophers would regard either as pretentious or naive. But the philosophy of the past three hundred years, from Bacon and Descartes onwards, has been distinguished by its determination to be sophisticated at all costs, and it is only now becoming finally clear that this sophistication has led philosophy into a cul de sac. In his *Theodicity*, Liebnitz arrived at the conclusion that before creating the world, the First Cause must have considered how to create 'the best of all possible worlds', and then gone on to do it. But, he insisted, there can be no contradiction between faith and reason; if an article of faith contradicts reason, then it must be abandoned as false. . . . This attempt to reconcile faith and reason met with no success; Voltaire apparently demolished the whole structure in his brilliant, but fundamentally silly (and ultimately boring) *Candide*. In effect, he accused Leibnitz, Descartes, Spinoza and all the other 'religious rationalists' of being either dishonest or weak in the head, incapable of pursuing their own logic to its conclusions. If you are honest, said Voltaire in effect, you can *see* the world is a meaningless mess. When the world is examined with the cold eye of reason, there is no evidence whatever for God or Purpose; all we can see are brutal, natural laws. . . . From then on, philosophers who wanted to reach out to positive conclusions—about destiny, universal purpose, meaning, etc—had to conceal the steps by which they did it in a thick verbal fog, which might be regarded as a smoke screen to baffle the pursuit of latter day Voltaires. The rules of the philosophical game, as evolved by Descartes, Locke and Hume could be compared to casting a man up on a desert island without any clothes, and insisting that he should learn to survive by common sense alone. And at the beginning of philosophical works, it became *de rigeur* for the philosopher to exhibit himself naked, showing his empty hands, before he settled down to the task of building his system from creepers and palm trees. . . . There was also an increasing tendency to solve the Cartesian dualism—of body and soul—by declaring that it doesn't exist; man *is* his body, and the 'soul' is a logical misconception. When Bergson tried to reintroduce it under the name of *élan vital*, Julian Huxley remarked that to explain the activities of living things by pointing to an *élan vital* is like explain ing the motion of a train by referring to an *élan locomotif*. Even poets like Whitman and D. H. Lawrence, who should have known better, tried to disinfect their mysticism by insisting that man is his body, and the body *is* the soul. When Gilbert Ryle finally gave an impressive philosophical formulation to this idea in *The Concept of Mind*, it had come to be regarded as a cornerstone of modern thought.

What philosophy had really done was to get rid of all 'higher' concepts by insisting that they can be quite adequately expressed in lower terms, in terms of the body and the chemistry of the emotions and our psychological drives. . . . But the trouble was that these new 'scientific' philosophies—logical atomism, dialectical materialism, logical positivism, linguistic analysis, atheistic existentialism—all ground to a halt, trapped in a net of their own making. All of them arrived at the conclusion reached by the American Hegelian W. T. Stace in his essay *Men Against Darkness*: that although man may long for purpose and meaning, this is ultimately wishful thinking; man has to recognise the fact that he is alone in a meaningless universe, and face up to it bravely. . . .

In book after book, beginning with *The Outsider*, I have tried to point out the logical and philosophical inconsistencies of these various schools. When *The Outsider* came out in 1956, it was attacked by logical reductionists like A. J. Ayer as a hodge-podge of half-baked mysticism and existentialism. But in the two decades since then, reductionism has ceased to have it all its own way; the criticisms of Karl Popper have undermined logical positivism, while a whole school of scientists, philosophers and psychologists of all persuasions have expressed their mistrust of 'reductionism'. And so what struck me chiefly in reading Bill Arkle's 'Letter from a Father' was that most of its philosophical attitudes would now be regarded by many as thoroughly up to date. And, amusingly enough, its theory of freedom and the nature of evil comes very close indeed to that propounded by Leibnitz in 1710 in the *Theodicity*. It has taken two and a half centuries for the wheel to come full circle, and for an error to finally lose its potency, like a dangerous germ left exposed to the air.

Arkle, then, expresses quite boldly the view that God's intention in creating human beings (and, presumably, living creatures in general) was to produce co-workers and helpmeets, creatures who would eventually become god-like themselves. In *Man and Superman*, Shaw makes Tanner jeer at Octavius's 'pious English habit of regarding the world as a moral gymnasium built expressly for you to strengthen your character in . . .', but this is precisely how Arkle *does* regard it ultimately. Like Sartre, he insists on the primacy of man's freedom. Sartre makes his Orestes say to Zeus: 'Yes, you created me, but you made one mistake: you created me free.' Arkle insists that this freedom, which can be so dangerous, is man's ultimate challenge, and he uses an interesting analogy to explain it. There are times when parents insist on acting on behalf of their children in a way that negates their individuality—perhaps apologising on their behalf to someone, as if the children weren't there. And when this happens, the child is quite right to consider it 'a devaluation of his nature'. In this matter, Arkle would agree entirely with Sartre's Orestes, who refuses to repent of the murder of his father and 'accept forgiveness'; Orestes says: 'If I disown my act, I disown myself and lose part of my essence. I prefer to retain my essence, and live with my guilt.' This, says the 'Father' in Arkle's letter, is why 'I have made your school in such a way that it becomes real to you and does not remain a game'.

As to evil, it is certainly real: it is the energy, or emanations, created by making the wrong choices, by trying to take the easy way out. But the lesson of evil is fairly clear anyway. (A thought that has often struck me in writing about crime: for example, people like Al Capone and Lucky Luciano seem to unconsciously will their own extinction . . .) And the Blakeian mystic emerges in his assertion: 'You do not know it, but I keep you and cherish you in ways that would amaze you.'

In the matter of the body-soul problem, he comes down squarely on the side of the Cartesian dualism, comparing man to a diver in a diving suit—the suit being the body. But the diving suit analogy leads to an interesting observation: that in restricting man within rigid limits, it also creates possibilities of discipline. This recalls a statement by T. E. Hulme—another religious philosopher who fought hard to escape the toils of reductionism: 'The bird attained whatever grace its shape possesses not as a result of the mere desire for flight, but because it had to fly *in air, against gravitation.*' The heaviness of the body slows man down, so that he can witness in slow motion the consequences of his acts of free will. And always, Arkle insists, the basic lessons are of 'integrity, affection, kindness, beauty and honesty'. He also seems to accept Shaw's notion of a God who is not perfect, but who struggles to evolve through matter, when he says that the difference between *conceiving* an ideal world (as Liebnitz's God did) and actually making it out of solid matter demanded the utmost ingenuity on the part of God and his mate. (Typically, Arkle conceives the Father as being supplemented by a Mother.)

He goes on to speak of the importance of the role of the family, pointing out that the disinterested love the parent gives to his children is the exact counterpart of the love God gives to human beings. He makes the interesting observation that if you want to understand God's relation to men, study your own attitude towards your children. It's a good point. The most affectionate parent has to recognise the limits of his ability to protect and insulate his children, since over-protectiveness cramps their own developing powers. The same point struck me recently in reading Michael Deakin's book *The Children on the Hill*, describing two parents who have turned their children into geniuses by giving them non-stop attention and affection; the trouble is that the parents have obviously sacrificed their own lives to developing their children. And it still remains an open question whether these highly precocious young 'geniuses' can grow into balanced adult geniuses, or whether they have developed the disabilities of hothouse plants.

The Letter ends with the statement that although the Fall was a reality, it was not an accident; man had to fall if he was to recognise his true potentialities. Omar Khayyam expressed a desire to shatter the world and rebuild it 'nearer to the heart's desire'; Arkle would insist that this is the comment of an irresponsible poet who can criticise without having to put his ideas into practise. If Omar Khayyam was really forced to confront the task of rebuilding the universe, he would have to acknowledge that it is more complex and purposive than he recognised. The shallow, defeatist philosophy of the *Rubaiyat* is typical of the man who makes no real effort to understand, preferring to strike a pose. The beauty of the world is more tremendous and terrible than hedonistic poets can understand; it can only be grasped by accepting the rigidity of the laws of our existence, the 'sternness' that is the basis of the love of God. 'What would my loving affection have been worth if it were lacking in this immovable strength and integrity?' This is a view that was expressed magnificently in that strange work of creative genius, *A Voyage to Arcturus* by David Lindsay, in which the name of the 'Saviour' on earth is Pain.

Hostile critics may say that Arkle's view is a return to a naive, Browning-esque Victorian optimism. This may be true. But we have tried erecting pessimism into a universal philosophy in the name of honesty, and found it self-contradictory. The stoical pessimism of Hemingway, Sartre, Camus, Beckett, collapses into self-pity when pursued to its logical extremity. Arkle's curious optimism may be Victorian, or Shavian, or whatever you want to call it; but it is ultimately realistic. It shirks no issues, and the final vision is imaginative and courageous.

It is a good thing that people like William Arkle exist—working away quietly, wholly preoccupied with the 'higher value experiences', belonging to no group. But it can have its disadvantages. It is important at a certain stage to communicate, to go through the second stage of Toynbee's cycle of withdrawal and return. A short time before I met Arkle, I met another remarkable recluse, who lived in a cottage on the edge of Dartmoor and studied the mystics and painted the cornfields around the cottage. Unlike Arkle, he was a violent world-rejector; modern civilisation struck him as a horrible embodiment of all the vulgarity and spiritual degradation that he hated. His temperament fascinated me so much that I put a portrait of him into my novel *The World of Violence* (where he is called Jeremy; incidentally, there is also a fictional portrait—or sketch—of Bill Arkle in my *Man Without a Shadow*, where he appears briefly as Bill Fletcher, in the entry for November 1st). I lost touch with my recluse friend for several years, and when I met him again, found that he had given up writing, and was running a puppet show at a seaside town on the south coast. This, of course, does not mean that he has abandoned his basic preoccupations; but certainly his total isolation, and the lack of interest in his ideas, had taken a heavy toll of his optimism. And if he does not return to writing books— he published a very good one on evolution—it will be so much the worse for civilisation. There can never be too many visionaries.

This is why I think it important that this book should be published and read. It represents an immense amount of thought and discipline, and it is the expression of a unique personality. Unfortunately, it is not a full expression of his personality; neither, for that matter, are his paintings or music. His temperament has a purity of obsession that makes it almost saintly; but he is also gifted with a sense of humour and an enormous tolerance and humanity. And these are qualities that require communication, human contact, for their healthy development. And, as you will see in the following pages, Arkle's is essentially a philosophy of human communication.

Colin Wilson, one of the most prolific writers of the 20th century, was the author of over one hundred books on philosophy, psychology, mysticism, history, and many other subjects. He maintained a correspondence with William Arkle for over thirty years.

PREFACE

We like to be loved and admired but we also like to love and admire other people.

When we love and admire other people, we are able to believe in the joy and merit of their nature. When we are loved and admired we are able to believe in the joy and merit of our Self. When we receive and give love and admiration we are in either case gaining something wholly delightful and desirable. But we do not take the trouble to look more closely at this situation, for the situation seems to be an end in itself. If it is examined, however, the sensation in question reveals that it is not so much the giving and receiving of love which matters but that the love and admiration helps to liberate an aspect of our nature which *is* joy and *is* happiness and *is* a sort of virtuous affectionate delight.

The trouble with life as we ordinarily experience it is that this part of our nature is always being suppressed and not liberated. Not only do other people continually restrict it but we find that we are restricting it ourselves. The problem however is not as simple as it looks. The difficulty is not simply liberating our Selves but the fact that in trying to do this we liberate our not-Selves. When we liberate a not-Self we are not freeing ourselves for an experience of great affection or delight but rather for an experience of misery, frustration and disappointment. The pain of this makes us think twice about any further attempts at liberation. We are inclined to leave liberation alone for we are not sure if we are going to liberate a God or a Devil.

The purpose of this book is therefore to help towards the understanding of these processes which are essential to life if that life is not to remain static. The theories involved are both old and new. Those that are not new have been found in the general literature of mysticism, religion and philosophy and no attempt has been made to identify the sources. The attempt has been rather to integrate them into some unified structure and to re-express them in another form. Not only will there be an attempt to map out the geography of the psyche and consciousness in general but also to describe the principles which are necessary for a journey and the best way to understand the 'Gods' and 'Devils' that we may meet on the way.

W.A.

FOREWORD

'Very suddenly there came back to my soul motion and sound—the tumultuous motion of the heart, and in my ears the sound of its beating. Then a pause in which all is blank. Then again sound, and motion, and touch, a tingling sensation pervading my frame. Then the mere consciousness of existence, without thought—a condition which lasted long. Then, very suddenly, *thought*, and shuddering terror. . . .'

This is Poe's description of the awakening of his hero in *The Pit and the Pendulum*—the awakening to the torture chamber. I quote it here because it gives a fair idea of our usual assumptions about consciousness. Consciousness is a kind of *light* that comes on when you wake up from sleep. It is not the same thing as thought—that comes later. It is merely awareness.

So how can we speak of the geography of consciousness? Is it not as absurd as speaking about the geography of sunlight? Surely, consciousness is so simple that there is hardly anything to discuss?

But no, this is untrue. The most interesting thing about consciousness is that it can *change*. It can be as cold as arctic sunlight, or as warm and glowing as the sunlight in Turner's *Golden Bough*. When you walk outdoors on the first spring morning of the year, consciousness leaps like a salmon. When you are hungry and you eat a good meal, it seems to sigh and relax. If you get deeply interested in a book or in a discussion, it seems to warm up, like a car engine, and becomes more efficient.

Imagine that you open your eyes in a dark bedroom. You know it is morning outside, because you can see the cracks of light at the edge of the heavy curtains; it looks a cold, grey light, and you suspect it is raining. You think of the things you have to do when you get up, and they all seem dreary. Finally, you yawn, cross to the window, and draw the curtains. Sunlight streams in, marvellously warm. You open the window, and the air smells warm and fresh. The feeling of dreariness vanishes. It is replaced by an eager desire to get your breakfast and get outside. A moment before, your consciousness had been 'hanging back', like a dog that doesn't want to go outside on a cold day. Now it is straining at the lead, pulling you forward.

There is another interesting point about this change in your mental state. When you were lying in bed, you felt *passive*, like a car waiting in the garage for someone to get in and press the starter. And now you suddenly feel active, like the *driver* rather than the car. You feel 'in control'. And why do you feel 'in control'? Because you are now getting a sense of *feedback* from the world around you. When you lay in bed, and looked at the dim outline of the clock and the dressing table, you felt nothing. It would almost be true to say they bored you. But when you look out into the garden, you begin to respond. The things you look at cause a feeling of pleasure, of interest, and this has the effect of making you 'reach out', like a child reaching out for a bright coloured toy. And the more you reach out, the more you notice things—that the grass is still wet, that a dog is barking in the distance, that the windowsill is warm and rather dusty. In fact, you are responding exactly as though you were eating food, and your stomach was reacting gratefully.

This establishes the first point: that consciousness has many levels and many ways of responding. It is not simple but complex. When you are nervous or upset—suppose, for example, that you are going for a difficult interview—you become aware that consciousness is somehow *divided against itself*; this is what causes people to stutter and blush. But for the moment, let us ignore these negative states, and consider the positive ones.

We might begin by talking about ordinary comfort—the feeling you get if you are tired and you relax in an armchair and pick up the newspaper. This is based on a feeling of *security*. If you expected the telephone to ring at any moment, or someone to knock on the door, you would not be able to relax completely, and the feeling of comfort would be weaker.

But assuming you feel secure and relaxed: let us now suppose that, instead of picking up a newspaper, you recall that one of your favourite pieces of music is being broadcast. You switch it on, and the familiar notes produce a feeling of *delight*. This is a word of which Mr J. B. Priestly is fond —and rightly so. 'Delight' describes an important and basic state of consciousness, which all healthy people should experience at least once a day. It may be the feeling you get as you walk into your favourite pub and see that the landlord has lit the fire; or as you pick up a happy baby; or as you start a new thriller by one of your favourite writers in the *genre*. It need not be a particularly exalted sensation: but it has the effect of giving you a pleasant 'lift'.

A stage beyond 'delight' is the sensation that Mr Priestly has called 'magic'. It would not be fanciful to say that 'magic' bears the same relation to 'delight' that a fine wine bears to a good beer. It has a feeling of *rarity* about it, of uniqueness: some peculiar smell, or sight, or sound, causes a tingling sensation in the nerves, a feeling of freshness and newness. It often happens on holidays, or in strange, new circumstances. There is always a certain 'sharpness' about this experience, and a sense that can only be called 'otherness', as if you suddenly smelled a wind blowing from some distant place, with a scent that aroused all kinds of memories.

You could say that 'magic' is a recognition that you have been underestimating the world, assuming that it is boring and limited when it is your own mind that is bored and limited. And this is important, for it brings the great fundamental insight, the insight that has come to all mystics and poets: that a large part of man's misery and pain is his own fault. For nearly three thousand years, cynical philosophers have been declaring that human life is disappointing and brief and miserable, and that the wise man has no objection to dying. But moments of 'magic' bring a clear recognition that the world 'out there' is infinitely interesting—so interesting that if we could 'turn on' the magic at will, we would probably live for ever—or at least, want to. The magic doesn't get in past our senses, which have thick filters on them. Blake recognised that it is as if man lived in a cold, damp cave, when outside there is warm sunlight and fresh air. 'Five windows light the caverned man, through one he breathes the air . . .'

Once this recognition has been grasped, there is only one important problem: how to get out of the cave into the sunlight. For Blake also recognised that through one of the 'windows' man can 'pass out what time he will'.

In saying that, I have defined the central topic of this book, and its purpose: partly to discuss that real, objective world 'out there', that we only apprehend in glimpses of 'magic', and partly to analyse the nature of this 'consciousness' that normally acts as a filter, preventing us from seeing the world of magic.

Consider the development of the consciousness of a human child. He is born into a warm, enfolding world in which his position is essentially passive. He receives food and kisses and warmth, and people try to communicate with him. He is very strongly aware of a *strange* world 'out there', a world of interesting meanings. It is a fascinating world in which older boys go off to the park carrying a cricket bat, or take a tent and go camping, in which fortunate engine drivers visit the seaside every day of the year, in which the mothers and fathers dress up in their best clothes and go off to dinner parties. In which sisters go dancing and get taken to the pictures. And from all this marvellous fairground of a world he is excluded because he is a baby. He can hardly wait to grow up and claim his share of the fun.

By the time he has been at school for a couple of years, he is aware that the world is not quite the carnival he supposed. There are many boring things, like geography classes and Sunday school and visits to old aunts. Still, the world is a marvellous place with delightful interludes like Christmas, summer holidays, birthday parties.

By the time he reaches his teens, he accepts that life is a difficult business. School work is suddenly harder; if he wants a new bicycle or a watch, he has to save for it. In order to cope with this harsher world, he has to throw up defences; he can no longer afford to be 'wide open' and wear his heart on his sleeve. And this is when 'shades of the prison house begin to close', and the world loses its newness and brilliance.

Wordsworth recognised that this 'prison house' is mental rather than physical. Let us look more closely at this process. Imagine a child at the seaside, on the first day of a holiday. His senses are wide open, because he is determined to miss nothing; they record the smells as well as the sights and sounds; the sharp, pungent smell of trains, the salty smell of the wet sand, the iodine smell of seaweed, the caramel smell of candy floss, the ozone smell on the fairground dodgems. . . . This is the intense kind of first-hand experience; he misses nothing. On the other hand, when he gets back home, and goes back to school, a second-hand quality creeps into his experience. His consciousness ceases to feed eagerly and hungrily; it now chews the cud of old experience. But the metaphor needs to be qualified. When a cow chews the cud, regurgitating and chewing the grass, the grass has some nutritive value. Regurgitated experience has almost no food-value.

There is an element of absurdity in this situation. After all, the experience of going to school is as 'real' as going to the seaside. But because he finds it less interesting, he erects inner-barriers against it, and it becomes 'second-hand'.

The deliberate refusal to 'get involved' causes an actual change in the quality of the experience. Imagine a children's party; one child is shy, and sits in a corner, watching the games, passive, rather bored. Then someone persuades him to join in a game; he immediately becomes livelier; he begins to enjoy it. The shyness vanishes. And *because* he is involved, the whole quality of the experience changes; it becomes richer, more nutritive.

The 'shades of the prison house begin to close' because we voluntarily close the senses, disengage ourselves from experience. We do this partly from boredom, partly from fear. We need security in this complex and frightening world, a place to live, a regular income. Like a bird or animal, we want to 'establish territory'; but the territory is psychological as well as physical: familiar faces, familiar words, familiar activities: in short, a daily routine. And this daily routine, with its low-value experience, becomes a kind of prison. When a man gets used to his routine—the family, the semi-detached with a mortgage, the office job—he ceases to live in the exciting, surprising universe of his childhood; he is in a universe of mechanical responses.

The process of becoming a second-hand human being, a kind of robot, may creep up on him so gradually that he is hardly aware of it. All he knows is that life is rather plodding and dull, and there isn't a great deal to look forward to except watching the football on television and having a couple of pints Sunday lunchtime. What has happened is that he has built up an automatic response system, and his true response system has become atrophied. But unless some new experience—pleasant or unpleasant—jerks him out of his dream, he will have no suspicion that he has turned into a kind of robot, and has somehow lost contact with his own life.

In order to understand just how much the adult has lost, we only have to make an effort to recall childhood, the *intensity* of experience, of toys, of Christmas, the smell of toast and mince pies. We then realise that a child cannot imagine finding life dull as an adult. There are so many exciting things that an adult can do whenever he likes: for example, jump in the car and drive to the seaside. How can a child understand that an adult lives in a kind of thick polythene bag that covers his senses, so that driving to the seaside would not be much more 'real' than sitting in an armchair and imagining it?

The reader may be inclined to dispute this statement. Surely things aren't as bad as that? But consider: at this moment, you could get up and go for a walk, or a drive, or perhaps even take a plane ticket to the other side of the world. Why don't you? Because you 'don't really want to', and you don't want to because it doesn't seem worth the effort. The experience would be second-hand—or at least, you think it *might* be. . . .

But although civilised life—and its evasions and short-term solutions—is partly to blame for this unsatisfactory state of affairs, the problem goes deeper than that. We are now speaking of deeply ingrained habits that have been a part of human nature throughout recorded history. Man has not yet evolved the ability to make the best use of his consciousness. He has certain stock-responses to certain situations which he takes completely for granted. These are the real cause of the trouble.

A child setting out on a train journey begins by being fascinated by everything, he cannot wait for the train to start, and when it starts, he stares avidly out of the window. But in half an hour or so, he recognises the over-all similarity of the experiences. He tries to vary these—perhaps by asking for something to eat, or asking to go to the lavatory, or walking up and down the corridor. And if his father asks irritably why he can't sit still, he replies 'I'm bored'. He is implying that interesting experience *ought* to come from outside; it is the business of the world to supply it.

Why does he get so bored on a train journey? If he was at home, he would manage to keep himself amused, even though the scenery there is totally familiar. The reason is that when he gets on a train, he switches into a relaxed, passive state of mind—the state of mind he experiences in a cinema as he watches the story unfolding. But the scenery from the window of a train fails to 'unfold'; it keeps repeating itself. And since he is in a passive and receptive state of mind, he finds it boring. At home, he would know that he has to amuse himself, and so he continues to make some kind of mental effort as he constructs a fort out of a cardboard box or plays with toy soldiers.

His father feels irritable that the child gets bored so easily; he resents not being allowed to read his newspaper or detective novel. In fact, he has no reason to feel complacent. His own capacity for 'paying attention' is hardly more developed than that of a child. He has simply learned to amuse himself in other ways: reading, smoking, drinking, studying the sports page. But he also makes the unconscious assumption that 'interest' should be supplied by the outside world. If he has to sit in an empty room for a couple of hours, and amuse himself with his own thoughts, his morale plummets; depression steals over him like a grey cloud. He feels he needs a stiff whisky to restore him to normal.

On the other hand, anyone who has ever ordered a book from the library, and had to wait months for it, knows that feeling of intense *interest* you experience as you take it home, the feeling that you are going to read it slowly, savouring every word. I recall an acquaintance of mine who loved Proust; he had read *Rememberance of Things Past* again and again; when Proust's early novel *Jean Santeuil* appeared posthumously, he deliberately rationed himself to a single page a day, so that it would take longer to get through.

When you are prepared to spend an evening reading a book and devouring every word, you summon an energy which could be called 'interest energy'. And this interest energy *is* yours to summon; you do it by wanting to, just as you open and close your hand. And here we are getting down to the essence of 'what is wrong with human beings.'

Imagine the following situation. You are in a strange town, staying in a hotel overnight. You know no one; you have nothing you want to read; there are no films worth seeing, nothing on television. You anticipate a very dull evening—and then you see an acquaintance. He is not a close friend; in fact, he is a man you normally avoid, because you find him rather a bore. But you now go and say hello, and feel delighted when he says he has nothing to do that evening either. You actually encourage him to talk about his boring affairs, and after a few drinks you begin to feel that he is not such a bad type after all. . . .

Because you were prepared for a wasted evening, you are willing to devote far more 'interest energy' to your acquaintance than you would on home ground. The consequence is that you do not find him boring.

We describe things as 'boring' as if it were a quality they possessed, like being red or square or shiny. But it is a quality *we* confer on things. And it is because we are only dimly aware of this—of how far we make things boring or fascinating—that we waste so much of our lives.

For to demand a very high 'interest' level from the world is as bad for the business of living as demanding high interest-rates would be for a moneylending business. A very greedy and rapacious businessman might succeed for a while, out of sheer delight in making money. But if he was always trying to get back twice as much as he was willing to give, people would soon begin to avoid doing business with him.

Now unfortunately, our childhood gives us entirely the wrong attitude to living, particularly if it is an easy and pleasant childhood. We get used to receiving, to being fed and protected and amused. And this passive attitude persists into adulthood. When anticipating some new experience—say, going to university or into the army or getting married—we ask: 'I wonder how interesting it will be?' And if it fails to interest us as much as we expected, we become sullen and resentful. And then we wonder why we feel bored and only half alive.

Examine the mental mechanism involved in boredom. Let us suppose you take down a book off the library shelf, and read a few sentences to see if it will interest you. You decide not, and it is as if an invisible hand reached out from your brain and pushed the book aside. You make a movement of rejection. You *lower* your interest, as a cinema manager can lower the lights by pulling on a rheostat. On the other hand, if something suddenly catches your attention, the 'invisible hand' seems to reach out and pull the book closer, and simultaneously, your beam of interest becomes brighter, as if you had increased the current. We are so accustomed to this process that we take it for granted; we imagine that it is the book that is responsible; it is an 'interesting' book. Even in giving this example, I have used a language that makes this same assumption, speaking of 'seeing if *it* will interest *you*', or of a sentence 'catching your attention'.

It is because this fallacy is in-built into our everyday attitudes, our habits, that life is so often dull. We are always making these snap decisions —about whether something is 'interesting' or not. And because we *automatically* dismiss so much as uninteresting, life *becomes* dull and predictable. But again, imagine you are stuck in a strange hotel, with nothing much to do. You glance at the bookshelf in the lounge and there is nothing you want to read—no detective stories, no spy thrillers. Finally, out of sheer boredom, you take a volume of Dickens, whom you have never read, and had never intended to read. And at first your misgivings seem justified; after ten pages, the story has hardly started . . . And then, as you plod on, you find you are beginning to enjoy it. The initial effort was greater than with a thriller, but the reward is also greater.

Notice another thing. If you start to describe the book to an acquaintance, outlining the lot, you discover that this has the effect of increasing your own interest; you want to go back to where you left off reading and find what happens next.

This matter of 'attention' applies not only to books, but to everything we look at. You may be walking down a familiar street. Instead about thinking about something else, try *doubling* your normal amount of attention, looking at everything as if you had just returned from ten years up the Amazon, or were about to leave on a trip to the moon. The immediate effect may be minimal; but if you continue to make this same effort for a few hours, you suddenly make the amazing discovery that you no longer have to 'pretend' that things are more interesting than they are. You are feeling more alive, and things have actually *become* more interesting.

Watch a dog sniffing at a plate of food. Some food scarcely interests him—cabbages and potatoes; first of all, he eats the meat, then laps the gravy, and only then, if he is hungry, turns his attention to the potatoes.

Human beings do this all the time; but we reject far more than we accept. However, what is important, for present purposes, is to grasp that we are 'sniffing' at the world around us every waking moment of our lives, unless we are merely staring blankly into space. This act of deciding 'what is worthwhile' goes on all the time. We have to decide how much 'attention' everything is worth, as if perpetually engaged in haggling with the outside world, deciding how much to pay.

What happens, obviously, is that we strike a certain balance. We decide, roughly, how much 'interest' most things deserve; and since we live the same kind of life every day, this becomes a habit. Unless some unusual circumstance forces us to devote special attention to something, we seldom venture beyond our usual limits. And we never discover that there are many 'bargains' that we are missing through these self-imposed limits—like discovering Dickens because there is no James Bond available.

Literally, we 'don't want to know' what lies beyond the bounds of our usual experience. We don't want to know because we are afraid of the effort —perhaps the pain—involved in extending these boundaries. Once we have learned to 'cope' with everyday experience, we prefer not to introduce further complications.

This is why the adult's world is so baffling to a child. The child can *see* that we are living in an infinitely fascinating world, and the adult apparently has the freedom to explore this world. How can the child possibly understand the barrenness and repetitiveness of the average adult's life? How can he possibly understand that most adults wear blinkers, like the blinkers horses wear in traffic? For who would *want* to wear blinkers when the world is so interesting? How can he understand the combination of fear, habit and boredom that makes the blinkers acceptable to adults?

Even intelligent people wear blinkers; we all do. People become artists, writers, musicians, because they are instinctively aware of these limitations of ordinary consciousness, and want to escape them. Art springs from a recognition that things possess an importance that we fail to accord them in the messy business of everyday living, and that this importance can only be grasped by 'standing aside', by looking at things calmly, with detachment, and without worrying about practical affairs.

But the artist has achieved only a partial solution. He is as prone to boredom as anyone else. In fact, he is *more* likely to drink too much, smoke too much, sink into depression and do something stupid to escape it. In the nineteenth century, hundreds of artists, poets, musicians, rejected industrial civilisation. All recognised, like Wordsworth, that 'the world is too much with us', and that the repetitiveness of everyday experience 'lays waste our powers'. Yet the suicide rate and the rate of early death through illness was exceptionally high among them.

The unsatisfactory nature of 'everyday consciousness' can only be altered through a full understanding of this consciousness. At the moment, we leave the operations of consciousness largely to chance. Our ideas about changing it are crude in the extreme. When we are feeling tense, we may light a cigarette or reach for the whisky. If vitality has sunk too low, we may take a long holiday. These are about the limits of our 'remedies'. Aware of their inadequacy, a younger generation experiments with drugs.

But this consciousness, which we take for granted, is a highly complex *mechanism.* It could be compared to a musical instrument—perhaps an enormous organ, capable of playing symphonies. We use it for picking out simple tunes, the equivalent of 'Chop-sticks'.

Before we can understand the capabilities of the organ, we need to know something about its mechanisms. I do not mean necessarily what goes on *inside* the organ; I mean that we need to know the *purpose* of its rows of stops and pedals. This can be discovered by trial and error and analysis. The present book is an attempt to present the result of this effort at analysis.

CHAPTER ONE

The Fields of Consciousness

This is an attempt to describe the field of man's consciousness in such a way as to relate intense experiences to the everyday world and to that system of universes in which it resides. Intense experiences come to many people and the record of them gives an indication of an order of consciousness quite different from that which we are used to. Between the two extremes of these orders of consciousness can be found a graded series of states which will be set into a structure and related to a theory of existence.

The first step will be to draw attention to the fact that although we find ourselves in a three-dimensional world with a three-dimensional body which is related to a stable time rate, the experience of this world when it is taken within our consciousness no longer remains three-dimensional and stable in time, but is multi-dimensional and multi-temporal. By this is meant our consciousness of physical experience becomes a package of quantitative and qualitative measurements which contains the relevant details of the experience but ceases to be the experience itself. Now this package can be related to other measurements from other experiences of different times in the past and it can also be projected into an imaginary future. The process of valuation, comparison, experimental construction and imaginative distillation goes on within a field of consciousness which, while it uses three-dimensional imagery, is no longer directly tied to this imagery or the time system to which it ordinarily belongs. Eventually it will be shown that our true identity, which is centred in consciousness, exists in other worlds which are related to the physical world and to another but which are nevertheless discreet and functioning under different conditions and with different ends in view.

Because, as previously said, the stuff of experience is multi-dimensional, basic dimensions will have to be found to which the whole volume of experience can be related. This is a difficult task, but it should be tackled in the hope of being able to build an effective structure which can be criticised and improved upon. We will try therefore to take as a basic dimension those conditions of separated unity which give significance to all our experience and which can be thought of as the masculine/ feminine aspects of events, experiences and attitudes. These can form a basis to experience of life and knowledge of ourself and they divide naturally into two aspects of human nature which is the nature we are most concerned with. The masculine aspect of consciousness and events is that which deals with the practical manipulation of forces to bring about specific results. The feminine aspect is that which gathers to itself and gives from itself through its sympathetic ability. The aim is therefore to try to classify consciousness in terms of these two aspects of experience and at the same time draw attention to the fact that it is experience of events which our consciousness and identity is concerned with, not the events themselves. Thus it can classify and orientate experiences in a two-dimensional field which is not a field of occurrences but which is a field of consciousness. For, as already said, experiences of events are the reality of existence for us and not the events themselves. In this way the basic three-dimensional world around us is transposed into a two-dimensional world of consciousness, the vectors of which are—

1. The practical, executive, quantitative, structural and concentrating aspect of events.

2. The sympathetic, unifying, qualitative, content bearing, and diffusing aspect of events.

It is the sympathetic part of our consciousness which brings us into touch with events on an ever widening scale and it is the practical aspect of our nature which manipulates the forces which surround events to influence them in the way we wish. If the practical, masculine aspect of our nature is poor we fail to communicate accurately our wishes to the field of events. If our sympathetic, feminine aspect of consciousness is poor, there is only a small field of events we are in touch with and we do not generate any strong wishes for our masculine aspect to be accurate and effective about. The extreme position in each case is that we may be able to do very little very well or do a great many things but do them very badly. We may be extremely interested in a minute aspect of life or we may be vaguely interested in a very wide field of experiences. It can be seen that the ideal conditions which we are consciously or unconsciously trying to achieve is the best of both aspects of consciousness which is to do a great many things well and to be extremely interested in the widest possible field of life events.

However, before continuing with the construction of the two vectors it must be understood more clearly how experiences reach our consciousness, or are formed in our consciousness. Our consciousness does not experience events themselves but it experiences the signals which our senses transmit which consist of coded replicas of the ingredients of the events which are transmitted along communication systems, the nervous systems, to the brain and thence to the seat of consciousness itself.

Experts know a good deal about the nervous systems and a little about the way they connect up with the brain, but they know nothing at all about the relation of the brain to consciousness except for the fact that certain areas of the brain deal with certain types of experience and certain types of nerve functions. It can be reasonably assumed that the information which reaches the brain is transmitted through some further system of communication to the seat of consciousness. It is because the seat of consciousness is intangible and the communication system to it also, that many people have been lead to try and form a mechanical theory of consciousness in the brain itself. Such theories are not successful for reasons that will be explained.

What concerns us as living consciousness is not the way in which information reaches us, but the valuation and response to information after it has reached our consciousness. If we confuse the function of the channels of communication with the function of consciousness itself, we are in a very different position to the one we are in if we consider that our real identity is detached and relatively remote from events and the signals that bring us the content of events. It is most important, if we are going to understand our real position, to realise that the time and space conditions to which events in the world around us conform have no direct connection with the conditions of consciousness itself. The 'geography' of consciousness therefore bears no resemblance to the 'geography' of the field of events. It is the field of consciousness which we are concerned with here and which it is hoped to map out and describe. This would be the more important field for us to deal with for the reason that it is the world in which we actually exist. We do not exist in the world of events at all, even though most of us consider that we do.

The value of the information received from the world around us is first of all assessed in terms of survival as a physical individual. When this factor is satisfactory we deal with the next line of valuation which may be hunger or physical discomfort. When this aspect is satisfied, we may value events in terms of personality satisfaction such as praise or blame, acceptance or rejection, personal affection or personal dislike, self-importance or unimportance. All these valuations can however be read as aspects of survival in the physical world and in the human group. But when we begin to value experience in terms of comfort we also begin to value things in terms of pleasing or most pleasing, until we slip away from events concerned with survival and measure them in terms of pleasure. At this stage we value things in terms of beauty and lovableness and this leads on to terms of rightness, fitness, goodness, kindness and so on. Later still we may measure events in terms of harmony, peace, serenity and the most ideal of our perceptions. Now this series of valuations shifts from the strictly physical position towards an ideal condition of consciousness which has no direct connection with survival in the physical world as a physical personality. This series of valuations will now give a third vector which is far more important than the first two which have been described, for this third vector is not so much concerned with the measurement of our abilities and fields of sympathy as with the direction in which these experiences lead and the purpose for which they and ourselves are in a condition of existence at all.

Experience of values gives a series of meanings which vary from those which are concerned with survival of the physical body in the physical world to those which are neither concerned with survival or the physical world as such, but which yet concern us deeply as consciousness. Now the third vector can give a gradual blending of these two types of significance which form a system of related experiences which we can verify within our own awareness. It is also possible that the process of growth of awareness consists of freeing ourselves from the attention we have to pay to survival in order that we are able to focus attention more and more on other values which tend towards a condition of idealism. The ideal awareness is not concerned with survival or with personality success, it takes these for granted and concerns itself with qualities which are not connected with time or space, but with the intrinsic worth of the state and condition of awareness itself. This state can be called the attitude of consciousness and it can be seen that this attitude conditions the valuation set upon all experience that reaches us and upon all responses which we in turn endeavour to communicate to others. The basic attitude is therefore like a filter and consequently the series of attitudes we create are also a series of filters of experience and response which give a specific world of existence at each level of attitude. While these levels are non-tangible and in a sense unreal to us, they are in fact the closest reality and form the universe which we actually live in, which is the universe of consciousness. What is called the physical world is of no real importance to us except for the fact that it is the medium through which we receive and transmit communications. These communications are primarily definitions of moods and states of consciousness and only secondarily statements of facts. For in the last analysis consciousness is not concerned with any fact except with the quality of its own state of awareness and the nature of its own filter. We are very interested in the nature of other people's filters for this is a way we can improve on our own attitude. The continuous improvement of this attitude would seem to be our basic concern although it does not appear to be like this, for the reason that we are caught up in the processes of communication which relate our attitudes to one another.

In Map 1, the first two vectors describe the size of the field of interest and the abilities we have to manipulate it and control it. However, these two vectors only refer to one level of our attitudes or our filters. If we wish to describe the whole volume of our experience, we must also include the third vector which describes the series of attitudes to which our interests and abilities belong. Map 2 combines vectors one and two and shows vector three at right angles to them, so that there is a plane of consciousness at each level of this third vector. In Map 3, the three vectors are in perspective so that they show the volume of our total experience which is partly actual and partly potential. In Map 1 the theoretical direction of growth of consciousness from the position of zero along the dotted line gives an ever larger reading along vectors one and two. But to get a more accurate picture of growth, one must imagine this dotted line in Map 3, starting from zero and moving outwards and upwards towards the opposite uppercorner of the cube of the figure (O - Z). In this way the line of growth describes an ever growing reading along all three vectors. This can be called a theoretical evolution of consciousness which is not merely towards a wider field of interest and more developed abilities but also towards an ideal attitude through which the interests and abilities are experienced. As these three vectors are all inter-related, it is probably difficult to progress along one of them without also making progress along the other two. It therefore indicates a type of balanced progression which will no doubt have limits of tolerance, and people wandering outside these limits will experience some strain of a negative type.

The position of zero on Map 3 is a theoretical point which cannot be described for the reason that one can never be sure that any identifiable body does not possess any consciousness at all. Human consciousness certainly does not begin at this point, and it is very hard to decide where along the line of evolution we take up our position. However, we know that from childhood onwards we definitely move along this path of growth, and we remember that there are occasions when we move forward with recognisable swiftness.

One can think of examples of development which are lop-sided and describe characters which result from this. There is the effusive, enthusiastic and over-busy doer of good works, who is also extremely

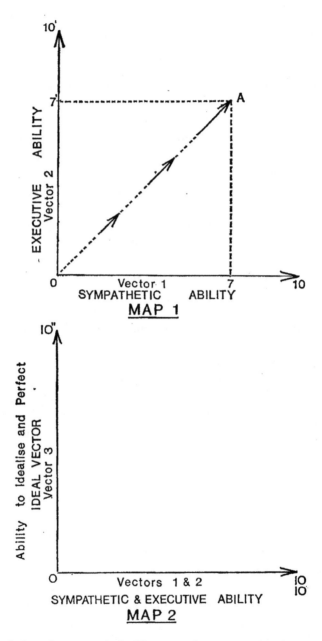

muddle-headed and impractical. There is the extremely clever technician who can manipulate the most delicate situations in the electronic field, but who is lost and helpless outside his workshop. There is also the widely interested and very able businessman who pays no attention to events in the fields of culture or intellect, religion or philosophy. And there is the

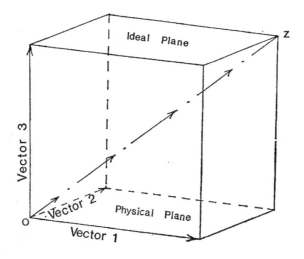

MAP 3

mystical person who endeavours to escape from all contact with the physical world and action of any sort. These extremes are unhealthy from the point of view of the ideal consciousness, for this consciousness should be able to interest itself and be effectively practical in the purely physical world, in the world of learning and culture and in the world of philosophy, religion and mysticism. The ideal consciousness should enjoy this whole volume of experience which the cube in Map 3 describes, and yet it must feel no compulsion to be a part of any of it, for any compulsion would indicate an attachment and therefore an aberration. One must place absolute consciousness and absolute identity outside the vectors altogether. Real being is in this case outside manifestation and one of the great secrets and values we have to discover through the experience of evolution is the realisation of this fact and the significance which it entails.

In order to make this point clearer, we will consider the physical personality and body as a factory and compare our consciousness to the manager of that factory. We know that normally the manager goes into the office of his factory to collect the latest facts about sales and production in order to control the activity of the factory. But we also know that if he is ill and cannot visit his office, he can telephone his assistant and by asking him for certain facts control the activity of the factory as though he were there himself. And of the manager had to go on a trip to America or Australia, he could still get in touch with his office and control the factory. In other words, if he were able to possess all the information he required he would never have to visit his factory at all. He does visit the factory, however, because it enables him to communicate more easily to more people on his staff. His connection with the factory therefore can be described in terms of communication whether he is at the factory or at the other side of the world. His success as a manager depends to a very large extent on the effectiveness of the communication system he has built up between all the part of his concern and himself. If one aspect of his business is in bad communication with him, this is the part that he would expect to cause him trouble. This is true of his production programmes and also of his human relationships among management and workers.

The manager of a factory goes to the factory himself, not to improve production, but to make sure that his channels of communication have been feeding him efficiently with accurate information. If he could rely on the effectiveness of his communication systems and the efficiency of the people involved in them, their honesty and so on, he would never have to visit the factory at all. The effectiveness of his management therefore would not depend upon any special relationship with the factory, it would depend upon his ability to observe all the information given him in comparison to all the information he already possessed. If the manager identifies himself with the factory it is very likely that some aspect of production will appear out of proportion to him. This will cause him to form a distorted picture of the situation in his mind and we can then say that he has become aberrated and less efficient. His best position as manager, as far as we can understand, is to be in a detached position to the production activity in order to see it all objectively and see it in relation to what the rest of the commercial world is doing.

Now we ourselves are like the manager in relation to our physical body and personality. We are in fact not connected to this personality function unless we choose to be. We can best observe and direct the function of the personality by being detached from it and by observing the situation it is in, objectively. So long as we are identified with the personality we must expect to experience its values in a distorted way. We will also get a distorted picture of our nature if our communication channels are inefficient or inaccurate. We will, in other words, only understand what we are and what we are trying to do if we experience ourselves as managers and our physical personality as a factory. However, even the manager is in a subtle sense conditioned by an inner consciousness which dictates to him how he will behave in ethical and other ways. And so with ourselves; we are detached from our physical body whether we like it or not, and we also possess an inner essential awareness within this detached consciousness which we may describe as a first order attitude or filter. The detached consciousness is thus a second order filter and the physical personality is a third order filter. The majority of people are identified with their third order filter, with occasional sensations of the second order. But the time has come when we can solve the outstanding problems of our civilisation by many of us achieving a permanent second order attitude with occasional sensations of the first order. This sensation is forced on us by virtue of the fact that there has been such a tremendous advance along the lines of the second vector which is the vector of practical scientific achievement among other things. If we do not match this sudden movement by a similar movement along vectors one and three, we shall lose our balance and heap misery and difficulties upon ourselves. The progress we must make along the first vector will result in our sympathies bringing us into a condition of unity with all the other peoples of the world and it will also tend to make us feel our world a part of the universal scheme. Along the third vector, the required progress will cause us to be more concerned with the essential meaning of life itself and with those factors which we usually think of under the term 'spiritual'. Of course, the meaning of life itself is for us the meaning of our own absolute existence; we cannot expect to understand any other reality until we understand something of this since this is our primary filter through which everything else is experienced.

It was said previously that we have a good deal of knowledge about the function of our nervous systems and the way in which they communicate information to our physical brain. However, unless we identify the physical brain with thought, feeling and consciousness, it is necessary to propose that our true being resides somewhere other than in the physical function of the physical body. One reason why we tend to identify our consciousness in the head is because our most valuable organs of communication are situated there. If our eyes were places in our left arm, no doubt we would tend to sense that we were behind them, and therefore in our left arm also. As the ears and mouth are also in the head we feel comfortably placed between them all and at the centre of our perception and transmission of information. When the nature of the communication processes associated with the human consciousness is examined, a system which is basically an electronic one is found. This, in its coarser stages, is associated with physical and chemical changes. Unfortunately, because men have not as yet succeeded in understanding much about the function of matter beyond the electronic stage, they are inclined to say that the electronic level of experience is the end of the road. The scientific type of study of these matters is so successful up to this point, that it has acquired an authority greater than that of the theologist, philosopher, psychologist or intelligent human being. When the scientist suddenly stops short in his description of the universe and of man, the temptation to stop short with him is very great. This, however, is most unfortunate, since there is good reason to believe that the level to which science has attained will be found to be very much on the perimeter of our true nature and our true reality.

It must be said, therefore, that something passes beyond the electronic level of function of the human brain and so must pass into a condition of matter which as yet science does not recognise and which it tends to be sceptical about. The scientist, having the authority which we have given him, tends to make fools of us all when it comes to the understanding of consciousness itself. The scientist is not to blame for this however. We are to blame, for the simple reason that we gave our filters to the scientist as soon as we noticed that he was uncommonly successful and full of 'magic and witchcraft'. We were only too pleased to find someone to give our filters to, since we knew they were very important but that they were a great deal of trouble to the owners. We must now face up to this situation and endeavour to create some sort of structure in our understanding, which will bridge the gap between the level of matter which the scientific instruments of our age has succeeded in examining and the stuff of consciousness itself which is the stuff we actually exist in. We must break with the temptation to allow our attitudes or filters to be governed by scientific facts and return to a position in which we remain fully responsible for our own attitudes so that they are the result of our own experiences, valuations and intelligence. The facts which scientists give us are still of great value to us so long as we do not see ourselves as identified with the world which they are taken from, for this world is the world of time and space which is of non concern to our consciousness as such, but is only a means of communication. We must no more identify ourselves with these physical modes of communication than we should identify ourselves with a telephone.

It will probably be a very long time before instruments are able to observe the stuff of consciousness and discover the seat of it. We cannot afford to wait until they do. We must therefore use our intelligent imagination to extend the processes which we have examined, towards the awareness which each of us knows exists. So long as we keep this in terms of a broad and tentative theory it cannot do any harm and may help us a good deal.

There is some connection between our scale of attitudes or filters and the scale of conditions of matter. The structure of matter stems from some sub-atomic level to that of the atom, then the molecule, the cell, the group of cells, to mineral, vegetable and animal structures. From the animal it leads on to the human and we must be prepared to discover that it goes on beyond the human. While all matter is a living 'substance' the substantial part of it is, in fact, non-substantial in the old meaning of the word. Instead of substance we find only organisation of energy. The value of such structure lies in the fact that energy is not pure force, but a composition of force and behaviour patterns. However, a behaviour pattern is not a mechanical function unless we are dealing with a pure machine. If we are dealing with living structures, then we must accept behaviour patterns as being the result of some form of consciousness and purpose. Therefore we must describe matter from henceforth as matter-consciousness, to remind ourselves of the fact that the old idea of substance has been superceded and that the mechanical idea of function has little or no ground left for it, and that it must shortly give way to a theory which allows for elementary occurrences to be the result of consciousness, perception and response to perception. This is an extraordinary situation for us to grasp, since we have been used to the idea that matter is a part of the living scheme of things we call nature but, at the same time, governed by mechanical forces in a purely mechanical situation. It is possible to describe the consciousness of matter as being very different to our own. To get used to this, we have to get used to the spacial proportions of the universe as compared with the spacial proportions of the atom and electron. We must get used to the idea that we have not yet established a definition of the upper and lower limits of consciousness any more than we have established the meaning of largeness and smallness in space. Unconsciously, we all like to feel that the electron is small enough and that nothing could possibly be organised on an even more minute scale. We also like to think that there is nothing larger than a galaxy or a universe. This is all a part of our conditioning as human beings, through which we like to establish the limits of our territory and the exact spot which we call home. When, however, we begin to sense that we are individuals who exist purely in consciousness, we shall be far more objective about our observations of the physical universe and we shall no longer look for a place in it which we call home. Our home will be our basic attitude. This can be a comfortable and happy one or otherwise.

It is necessary to propose some more ethereal order of matter-consciousness, which goes beyond the level of the electronic state; which carries the forms and matrix for communication channels which continue the process of transmitting information from the physical senses to the individual awareness. We may reasonably suggest, also, that this is not just one stage, but, as in the observable world of communication, a process involving many stages and transformations. In our own methods of artificial communication, we use the electronic impulse process in copper wires which we transpose into modulations on radio waves for finer and more remote types of communication. So we may well expect that the more direct impulses of the nervous system are transformed into more ethereal signals in more ethereal conditions of matter-consciousness during their journey to the seat of consciousness. The remoteness of this consciousness depends on the level at which the individual has identified himself and believes himself to exist. If he is identified with his physical body, he will be less remote than if he identified himself with his intelligence/feeling filter and far less remote than if he identified himself with his Absolute Being filter.

The physical nervous system, even though relatively coarse and restricted in its function, is able to supply information to us from the surface of our skin in such a way that we feel we are covered with a sensitive film. When this sensitivity is taken to a higher stage beyond what we can observe as the physical system of communication at the electronic level, the effect will be another, finer network of communication. This super-physical network will be more in the order of radio communication and will therefore be wider and more homogenous in its application. It is not equivalent to a radio network, but it tends more to that order of communication of signals. Similarly, as this network is transposed into an even more ethereal one which is nearer to the absolute level, so the body of communication, or film, will be finer and even wider in its coverage. This system not only makes for more efficient and delicate types of communication, but it also makes for a universalisation of communication. This includes incoming information as well as outgoing information and in this sense it links up with the first two vectors in that it implies a wider field of sympathy and interest, as well as a more developed and efficient executive ability. There is thus a reference between the area of experience at each level of attitudes on the third vector which corresponds to the ethereality of the body of communication. Thus, if the physical body is associated with a number of other bodies of sensibility or communication, they form a chain of exchanges, similar to telephone exchanges, which enable us to be in touch with a whole universe of experiences and valuations at each level of matter-consciousness to which they belong. Our sense of our own identity therefore depends to a great extent on which of these exchanges we are using and which ones we are unconsciously identified with.

CHAPTER ONE: Summary

We receive experience of events as a package of signals. These signals are valued and responded to from the 'inner' worlds of consciousness which are multi-dimensional and multi-temporal. They are discreet worlds, while functioning in a related way, to which a scale of attitudes can be attached. The main theory of this description of the condition of man is built on the strong basis it has in a Masculine-Feminine, Father-Mother current which is concerned chiefly with the creative act of evolving 'children' in order that they should mature into 'friends'. The vectors describe this structure within the field of consciousness or awareness. The third vector shows the scale of evolving attitudes. A scale of matter is also proposed which goes 'beyond' the conditions of matter which we can observe at this time. Matter and consciousness are then tied together as matter-consciousness. A series of bodies are proposed which belong to each level of matter-consciousness and which are a proper part of the whole man. These are called bodies of communication, and we should use them for this purpose rather than identify with them. Successful evolution is thus seen to be a very complicated process which requires great balance and the best of our attention and effort. Fortunately our real nature is so much more able than we give it credit for that the situation is still an optimistic one.

CHAPTER TWO

Bodies of Communication

As the idea of bodies of communication is most important to this theory, and as it may be a difficult proposition to grasp clearly, it will be described further in terms of the diagram called Map 4. At the top of this Map there is a figure of the human body. This body, which is called 'A', is the near physical body of communication which we know as the nervous system and which conforms in shape to the purely physical structure.

Next there is figure 'B' which represents the next highest body of communication and which is composed of a higher frequency order of matter-consciousness but which is still close enough to the nervous system to connect into it and to conform to the outline of the physical frame. The next body of communication 'C' is of a higher frequency matter-consciousness again, but is finer and more diffused than 'B' and has virtually lost the shape of the physical frame. Similarly, there may be further bodies 'D' and 'E' which communicate our awareness to higher frequency levels and which tend towards a wider and more universal consciousness of events. In the lower part of Map 4, these various bodies are seen separately and also related to the levels of matter-consciousness of which they are composed. To visualise these levels of matter-consciousness and bodies as one above the other is misleading, since they interpenetrate by virtue of their widely varying frequencies which may be as difficult for us to grasp as the variability in size of atoms and galaxies. When, however, we do succeed in visualising these bodies as being superimposed upon one another while at the same time being discreet, we will have a picture of the human situation which for our purposes is essential.

Our true awareness as individuals, therefore, stems from the absolute which is free from time and space considerations. Thus the lower the reading on the third vector to which the particular body of communication corresponds, the more the attitude of that body is coloured by the conditions of time and space. The content of time and space considerations in any of our perceptions will therefore be a very helpful indication of the level of the body through which they were communicated. This body is thus the equivalent of a filter to our perception and is also equivalent to an

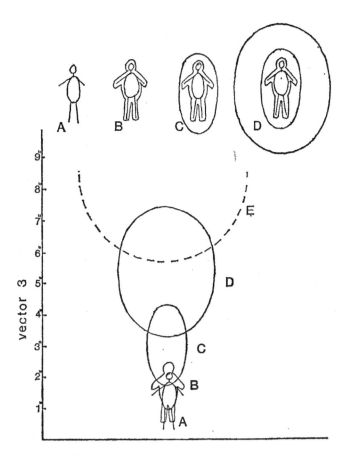

MAP 4

attitude of our awareness. It also tends to capture completely our sense of identity. The reading on vector 3 which corresponds with the quality of our perceptions will indicate to us the type of body that in the main we are using and also where we stand on the scale of evolution. It will help us to identify our possibilities of further evolution and also some of the old attitudes which are holding us back.

It should be remembered that in using diagrams the factual side of the theory is bound to be inaccurate and is not to be taken literally. It is not known if there are seven or seventy bodies of communication between events at the physical level and the seat of consciousness, but probably there are a number and the number depends upon the attitude of the particular individual involved. Since the attitude of the individual corresponds to the time and space content of his perception filters it can, however, be said that the number of bodies of communication an individual is using at any time varies inversely with the time and space content of his perceptions.

The usual or chronic attitude we have to space and time content in our lives is therefore also an indication of our chronic level of consciousness and our position on the scale of evolution. While our position in human society seems important to us and we give a great deal of our attention to it, our position on the scale of evolution is far more important even though we may not give it any thought at all. For while the values of society are mostly man-made and of moderate significance as far as the quality of consciousness is concerned, the values of the scheme of evolution are based on the reality of the Absolute Awareness and they are therefore of the utmost significance and concern our most fundamental intelligence, instinct and well being. When we are aware of numbers, measurements, distances and durations of time, we are caught up in the communication processes which relate experiences of qualities to us and through which we ourselves communicate qualities to other individual consciousnesses. Since our absolute reality is concerned first of all with the quality of its attitude and filters, it is not fulfilling its real need so long as it is paying attention to the means of communicating qualities rather than the qualities themselves. Fortunately the process of evolution tends to overcome this condition by the fact that the higher the body of communication which is reached, the more universal and delicate is the information which it filters into its system and the more partial and coarse the information it filters out of its system. So while the effort is required to reach a higher level of consciousness, when it is achieved it may reinforce our efforts and tend to establish them at a certain critical level. This level is the norm for the particular processing which any discreet body of communication involves and it is dependent upon the frequency of the range of matter-consciousness involved. However, the very long and the very short durations of time, like the very vast and very small distances, do not really penetrate our understanding, and this immunity tends to make us aware of the Absolute state of consciousness in these types of perceptions, which is why we sense a great significance in the experience of eternity and of the split moment of the now. This correspondence is also true of perceptions of the vast Universe and of the tiny atom. Experiences of this sort tend to numb the rational processes of consciousness and prevent us placing upon them the man-made values by which we are largely conditioned.

One of our major conditionings is the idea that there is solid substance on which our physical world is built. It used to be considered that the atom was an indivisible unit of substance which was built up into more complex structures to create the mineral and vegetable worlds. It is now realised that this atom is itself a complex conformation of energies whose paths constitute its 'size', but whose interior is largely space through which various energies inter-relate. Today substance is not a solid but a temporary structure of energy which gives the impression of solidity because it communicates to us something of its nature. If it was not within the boundaries of our perception of communication, then we should say it did not exist. This sort of communication must not be confused with our own human ones, for these communications are in terms of elemental qualities and of energy, and it is in these terms that atoms are communicating to us and one another. We are also conditioned to consider that communications which are not in terms that have meaning for us as humans are not valid communications and do not arise from anything we can class as consciousness. But this again is one of the things that has to be adjusted if we wish to understand the background to human activity. We must be more objective and open-minded about conditions of consciousness other than our own, and we must be more aware of the possibility that categories of matter which we used to class as non-living are not only living but retain their nature and function through very efficient forms of communication. As was said previously, we must not only be prepared to consider that an atom is an entity but we must also be prepared for the fact that it is an entity with a purpose and a responsive awareness.

The position reached when reality is looked at from the point of view of this theory is that what is normally referred to as matter is first of all essentially communication and only secondarily a structure of energies. This is to say that the value of any particle of matter is the quality which it is communicating. This quality is not only the important aspect of the situation to us as conscious individuals, but also to the particle of matter as an entity in its own right. It follows from this that we will be in a much better position to understand the significance of matter and the general ground of the experience we are in if we study and classify occurrences in terms of their possible communication content, rather than in terms of their structure and apparently mechanical function. It may be found that all matter is communication as far as we are concerned. For we are essentially receivers, valuers and transmitters of information and our true nature is awareness itself and in no way directly involved with that part of manifestation which we think of as matter. As far as our true significance and reality are concerned, matter is synonymous with communication. So here we can also say that when we are conscious of matter as such, there is something wrong, for we are not observing the reality of the situation; we have got the wrong set of filters in circuit. When, however, we observe events in terms of their real content, then we shall not be aware of matter but only communication. This means that we are employing reasonably suitable filters for that situation.

The universe of matter-consciousness, which is thought of as the universe of non-living matter, is therefore more accurately a universe of communication. However, the subject cannot be left there since the fact that communication is the chief reality of each individual structure of matter at each level of formation implies consciousness, which in turn implies purposive response and rudimentary desire. But this is what would be expected and looked for if the premise of the theory is near the truth, for it proposes an evolution of consciousness which starts from a point of zero consciousness and progresses from there to what is termed absolute consciousness. We know that human consciousness is well above the zero position. We must expect that animal consciousness will be closer to it, then vegetable consciousness and then mineral consciousness. It would be arbitrary to stop there simply because we are approaching the limits of our observation. Therefore it is necessary to visualise a type of consciousness related to the sub-atomic level of matter and of levels more minute and fundamental than this again. But here there is something of a contradiction, for these sub-atomic levels of matter will be approximating to the high frequency type of matter-consciousness which was proposed as a connecting link between low frequency matter events at the physical level and individual human consciousness at the level of frequency on which its awareness is identified. This creates a very interesting situation, for it indicates that somehow the processes of living consciousness have been made to double back upon themselves, in that we as units of the absolute consciousness are creating bodies of communication and communication channels in matter-consciousness which itself is evolving; but paradoxically, the higher the level of the body we achieve, the more elementary the level of awareness is of the matter-consciousness which composes that body.

To explain this more clearly, a theoretical track of evolution will be drawn against the three vectors. This will be seen in Map 5, together with divisions of this track into consciousness which is sub-human, semi-human, human and super-human. The proportions of these divisions are not important to us at present.

Now in Map 6, the level of the frequency of matter-consciousness is plotted against this evolutionary track and the track of the dotted line which results is called the Life Cycle. This Life Cycle represents a series of conditions of matter-consciousness which are discreet and yet which unite with one another to form a chain of strata of manifestation from the highest level of the Absolute to the lowest level to which it falls. As we see,

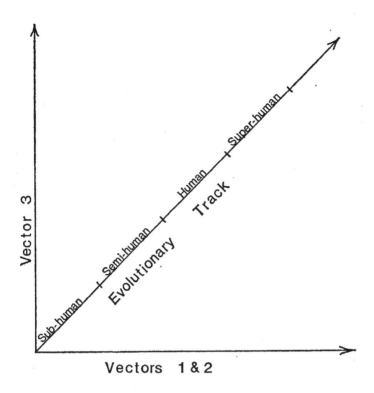

MAP 5

the cycle doubles back from a certain low level towards the level of the highest frequency. The whole of the Life Cycle in this map has not been shown, but in Map 7 Figure 1 it can be suggested that it descends and returns along a rebounding curve with the passage of time. If now the Evolutionary track of Figure 2 is superimposed upon the point of lowest descent of the Life Cycle, Figure 3 is arrived at, whereby we can identify the second half of the Cycle with the Evolutionary Track by allowing it to become curved. Similarly, the first half of the Cycle takes on a movement of the Life Cycle which can be called the Involutionary Track.

From knowledge of physics it can be suggested that this critical point of rebound is the experience of greatest resistance, friction, compression and limitation which life is able to withstand. Beyond this it has not the ability to go, but at this level it experiences the maximum opposition. We can imagine that this level of experience has a great significance in our understanding of the processes of life. The imagination immediately jumps

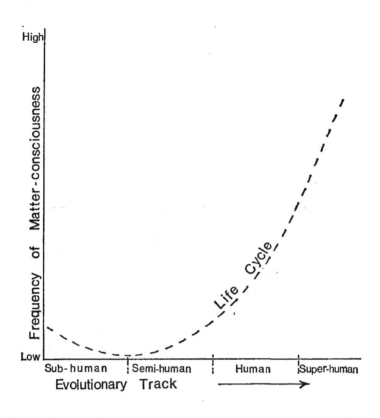

MAP 6

to the possibility that this experience of maximum density is in some way connected with the beginning of Self-consciousness, which is consciousness of the Absolute, which is what is called the beginning of evolution. This process is not unlike the process of spontaneous combustion which occurs at high temperatures and pressures, but in terms of consciousness it would indicate an experience of such magnitude that, although elementary, it is sufficient to spark off the dormant potentiality of a unit of matter-consciousness of that frequency which converts it to a significantly different unit, one which can be called a unit of matter-Self-consciousness which is the beginning of that process in which we find ourselves. When the Absolute has thus achieved its opposite condition from that of Absolute as awareness and purpose, to what we might call absolute non-awareness and non-purpose, it is still in fact completely united with the Absolute but has suddenly ceased to know it. Instead, it knows only an urge towards lessening the restrictions which confine it.

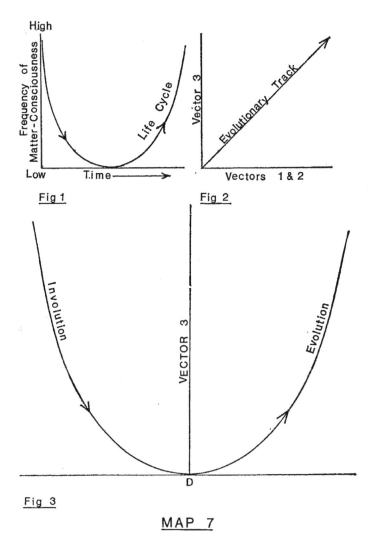

Fig 1

Fig 2

Fig 3

MAP 7

To recapitulate, it was said that matter-consciousness descends along the evolutionary track into conditions of greater density. At the critical point of maximum density it is either unable to survive an increase in density, or the experience is such that it generates a new factor which reverses the process. In terms of consciousness, what changes is the desire. It can be imagined that the desire for greater density is not simply a desire for restriction. This is the negative factor involved. The positive factor is a desire for crystallisation of intention. We ourselves know this to mean that our motives are not clear until they have been involved in action, in which case we find that there is a content which we did not allow for or did not realise existed. It can be suggested therefore that the Absolute is keen to observe the result of its intentions worked out in the greatest detail in conditions of acute differentiation. It is possible that this 'thought' motivates the involutionary process of matter-consciousness, the units of which process are called units of matter in atomic physics and which it must be assumed exist also in sub-atomic states. These units have no tendency to become autonomous and are aware only of the intention and desire of the Absolute.

After the critical experience of maximum density, however, the instinct of autonomy is aroused, although there is little or no room for its expression. Matter is therefore conscious of its condition but is in no way conscious of its-self. Only much later when a great deal more movement is available to it does it begin to achieve rudimentary self-awareness but only in terms of identity as matter. Later again, there is a balance achieved between consciousness as matter and consciousness as a self. This is the stage which we become aware of as the human stage. The next part of the process can be understood to be the elimination of the matter part of our identification complex so that we can become more simply units of Self-consciousness. This would seem to be achieved in the secondary section of the human evolution, the later sections are thus designed to deal with the identification we have with many different selves.

This is the stage that we are at and with which our science of psychology is dealing. The levels of the self associated with here are mainly those loosely called the personality, which are created by our tendency to be identified with our physical response systems. There is also here some consciousness of a higher order which is called the Soul consciousness and which creates a sensation in us of being a very different self to the one of which we are normally aware. However, this is not the end of the process as has already been indicated, and we must later move through an experience of greater certainty about the Soul level of consciousness and from that much more evolved state begin to sense the Absolute identity which is the final and complete experience as far as the evolutionary track is concerned.

It must not be assumed too easily that each evolving unit of matter-consciousness is capable of that ignition experience which causes it to develop towards self-consciousness as we know it. Little of the many factors involved in such a condition is known even if this theory is approaching the truth, and it is also possible that there are other forms of evolution which are not taken into consideration. It would seem that the seeds of Divine Self-consciousness are sown, or have been sown, in amongst the units of matter-consciousness and that the proportion of these seeds to the units of matter-consciousness is very small indeed.

An interesting point to consider here is that it may in some way be possible to connect this idea of evolution with the theory of creation which astronomers hold. At the present time there are two main theories: the steady state theory, and the expansion from a single point theory, and on the face of it we would expect this theory to be associated with the expansion theory, which would be followed by a contraction. This is all a part of a cyclic programme which can be associated with involution and evolution. However, it is possible that cycles of expansion and contraction could occur within larger cycles of expansion only. It may thus be possible that there are many such pulsations as this occurring in the Universe at different stages and on different scales, so that our particular evolutionary scheme may be a relatively local affair in which case we may look for some local contraction in our Solar system while our Galactic system may be in a state of expansion.

CHAPTER TWO: Summary

The idea of bodies of communication is elaborated and the scale of matter-consciousness levels described in terms of frequency. The higher orders of matter-consciousness being associated with higher frequency in the structure of manifestation. The term frequency can be taken to mean vibration or speed of cyclic activity. This structure of bodies of communication is a difficult idea to get used to if it has not been considered before. It may very well take a number of years for the idea really to sink into consciousness even if the reader is sympathetic to it. This whole geography is therefore a system that one must expect to have to adjust to and the adjustment will have to happen in its own proper time. Gradually the system will appear to be like a college of education where each body of communication provides a classroom for its own level of understanding. The idea of matter which is not living in some way, is rejected. It is proposed that the life effort starts at the most ethereal level of creation, descends to the most dense and then returns again to the most ethereal, gathering its harvest as it goes. This is called Involution and Evolution and the harvest is our own fully conscious individuality. The value of the dense level of experience is that it creates for us the greatest opposition and possibility of diversity or uniqueness. Since there are so many units in existence we must assume that only a very small proportion of them are truly Divine Seeds destined for autonomy.

CHAPTER THREE

The Self

Let us consider that unit of the Absolute which is engaged in the Evolutionary process which has just been described. This growth begins from a state of relatively little awareness and continues until it becomes possessed of the consciousness and ability of the Absolute. Since it is in fact a portion of the Absolute all the time without at first knowing it, some theoretical construction must be proposed which can take account of this fact. One way to do this is to use the analogy of a musical instrument which is composed of strings. The classic and simplest variety is that of the harp.

Let us consider that the frame of the harp is 'given' by virtue of the fact that some portion of the Absolute is detached and sown into the field of matter-consciousness, but let us assume that the frame of the harp at first does not possess any strings and is therefore soundless. The analogy consists of likening the process of evolution to the process of placing strings in the frame of the harp and learning to sound them and eventually play music on them. Probably this process is very slow and tedious at first, for until we begin to realise the significance of music we will not have any idea why we are in a condition of consciousness at all. However, once we have 'read' and understood the sublime quality that reaches us through music, then it is possible to sense that we are connected with a purpose, and a delightful one at that. Unfortunately the change between a life which has to be endured and a life which is delightful and creative is one which we have to bring about ourselves. Without the necessary incentive, therefore, this seems like a case of the cart being placed before the horse. One assumes then that if evolution is working among us we are in fact experiencing higher orders of awareness which possess these attributes of delight without always being consciously aware of the fact. This should occur through the faculty of the higher bodies of communication which we are gradually building up and becoming associated with. The information which these partly-formed bodies receive will be of the highest order and will possess something of that delight which is required for progress. The experience of this, however, only reaches us through the fringe of our everyday attitudes and is a part of our awareness which we term instinctive or unconscious. As far as we are concerned, this signifies the fact that the higher order signals are largely 'drowned' in the noisy lower order signals which are not unlike the jamming devices used in radio broadcasting. If we wish to hear what these higher order signals are saying, we must therefore train our lower order bodies to be quietly responsive instead of noisily responsive. This is a way of saying that we must not let our more physical channels of communication become over-excited, for if they do they run away with us and we tend to become completely identified with them.

In the analogy of the harp, the strings which we have to build into our instrument represent an ability to respond from the level of the Absolute to a certain category of experiences. Where these strings are missing, we are consequently weak in our response and likely to transfer the whole occurrence to another part of our harp where strings are in operation. It must be expected that the preliminary part of our evolution will be full of mistakes concerning values and identities for the reason that we simply do not as yet possess the understanding to cope with the situations. The result of these mistakes will be some form of pain and suffering and this seems inevitable unless some direct conditioning or supervision is received. This raises a most fundamental point which concerns our autonomy. Common sense and intelligence tells us that our real value lies in a separate unique identity, even if this is still only at the stage of potentiality. If the scheme of things was not concerned with this individuality, then the ordering of the human world would be much simpler, for we would all be puppets or automatons and do precisely as we were ordered. If God or the Absolute Cause did not choose this way, then it is either because our uniqueness is important to Him or because He enjoys our suffering which is the result of our autonomy. The latter proposition cannot be held seriously. Our intelligence naturally assumes that the attitude we have towards our own physical world, families and children, is not just a chance affair, but stems from some supreme attitude on the part of our Creator. It can be imagined, therefore, that our relationship and value is to our Absolute Parents something like that of our children to ourselves, but since it occurs at a much higher level, it must be more ideal and detached from space/time considerations.

The analogy of the harp, taken with the fundamental idea that the purpose of manifestation is to preserve as well as to bring to life separate individuality as a self-conscious experience, gives us some reasonable cause for the fact that God allows suffering and evil to exist. It also explains why so many mistakes are made and why it is so hard to believe we possess Divine instincts. It can be suggested that there is some sort of Divine permutation taking place, through which all or many of the qualities of the Absolute are being mixed and re-mixed and that the results are to be established in Reality in terms of living individuals. This would be a fair assumption and would account for many of the facts, but it would presuppose that there is some continuation of experience after the occurrence of physical death. However, we have established a reasonable system which can take care of this in our theory of bodies of communication at various levels and frequencies of matter-consciousness, for while the physical body of communication obeys physical laws of disintegration, the next higher body is not subject to the same laws and we can expect it to be not only different in attitude but also different in time scale. Similarly, the body of communication which is more ethereal than that again, we must expect to be more ideal in the nature of its filtering processes and less subject to our concept of time. The number of abilities of response possessed in our True Being or Harp is therefore connected to our level of evolution and the type and number of bodies we are filtering experiences through. When the physical filters are dissociated from our identity at the change called death it will be natural to gravitate to the next highest body of communication and to identify with its attitude and worlds with which it is in contact. If the chronic attitude is relatively low, then one must expect to remain attached to bodies and conditions approximating to the conditions of Earth. If the attitude is relatively high then one can expect to gravitate to a higher body of communication at the level approximating to what is called the Soul level where our ideal and spiritual inclinations will be given means of expression and fuller and more responsive conditions. If, however, experience in the physical world is not complete in that it has not enabled us to build in those responses which can only be gained at the physical level, then it is possible, consciously or unconsciously, to wish to return to Earth conditions and be drawn to a certain type of situation depending on what one merits and what one is attracted to. If the evolution is not very progressed, almost any situation will do, but if it is well progressed then the type of parents and type of opportunity available will be most important because we will be attempting to master certain specific experiences and abilities. It can be understood that we will tend to be associated more and more with a certain group of people who possess certain qualities. If these people ill-treat one another, they will take it in turns to bear the brunt of such treatment until they learn better. Similarly, good parents will attract higher-level children and give to them high-tone potentialities of which the children are able to make good use. Although it would seem right for all children to have the best parents, this is not possible and would in any case be a wasteful process, since it would reduce the quantity of experience available. Children who are not highly evolved are not able to take advantage of certain conditions which more evolved souls are able to do. If, of course, a large number of ideal parents were available, this would be the best possible thing, but we know that this is not the case. While all children look much alike and behave similarly, it cannot be allowed that they all have the same potentialities available. The potentialities are there in every case but if they have not been made responsive, they appear not to be present. Only so much can be done in each life time and we are only able to educate responses which in fact have begun to show life.

The idea of evolved and more ideal families must not be confused with human aristocracy, or with wealth, for these are only a measure of certain values which do not relate to True Reality at all. But probably nature produces an aristocracy of its own which is measured in terms of evolution and has none of the conceit and pride which is a part of any human aristocracy. The true aristocracy is measured in terms of understanding and responsibility and may appear in any level of our human society.

The process suggested, whereby responsive abilities are built into identity at the Absolute level which can be called the True Self, will enable us to understand and accept more easily the concept of sin. Whether we admit it or not, the sensation of sin affects us all profoundly and if we are to accept the teaching of original sin which the western churches give out then we are in danger of putting ourselves in a very wrong and negative position. The process of learning by mistakes, which in science and engineering is called the process of trial and error, is confused with the notion of sin and wickedness. This presupposes that we are either put into the world as perfect beings who should know better or we are put into the world by a sadistic God who knows we are imperfect but who punishes us for being so. In the first case there would seem little point in going through the process if there is nothing to learn. In the second case one is confronted with a dichotomy which is so absurd that it could only be the result of human aberration. Instead of the teaching of original sin, it might be well to substitute the teaching of original fallibility. The difference between fallibility and sin is that the first is expected to be indicated by suffering imposed by our surroundings, but the second is expected to be indicated by suffering imposed by God. Obviously the two are liable to be confused and if the second is chosen, the person concerned is in a most difficult and hopeless position, for he is confronted with a Divine example on a cosmic scale of his own immature understanding and development. We cling to the idea that God is concerned with us as individuals who are responsible for their own actions and we cling to the idea that we are not perfect but are in the process of attaining perfection. Yet we cannot bring ourselves to conceive of the fact that we were born with shortcomings instead of sins. This idea of sin is perhaps applicable to those of us who deliberately repeat actions which we know are wrong and which we know will harm other people and which we are in a position to prevent. But if we have reached the stage of knowing an action is wrong it may not be realised how it is harmful to others and even if so, we may not be in a position to prevent it. If, on the other hand, we do something harmful and wrong because we know no better and are unable to respond with Absolute Awareness to the situation, we can hardly be blamed and we would certainly not have opened ourselves to something akin to Divine wrath.

The main trouble with the idea of original sin is that it consciously or unconsciously causes us to associate the very core of our being with something rotten, and this something in turn is unavoidably associated with the act of our creation on the part of God. Since the core of our being is where our Absolute potentialities lie, and since this highest and truest part of our nature is the source and mainspring of our effort and 'salvation', the idea of original sin replaces that part of our nature which should be looked to for the solution of all our problems, with some negative and evil presence. If this doctrine is seen from such a point of view, it becomes apparent that instead of influencing us to become humble and repentant and aware of our natural shortcomings, all the teaching of original sin does is to make us bitterly aware of the unjust and hostile attitude of the source of Being. Since it is realised now that the unconscious and deeper consciousness of our nature has a profound and overriding effect on all our conscious deliberations, and since it is also discovered that this unconscious part of our nature has a very strong sense of justice, right and wrong, sin and punishment, virtue and reward, one can see that this fundamental conditioning aspect of our awareness is thrown into a hopeless and distorted state by prevalent religious ideas. Until the idea of sin is replaced with the idea of shortcoming, we will be destroying effectively the very purpose of religious and spiritual effort, which is to become trustful of and acquainted with, first of all the Divine qualities of God and secondarily the Divine qualities of our own real nature. It is quite obvious why God is described as forgiving our sins before we commit them—it is because He realises only too clearly that we must continually make such mistakes before we can be of any value to Him or to ourselves. It is not God who has suggested to us the idea of original sin and the necessity of being punished for the results of such sin, it is our own superstitious and unintelligent interpretation of the world around us that has led to this state of affairs. It is our own lack of forgiveness and our own inability to feel responsible for our actions and efforts that have led us to this point of view.

Our indolence is fully borne out by the fact that we link the idea of inborn sin to the idea of Divine intervention (in the form of Grace for our salvation) in such a way that we put the whole process of our qualitative and spiritual development firmly into the hands of outside agencies, so that we can sit back and do nothing for ourselves and still blame someone else for whatever happens. Unhappily, in this respect the purposes of our Creator would appear to be just the opposite, for in order to become and remain true and autonomous individuals who are alone capable of sustaining anything but mechanical values, we have got to develop through the results of our own spontaneous actions and desires. Whereas we are quite willing to believe that, in the world of our western civilization at the physical level, we will only acquire what we want through taking a businesslike advantage of the opportunities that arise and by seeking to create such opportunities if they do not arise, when it comes to spiritual matters, our attitude is totally different and passive. We even wait and hope for 'something' to happen to us in this respect without even having a desire for such a happening, so that our 'hope' is in a peculiar way an inverted one. This inversion is very significant, for it seems to stem from the fact that spiritual and religious effort is associated with pain, suffering and punishment, for the image of such a life is founded on the fact that we try to believe that God tortured and punished His own Divine Son for the sake of our spiritual progress. If God would do this to His own Son who has actualised His Divinity, how much worse will He not do to us who have actualised very little of our Divine potential. Again it does not occur to us that it was we ourselves who punished this Divine Son of God, as we continue to do so in ourselves and in others, when the fact of its 'difference' to our normal attitude comes to our attention. The fact that God 'allowed' us to torture His Divine Son is the true significance of the crucifixion symbol, for it indicates clearly to us that the principle of non-interference must be somewhat more than a little important, and that this freedom we are forced to possess and keep, even though many of us would gladly shed it, is the basis of our intrinsic value. It also shows that this principle allows us not only to attain our Divine potential but it also allows us to destroy this Divine potential. The choice will constantly remain ours whether we like it or not.

The nearest it is possible to come to an understanding of the idea behind the teaching of original sin, is to understand that the shortcomings of each generation are built into civilization in terms of habits and attitudes. These create an atmosphere which we are born into and which we absorb before we can criticise and reject it. In this way we do indeed act as though our wrong behaviour was in us at birth, but in fact this is the result of the distorted atmosphere of our way of life combined with the natural weakness of our True Being which has only partly actualised its potentially Divine capacities. Wherever situations of physical experience should have been dealt with by a portion of our harp which does not possess strings, there we must expect to find wrong response and apparent sin. Those who have a relatively full set of strings can fight against the wrong attitudes they are born into and overcome them. Those who have very few strings are bound to become victims of these wrong attitudes.

There is one more factor which must be considered, although it may seem at first to be rather involved. This is the factor which concerns the term of existence or life of the lower bodies of communication and their possible influence on a recurring life at the physical level. This factor rests upon where our chronic attitude lies on the third vector and how much aspiration we possess towards ideal values. If our chronic level of consciousness is low and our aspirations feeble, then at the transition of physical death we will gravitate to a level of matter-consciousness almost identical with the physical level we have been used to. In this case we will continue to live and experience much the same conditions and the same wrong attitudes and emotions. If all our attention is given to such low-level bodies of consciousness they will be greatly vitalised so that when the next transition occurs, which is caused by us requiring to return to physical level experience, these lower bodies will still be active and the new-born child will tend to become associated with them and carry on the more automatic responses which are also associated with them. Ideally, when death at the physical level releases us from the physical body of communication, aspirations in the physical life should have been strong enough to enable us to gravitate to the level near that of the Soul or higher. In this case, the lower bodies of communication will be de-energised and will have time to become dissociated and return to the background material from which they were made up. Thus the individual involved is able to shed all those wrong attitudes which are rife in the world and which act as a perpetual barrier to progress. Consequently, when another physical life is entered into, it is done so with comparatively unhindered bodies and with a greater chance of making progress. This idea reflects the Eastern Doctrine which concerns the wheel of life and death to which we are tied. When looked at in this way, it is possible to understand how in fact one can become enslaved by this process and that the cure for it is to attain an optimum level of consciousness, idealism or aspiration through which enough time is given the lower shackles, between births, for them to become deactivated and harmless to our next physical life. In this respect, we can become almost unable to help ourselves, due to the fact that we are steeped in wrong modes of thought and emotion from which no respite can be gained through what should be a natural course of elimination. When the tone of a whole civilisation sinks below this optimum level, it signifies that to a large extent evolution of consciousness has ceased, even though the evolution of the man-made culture concerned may continue. This man-made aspect of culture can become very wide and complicated as well as seemingly sophisticated without the consciousness involved moving either upwards or downwards on the third vector. As far as reality is concerned, a Saviour is a highly-developed individual who is capable of showing and infecting us with high-tone attitudes. If we absorb these attitudes, they do in fact save us from what would otherwise be an endless, painful and useless situation. Such rescue operations would not be necessary if a large number of people had not at some time consistently chosen wrong attitudes, so that the force of their way of life became strong enough to amount to a psychological infection and disease which later spread to the whole world. For fundamentally, the potential consciousness which we possess is pure, in the sense of being free from conditioning circuits, and is just as capable of developing towards an ideal way of life as towards a distorted and conflicting way of life. The difference to us is most important, since it indicates whether we are going to progress with great suffering or little suffering. It can be understood that the natural background of our world is designed for progress in evolution, so that if we resist such progress, the tensions we build up at all our levels of consciousness will grow progressively more severe and uncomfortable.

CHAPTER THREE: Summary

Each individual Divine Seed or child is engaged in making actual the abilities it inherits as potentialities only. To try and describe this process, the analogy of the harp is used, because it helps us to understand the significance of the blank spots in our nature which seem to us to be like original sins but are in fact more like unawakened aspects of our nature. This goes on to excuse us our sins and makes them appear more like an honest endeavour to learn by trial and error. While error has repercussions, these simply draw our attention to error and are not to be taken as a form of punishment but more as a form of help. It often feels at the time more like punishment but this is because we have failed to understand the long term purpose of our existence. At the time of physical death, our physical body is taken from us and we are left with the remaining bodies. Some of these may also be taken from us later so that we understand better how not to identify with them. At a certain point in this process we are high up the scale of evolution and really beginning to understand what reality is about. This causes us to see the value of physical level experience and we set about returning to physical birth again, for we see that in 'heaven' there are many things we cannot do which we wish to do and learn about. We return to a special parent at a special time to get a special experience. Eventually we touch upon the Christ consciousness which is the touchstone or catalyst of our system. This gives us special help to understand.

CHAPTER FOUR

Circuits

An example of the complexity of the transformation of signals which communicate the content of events to consciousness is shown in the construction of the human ear. Instead of being able to hear sounds directly, what we discover is that there are at least six distinct phases in the communication process between the sound waves in the air and the physical brain. How many further processes there are between the physical brain and our consciousness we do not know, but the number is in direct ratio to the degree of idealism which the particular individual has achieved which results in the chronic level of awareness.

These phases are:

1. Sound waves are channelled through the trumpet of the outer ear to the ear drum.
2. The ear drum vibrates against a structure of three very small bones in the middle ear composed of what are called the hammer, the anvil and the stirrup.
3. The stirrup, which rests against the inner ear, transmits the vibration to the liquid which fills the shell-shaped inner ear.
4. The liquid transmits the vibration throughout the inner ear to the nerve ends of the auditory nerve.
5. The auditory nerve ends translate the vibrations into electromagnetic signals.
6. The auditory nerve transmits the signals to the brain.

This process is shown in Map 8 and is further complicated by the fact that there are three mechanical movements in the bones of the middle ear. On reaching the brain, the signals enter into the structure of brain cells of which there are a great many and about which relatively little is known. Only after the physical brain has dealt with the signals do we eventually hear the sound being transmitted. But of course we, as consciousness, never hear anything. All we are really aware of is the signal stage of the signals which indicate to us that a sound has occurred at the physical level. If there is some distortion in the channels of communication, we will thus get

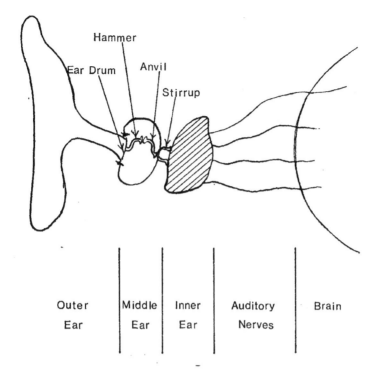

Outer | Middle | Inner | Auditory | Brain
Ear | Ear | Ear | Nerves |

MAP 8

a distorted impression of the occurrence. If the signals are side tracked or if they are dealt with by some sort of automatic response, then our real consciousness may not be aware of them at all. This process applies to all the other senses as well as hearing, but it applies in particular to that type of hearing which is concerned with the reception of speech communication and that type of visual communication which is concerned with our personality level of experience, for these particular communications we tend to label and sort into categories which are covered by automatic and compulsive responses.

Psychologists have discovered that a great many responses to experience or occurrences are dictated by mechanical activities in our nature and that such activities cannot be said to be under the control or valuation of the real individual consciousness concerned. What has happened is that at some time the individual has had to deal with a type of happening which has been associated with a strong sensation of pain or pleasure or some such basic valuation. The occurrence was such that the factors involved prevented the individual from making the response in a confident way from the centre of awareness, according to inherent capacities. The response was in some way enforced and was valued as the safest or most reliable response, whether painful or otherwise. Because this process occurred without true valuation but was the result of enforcement, there was no suitable place for it to be stored in the nature of the true consciousness, for this can only store intelligently understood responses. This intelligence stems from the nature of absolute consciousness itself. Therefore this enforced reaction was stored as a source of response somewhere in the system of circuits themselves. This reaction can be likened to an enlarged and overactive channel, which not only connects directly into some response pattern but also tends to channel stimulus which is not connected with the original occurrence or even with closely related occurrences. The size and sensitivity of this particular circuit tends to cause it to be activated by and consequently to interfere with a host of unrelated occurrences. Let us try and clarify this point by looking at Map 9. In Figure 1 is shown a point C which represents the individual consciousness against a certain reading along Vector 3. The base of the figure represents the passage of time and the point A represents an occurrence at the physical level whose content is transmitted along channels of communication in matter-consciousness of different grades until it reaches consciousness at C. The content of the occurrence is then valued by C and a suitable response formulated which is sent back along the communication channels to the physical level at B. This could be a normal unaberrated response to a physical level situation. However in Figure 2 is shown what would appear to an observer to be the same situation as Figure 1. But in this case the transmission of the content of the physical occurrence has stimulated an automatic circuit which is energised into operation at S.S. and thus translates the stimulus into a conditioned response which returns to the physical level at B and appears to come from the True Consciousness at C. This, however, we understand to be a false circuit, and it is in fact a short circuit, for it has cut out the real individual consciousness from the situation. If there are many of such false circuits in the bodies of communication of the individual, then these form a personality of their own which is not directly connected to the true person and not under the control of the individual. In Figure 3 are plotted a series of types or categories of experience from 1 to 7 against readings along vector 3. In the vertical column of each of these categories is drawn a line or lines which represent barriers or false circuits and the size of these barriers indicates just how much of that category of occurrence they filter off into an automatic response. Type 1 is half filtered at a low level of matter-consciousness and attitude, which also indicates that it is diverted to a

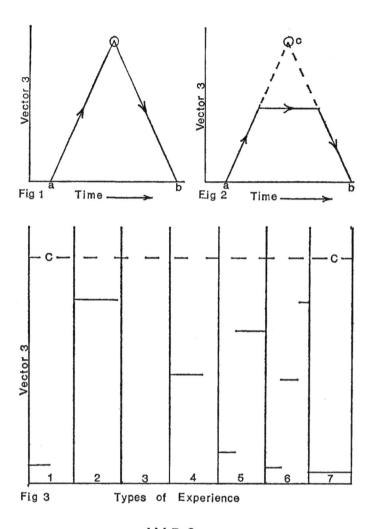

Fig 1   Time ——→

Fig 2   Time ——→

Fig 3   Types of Experience

MAP 9

mechanical response close to the physical level of occurrence and remote from the chronic level of awareness of the true individual consciousness at C.C. Type 2 is badly affected but at a much later stage in the process of communication nearer to the level of proper consciousness, and Type 3 is a clear variety which is dealt with from the true centre of consciousness and which produces relatively high tone responses. Type 4 has a half block half way towards the chronic level. Type 5 has two circuits which come into play at two different stages of transmission and which between them cause a complete blockage to consciousness. Type 6 has three such distorting circuits and Type 7 has a very heavy and complete block at a very primary level of communication close to the physical level, perhaps in the very nerve system of the physical body itself, which would produce very basic distortions. The ideal is to have very clear channels of communication in all seven categories of occurrence. But even when these channels are undistorting, the true consciousness itself has still a partly undeveloped response system, since it has not yet built in all the strings into what has been called the harp of its Absolute identity. We are thus able to visualise just how far away from the truth of any situation we can get, when not only the attitude of our consciousness is wrong but, in addition to this, the circuits which bring information to this consciousness fall down on their job and produce distorted and garbled versions of what has occurred.

To explain further what is meant by Personality, Soul and True Self, there is in Map 10 Figure 1 a diagram which suggests for our purpose the position of Personality. This is a transforming and communicating set of bodies which are a combination of the physical body and the Absolute consciousness of the individual identified with the physical body. This brings together the physical flesh and bone structure, the nerve system, the brain and the lower frequency order of super-physical matter (This has not yet been identified with scientific instruments.) These lower order bodies can be called the lower emotional and lower mental bodies for the sake of convenience, but too much importance must not be attached to any of these labels, for one must expect them to be found to be incorrect in practical detail. Figure 2 is an indication of the Soul complex which is made up of the middle frequency bodies of communication. These are formed by the interplay of True consciousness with Personality. This means that the individual is identified with a strata of attitudes and qualities which express the idealism of the Ideal and Divine levels of consciousness as a compromise with physical world requirements and habits of thought as they appear to the everyday experience of the Personality. It might be said that the attitudes of the Soul represent the Quality of the Absolute expressed in terms of physical level experience, so that they lose something of their innermost meaning while gaining ease of application to physical situations.

What is termed the Absolute Self or Real Self can be represented for this purpose in Figure 3 of Map 10. While this shows the position of the complex of bodies of communication at the higher levels of vector 3, it does not explain that the Absolute exists outside what is considered to be manifestation, so that in this diagram it is either consciously or unconsciously still identified with manifestation. However, if the position and nature of the Absolute individual were explained further, there would be no means with which to do it and for these purposes the diagram shows

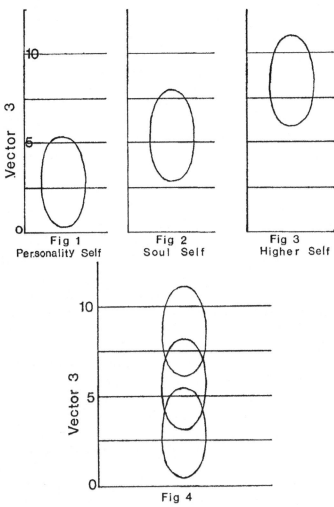

Fig 1
Personality Self

Fig 2
Soul Self

Fig 3
Higher Self

Fig 4
Whole. Consciousness Complex

MAP 10

what is of practical interest. This Absolute self is in a position on the Ideal vector to experience and express the highest qualities and attitudes without distortion or compromise, for the nature of matter consciousness at this level is extremely fine, responsive and vital and almost devoid of the density and friction which is associated with physical matter. The experience of existence at this level of manifestation must consequently be blissful, exhilarating and free in the sense that will be explained later. Since time is the result of friction, viscosity and inertia which results in opposition to movement, communication and adaptability, and since the actual experience of time as it comes to us is the same experience as space, it is the essential content of movement and the experience of movement. If we, at the physical level, cut ourselves off from all movement in the world about us, we will cease to get any sense impressions and shortly experience the feeling of 'being' as distinct from 'living'. This sense of being, without time or space considerations or movement, is close to the true condition of Absolute consciousness. For while we still get some sense of continuing identity in some form of time sequence, this time sequence is not linked to anything which we can identify. The result of this experience is that we are made more aware than usual of the fact that the innermost consciousness is concerned with qualities and attitudes which it has to learn to generate on its own without outside stimulus. When it has learned to do this, it has also learned to be truly creative and may be said to be God.

Figure 4 is a diagram which represents the chain of the three main transformer complexes and thus the three main sources of identification which are available to the individual when he is in touch with a physical body. It is misleading, however, to imagine these bodies related in this drawn out fashion since they are amalgamated in a far more subtle and interpenetrating way, but for the sake of clarity, their relative structures must be indicated in some distinct way.

To go one stage further, in Map 11 these three complexes are shown in terms of their partial development and partial reactive conditioning. If the dotted lines are the possible development of each body and the firm outlines are the actual capacity for response of each body, then the shaded area in each actualised body is the amount of response which is liable to be governed by false circuits. The unshaded area shows the relatively clear and unhindered capacity of each body. The higher body may be relatively undeveloped in relation to the lower body and consequently more tenuous and divorced from lower order experience. Also, each body, while it can be more or less developed, can also be classed in terms of conditioning which results in compulsive and mechanical activity. The Personality can therefore be called the True Personality if it is clear of compulsive circuits, or it can be called a False Personality if it is largely conditioned by compulsive circuits. In the first case, the personality is an appropriate and very valuable part of the whole individual. In the second case, the false personality is not only a distorted aspect of the individual but can either cut itself off from the True Consciousness or so enslave this True Consciousness that it virtually has no more control over the situations it is in.

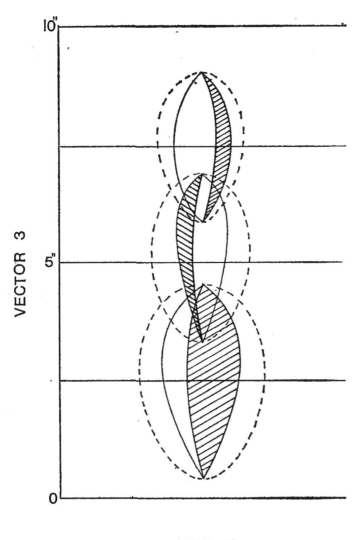

MAP ll

As Evolution proceeds, so the higher bodies become more developed and free from false circuits and perhaps the lower body eventually becomes smaller again. But to begin with, the individual consciousness believes itself to be identical with, firstly, the physical body, then the physical personality, then the Soul personality, then the Soul, then the Divine Soul and lastly the Divine Self. However, throughout all this process of changing identity, it belongs in fact to the Absolute level of consciousness without being aware of the true situation. The process of awakening and

Self discovery is one which we are not unfamiliar with, but the extent to which this process goes and the scale on which it exists as potentiality are something which is hard for us to believe. It is hard enough to grasp the meaning of the astronomical discoveries which scientists are making. The tremendous distances and numbers of enormous galactic systems are things which our rational minds cannot really take in, for these quantities do not have any experienced significance for us as human beings. Similarly, faith in the potential of our own Divine Nature does not have any sufficient meaning for us until we begin to have experiences of higher orders of consciousness. However, once the more sublime responses in our nature are sensed, then this does not help us to feel also that, through the scale of the atomic universe and the astronomical universe is numerically and physically fantastic, the qualitative significance is not so great as that which we have access to within our own living consciousness. This experience helps to reverse the domination which the physical universe has over us.

Another, more graphic, way of showing the position and function of false circuits and the way they create a False Personality is found in Map 12. Figure 1 is another expression of Figure 3 Map 9, in which circuits on several categories of experiences or events are shown in their state of severity against their position on the the third vector. In this particular case, there are several more false circuits but they are focussed on to the position of the True Centre of consciousness at C. The false circuits are indicated by the lines cut short. The whole is outlined in a triangular shape to indicate the outline of the personality-soul complex which is more developed the lower it relates to the physical level. If it can be imagined in Figure 2 that these false circuits can reach a stage of complexity and sensitivity whereby they begin to activate one another through the cross connections lined in on the drawing, it can also be imagined that they readily make up a comprehensive reactive unit called the False Personality which takes over a portion of experience and response from the True Centre at C. In this case, the outline of the personality-soul complex is shown with a restriction forming towards the apex. This signifies the beginning of separation of the True Consciousness from what had previously been its proper personality under its proper control. Figure 3 goes a stage further and indicates an almost entirely separated Soul and Personality. When this happens in life, that life is wasted from the point of view of evolution since the valid centre of consciousness has been divorced from life experience and may as well not be present at all. Worse than this, such a divorced personality still appears to others to be valid since its responses seem to come from some centre of consciousness within. However, the diagram shows that this is not the case and that such a

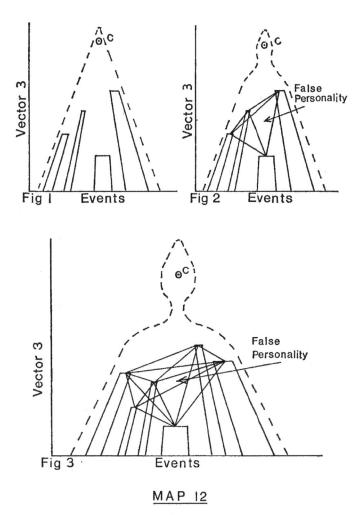

Fig 1   Events

Fig 2   Events

False Personality

Fig 3   Events

False Personality

MAP 12

personality is virtually dead. A personality of this sort can be understood to have a very bad effect on its surroundings, in that it destroys other people's faith in the validity and possibility of human nature. It would not be difficult for such a person to commit atrocities, since its proper qualitative judgement simply does not exist. This type of separation can be called compulsive or accidental, but there is another type which is the result of the Soul consciousness deciding to withdraw or separate from its personality deliberately. This can be due to a false circuit forming in the Soul complex itself. It can be readily seen that the higher the level of the false circuit and the higher the body of communication it forms in, the more severe and comprehensive is the effect. This severity relates more to the individual consciousness concerned and is not always obvious to other observers, since they only see the physical results. The habits of the physical personality can maintain it in activity long after the higher and True Consciousness has been cut off. When dealing with cases of psychological illness, it is difficult to tell whether the condition is an effect of the higher nature deliberately refusing to participate in the life of the physical personality, or whether it is the result of physical disease or false circuits. If the difficulty is the result of a higher-level decision, then this may not be anything more than a wrong valuation from the process of trial and error, but since it occurs at a higher level, such a wrong valuation has a very sweeping effect. This sort of condition is one which responds well to therapeutic discussion, but if it is treated as a form of illness or 'insanity' it may lead to this condition as a result of shock and as a result of the treatment implying 'insanity'. To treat a high-level decision as a form of insanity is bound to be the worst possible thing to do. When we realise that a whole civilisation can be suffering from certain delusions, then we must be very careful not to confuse normality with sanity. The decision to opt out of the physical-plane life is not always the result of wrong decisions as such, but is more likely to be the result of powerful emotions of injustice and futility which may have a very reasonable basis. We must not allow ourselves to think of a physical personality which has become aberrated or peculiar as being the outward expression of a wrong mode of consciousness. It may be the outward expression of a very powerful feeling of revolt which is based on noble and high-tone values and a sensibility to perfection and idealism which have been found too rare in the physical environment. One must expect, on occasions, to be able to rehabilitate such a consciousness through tactful approaches. It must be remembered that any low-tone behaviour shown to such an individual will only reinforce the correctness of the decision in question. It would be true to say that much of our treatment in these sort of cases is low tone and mechanical because we cannot believe that there is a proper consciousness present which is valuing our behaviour towards it. Unfortunately, there are many conditions of a similar nature which are the result of physical and brain abnormalities which need a great deal of study before they can be separated out from one another. Until we have far better facilities for dealing with mental illness, we cannot expect the time and effort to be available for such treatment. One of the many problems we have to face in dealing with any condition is to assess the workings of the unconscious which may be either of a higher level or lower level order compared to the level of the conscious rational nature. This problem will be studied through a closer understanding of the bodies of communication with which consciousness identifies itself either correctly or incorrectly.

CHAPTER FOUR: Summary

When we follow through the processes by which physical sound reaches our nervous system, our brain and then our awareness, it becomes obvious that we must expect a large number of transpositions. This change of one type of signal into another must continue to some final stage which we call the Absolute and it is here that our real identity resides and it is from this identity that we get our true understanding and response to events. If at some stage there is a fault in the linkage of the signals, then the message does not reach the real individual and a preconditioned response is substituted for a real one. Such a fault and its automatic response is called a false circuit or short circuit. If many of these circuits build up, due to unpleasant things happening to the person or due to some malformation of the bodies, then these circuits can interact between themselves to build an entire false personality front. The real self is unable to break through this and often gives up trying. To the outside world, the false person can appear to be the same as a real self because the real self makes mistakes too, but not automatically. In psychotherapy we must bear this in mind and talk to the real self in a high tone way, in order to entice it back into the bodies and circuits it has given up trying to control.

CHAPTER FIVE

Entities

The fact is now accepted that the single biological cell is the primary form of life which combines in many and complex ways to produce vegetable and animal forms. It is said that the living cell is born and dies and also divides. It also has a purpose of some sort, which it fulfils in different ways, depending on its type. One must, therefore, in allocating life to this cell, also allocate consciousness of some sort.[2] But while, as has been said, matter at the atomic level and at other very fine levels is also associated with consciousness, in cellular consciousness it is possible to differentiate between the condition of matter-consciousness and conscious matter. For while atomic bodies are not associated with separate consciousness, in that their consciousness is classed with some sort of absolute control from the level of Absolute Reality, the living cell indicates some new and important factor present in the situation which allows for a certain autonomy and a certain separate function of intelligent purpose and ability. The level of molecular structure seems in a peculiar fashion to be a compromise between the separate life of the cell and the universal controlled function of the atom. While the consciousness of the atom is possibly the consciousness of the Absolute in a permanent and rigid form, deliberately restricted for its own purposes, the consciousness of the cell would seem to show signs of an individual awareness which only become obvious at later and more evolved stages. The molecular level of manifestation achieves the highest possible degree of complexity and qualitative content able to be manifested by the method of universalised and complete control from the level of Absolute Origin. This molecular condition of matter produces those multiple expressions or communications of qualities which are, as it were, permutations from the atomic qualities which pave the way for cellular life and carry units of matter to the brink of elementary self-consciousness. The cell is beyond that brink and must be placed by us upon the upward or evolutionary part of our life cycle.

---

[2] The Virus is possibly a more elementary unit in this respect.

By self-consciousness in this context is meant that there is some sense of instinctive function and self-preservation, but in no way implying that there is present anything remotely as developed as human self-consciousness. The implication here is that there are degrees of self-consciousness ranging from zero to maximum and that the cell is close to zero but not identical with it. It would not seem to be wise to make an arbitrary boundary to this field of self-consciousness somewhere in the animal or even vegetable kingdoms, because this boundary is based on our ideas of human consciousness and is therefore not an objective definition. It must be expected that the phenomenon of self-consciousness tails off very gradually to the condition of matter-consciousness which is, as was said, a manifestation of Absolute Consciousness in a highly restricted but highly efficient form. To make this relativity of self-consciousness clearer, it must be realised that in our own condition of human self-consciousness the process is still only partly complete. Thus we are as far from full self-consciousness as the vegetable kingdom is from human self-consciousness, for full self-consciousness is the realisation of ourselves as individuals at the Absolute or Divine level of consciousness. This is only achieved through the development of higher bodies of communication and by the elimination of false circuits from these bodies. The way is then clear to engage in life at any level with undistorted communication to and from the fully responsive awareness. Until this is achieved, we must swallow our pride and accept the fact that we are incomplete, subject to error, subject to mechanical responses, not in a position to make proper judgement and in need of all the assistance we can get which does not take away from us our own initiative.

The single biological cell combines with other cells to create larger organisms or cell groups. These groups combine to create larger groups again and so on. This process is another which seems to continue endlessly and one which we should again be wary of fixing boundaries to. When cells combine into a larger group, to make this group a proper one, a combination is necessary which is more than the mere sum of the parts. This means that the congregation of a number of individuals can merge into a group or remain a number of individuals. If they merge into a group, a combination of consciousness and function takes place in which part of the individuality of the members is given up to create a central and dominant consciousness, which is more than, and different from, the sum of the parts. This collective consciousness can be called the group consciousness and seen as a form of life and consciousness which has come into existence because of the amalgamation of the members. However one can also reverse this thought and say that the group consciousness existed prior to the amalgamation and was the cause of the amalgamation. In this case, the consciousness which becomes that of the group can be visualised as a unit of evolving consciousness similar to or identical with that shown in the maps as being the evolutionary species of self-consciousness working on the evolutionary cycle of life. Whether the group consciousness is the cause of the group combining or whether the combination of the group results in the group consciousness need not be decided here, but the resultant consciousness which has authority and purpose can simply be called an 'Entity' for the sake of convenience.

This entity is essentially a monitor which supervises the function of the group of cells. Such groups are a part of larger groups which must be under the influence of a more developed and more authoritative monitor, and this process must continue not only up to the level of the human physical frame, but beyond it, in ways which are difficult to imagine. Therefore every group, whether in the microcosm or macrocosm, can be expected to possess an associated consciousness which can be called an entity. The Human Being is thus a specialised form of entity, functioning along its own line of evolution. But there are other lines of evolution that entities are engaged in which are non-human. It is these entities which not only create and maintain bodies of communication for us as a part of their own purposive function, but also function instead of us if we refuse to take the initiative.

Therefore we are not only liable to be ousted from our true position of conscious valuation and response in life by false circuits, but also by the monitors who are associated with the many and complex groupings in our make-up. These are bound to act if we do not take the initiative ourselves, as manager of our own individual universe. While many functions are best left to these group monitors or entities, some of these functions are a vital part of the understanding and expression of our True Self and as such we must capture and maintain our authority in these fields or lose the opportunity of proper experience and progress.

The monitors concerned with the building and maintenance of physical bodies we should value and leave to their work unhindered, for they perform their task better than we could do and this leaves us free to develop our own special capacities. But the entities which are concerned with the building and function of our Personality and Soul bodies of communication we must monitor ourselves, and see to it that the function of the entity is confined to its proper field and does not overlap into those experiences and activities which call for our own evaluation and response. If we allow this, we will again arrive at the position of atrophy indicated in

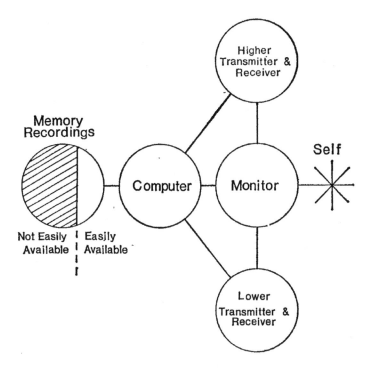

MAP 13

Figure 3, Map 12, only this time the cause will not be false circuits but over-dominant and monitoring entities.

In Map 13, a diagram suggests the theoretical make-up of an entity. Here the essential consciousness of the entity is separated out as the Monitor. But this Monitor is also connected to a computer type of consciousness, which in turn is connected to a memory store where patterns of behaviour and their causes and effects are kept and can be played back or recalled. This memory store is divided into two compartments which divide off the memories which are in constant use and easily recalled, from those which are not often used and not easily recalled. Connected to the Monitor and the computer are a higher and lower transmitter and receiver of signals and communications. These latter can be used either by the Monitor or the computer and enable the entity to combine with levels of matter-consciousness above and below its own frequency and with other entities larger and smaller than itself. The True Individual Self, which is the true identity of each Human Being, identifies with one or several of the more advanced entities by dominating the

Monitor and connecting its own consciousness through the Monitor to those worlds of matter-consciousness which the particular Entity is in touch with and concerned with. The Self is a unit of Absolute Consciousness and it attaches itself automatically to whatever level and nature it believes itself to be. The Self is none of these Entities or levels of matter-consciousness but, until consciousness is more complete and stronger in Self-identity, it is bound to compromise and identify to some degree with the Entity Evolution.

When the particular body with which an entity is concerned is finished with, the particles break down and return to their natural background of matter-consciousness. But the entity itself belongs to that order of matter-consciousness which does not disintegrate but which is on the evolutionary track. The entity gravitates to a common pool of such entities as its own level of matter-consciousness which in loose terms can be said to be a part of that atmosphere of life which surrounds our physical earth. This common atmosphere of entity intelligence possibly functions as a whole and evolves as a whole and is monitored by highly evolved and individualised entities in its turn.

The highest monitors associated with us as human beings are those in charge of our higher mental and spiritual bodies of communication. These Entities we can expect to be individuals and in the process of growth as we ourselves, but along a different line of development. The lower level entities will not have become individuals but will work and exist as a group function, even while attached to a particular cellular structure. The higher entities will resemble ourselves more and more as they approach the Ideal level of matter-consciousness and thus we will expect to find ourselves associated with what are virtually Brother Beings, whom we are destined to know and understand more completely and work with more consciously. However, this side of development will not affect us yet as we are still at the stage where our contact with this evolution is likely to be unconscious and completely unsuspected.

To return to the structure of the entity itself, a very important part of the function is that which is governed by the computer. This is a mechanical part of life which runs the structure of cellular life it is in charge of according to its recorded experiences and patterns of response which the monitor has valued as good and reliable. The ordinary running of the cellular body, such as a gland, which the entity is responsible for, is thus done automatically by this computer through its higher and lower frequency receivers and transmitters. Normally, the monitor will not be attached to a 'Self', as shown in Map 13, but will be monitored by another entity of a higher order. The Self only attaches to a very few entities; the main ones being the one in control of the physical body, and the ones in control of the bodies shown in Map 4 which are those of the Personality, and the Soul. When, however, something unusual occurs in the field of responsibility of an entity, then the monitor has to take over from the computer and resort to unusual responses and perhaps ones which have not been tried before. When the whole physical structure of the human body is under stress, then all the monitors are brought to a condition of active work which is governed in the last analysis by the major entity present. The concern here is not so much the detailed knowledge of how the various parts of our make-up function, but the fact that there is a hierarchy of entities which normally function very efficiently but which are within the effect of the psychological attitudes. This means that if we will live with and value the function of our entities properly they will work together very well, but if we ourselves become aberrated or wrongly identified, then we can force on to those entities our own psychological stresses and wrong valuations and consequently upset their work and their well-being. When this happens, they object to us by sending us messages of pain and discomfort of one sort or another. If the situation is not remedied, it can deteriorate until the responsible entities are paralysed and put out of action. An example of this is when a limb of our body becomes useless through some psychological stress. The limb can appear beyond hope of remedy but can be restored to proper function by recalling the situation which started the trouble and revaluing the elements which composed it and which caused the feeling of grief, anger or futility to arise and to be transferred on to a physical limb as blame or punishment.

This is a simple example of wrong identification and interference with entity work, but there are many more which result in physical and nervous disorder and which are caused by giving orders to entities which are outside the proper field of identification and experience and which are mostly below such fields. But when a wrong identification occurs at a high level of consciousness, then the effects can be very severe and far reaching, because of the number of entities which it in turn is supervising and which it can therefore wrongly direct as well. It is not uncommon to be angry with one of the entities, for example the entity managing the emotions of the personality, and to punish it by withdrawing from its circuits or by pushing it out of its circuits. In either case, the personality responses to emotions are inhibited. An obvious case is to be deprived of affection as a child and to punish 'the need' for affection by trying to destroy the activity of all affection in the nature and even replacing it with hostility. In this way we not only stop our conscious affections but we will also prevent unconscious affections functioning which are not merely a means of communicating to people but are a vital network which binds all our many parts together into an harmonious whole. When this unifying feeling is lost, all our many functions will tend to separate out, thus causing us to be aware of many separate identities which all try to be ourself but which all want different things. The resulting confusion will destroy our psychological nature. The remedy is to release the entity which is controlled by the decision to withhold proper emotional and affectional responses. This can only be done by getting the True Self into conversation and communication and revising the decision at the highest possible level. To try to cure this position by communicating with the personality level will do no good since the decision was made and can only be understood at the level of the real Self. The essential problem with a large proportion of these situations is not so much to change the decisions and attitudes, as to contact the Self which formulated the decisions and attitudes, for this Self may have withdrawn a great deal since the harmful attitudes were taken up and made automatic.

One way of helping stress as far as false circuits are concerned is to rest such circuits for as long a period as possible. In this way they are not re-energised and their inflamed and exaggerated function can subside. But if such circuits are the result of decisions of the Self, then this remedy will only be a respite and the circuits will shortly build up again. However, sometimes if the rest is accompanied by a complete change of environment the cure may be complete, since the stimulus of the false circuits may have been removed and the habit patterns forgotten. But to rest the person so that these circuits are not activated is a very difficult task and requires very careful nursing. The chemically induced coma is the well known example, and the electric shock treatment a short cut which we can visualise as being a drastic interference with delicate psychological circuits, which may break up cross linkages, but which also 'blow' vital fuses and connections. Today sedative drugs are generally used.

Ideally, the perfect treatment is one of conscious discussion which can result in revaluation of wrongly assessed experiences. Such discussions, however, require experienced therapists who have the right type of personality approach and who have plenty of time to devote to their cases. Unfortunately, this is what we do not possess, so an effective alternative has been found, by which the cases are brought together as a group and encouraged to enter into group communication. In this way the sometimes abnormally keen insight of suffering patients is brought to bear upon each other's problems and is able to probe with an effectiveness and immunity to opposition into matters which would take a therapist a very long time to reach. It has been found that such group work can have very helpful results.

Many inharmonious conditions of personality are the result of physical disease which may or may not have been induced by the attitude of the Self but which is, in any case, so far developed that it can only be treated in physical and ordinary medical ways. But when the stress is caused by less physical situations, then the primary objective is:

a. To increase communication between the patient and all levels of consciousness and experience.

b. To reassociate the Self with its chronic level of awareness, to validate this awareness and, if possible, to raise the level of this awareness.

To accomplish the first objective, all types of occupational work can help, as well as social and artistic experiences. In this context, it is necessary to treat the patient as a high tone Being as far as possible and put qualitative experiences before him which are higher than the average or higher than those chosen by people who are fit and busy simply enjoying life. For instance, a person under stress may get a great deal of value from a fine picture or a fine piece of music which under normal conditions he would get no value from at all. Similarly with conversation subject matter. The patient should be, if possible, confronted with high-tone concepts, morals and ideals which would be far above what is normal for the ordinary person. This focusing on high-tone values is the only way to get the high-tone part of the personality into effective communication, and through this aspect of the personality to get some communication with the real Self, which the patient may not realise exists, but which the therapist must believe exists and which he must court. If communication with the Self is achieved, then some real progress is possible, for there are potentialities and responses latent in this Self which are of the Absolute and carry with them the understanding of the Absolute. If this understanding can be liberated, then an impossible situation may be seen through and reappraised in a moment, thus releasing the whole complex of associated entities from some crippling distortion. But let it not be thought that all people under stress respond well to high art and high-tone conversation. Disturbed personalities are difficult to communicate with in any case, but there may be more occasions than are imagined when some such high-tone attempts will succeed where ordinary level approaches will fail. This is because the True Self of the patient may be attracted to and tempted by qualities of thought and aesthetic experience which are out of the usual run and which may, as it were, contain some elements of deeply significant Self-recollection which act as a saving grace. The patient may realise that such communications imply a sensitivity in others which has been so shocked, for some reason, in himself. Where the chronic level of the patient is low, one cannot expect a great deal from conscious therapy for the level of being will be that of the Personality itself and consequently the higher forms of intelligence associated with the Soul are not available.

What has to be faced up to is the fact that we possess very little proper identity, self control, freedom or choice; for what is normally thought of as our own activity is either the activity of false circuits or the activity of entities. This is a hard situation to accept or get used to. It hurts our pride to contemplate it, and it damages the idea of purpose or effort and takes away from us the sense of having a will and being able to use it. Nevertheless, a clear realisation of this situation can result in a rewarding change of attitude which can restore in fact what was previously only possessed in fiction.

CHAPTER FIVE: Summary

In thinking of matter and consciousness as united, we come to the structure of the hierarchy of units of this combination which are called Entities. Entities function as individuals within groups which themselves become entities, so that control and responsibility is fully portioned out in a unified system. At a critical stage in the process of involution and evolution, some of the entities become more than units of matter-consciousness and we can refer to them as units of matter-selfconsciousness. These units seek greater and greater autonomy and de-restriction. As they achieve this, they rise up the scale of the third vector and change their status. Some of these become human, some remain part of an entity evolution which we might think of as nature spirits of various degrees. The physical body is built up of these entities of an unself-conscious nature who work together to help the whole organism function efficiently. They also help us at the psychological levels and do everyday chores for us. The basic structure of an entity is suggested which incorporates memory banks and a computer-like ability to repeat known patterns of behaviour. They can be a mixed blessing to us because they can also live our life for us if we let them. When we are incorrect in our psychological response to life, we can damage the working of these entities, so that they too are crippled by false circuits, punishment and blame. Therapy tries to remove wrong pressures of blame, fear and apathy from the vital centres of our physical and psychological bodies. This may be better done if we enlist the support of the subjects highest nature, by offering high tone communication to him. The higher part of the person's nature may then be able to understand in a moment what the lower levels of consciousness would always find very difficult to cope with, thus quickly sorting out tangled and aberrated circuits. We are faced then, with the knowledge of how little we know, understand and control in what we fondly think of as our own nature. But at least at this point we are in a position to do something about it. Until we understand the situation, we are living in a fools paradise.

CHAPTER SIX

The Problems

Map 14 represents a more complete version of Map 10, only this time the three entities are shown associated with the three bodies of communication which to us at our stage of evolution are those of most concern. It will be observed that each entity is connected through its transmitters and receivers to higher and lower levels of matter-consciousness and that the Self, which is the individual true identity, is connected to the monitor of the Soul level Entity. This Self is shown as being outside the boundary of the individual's body complex, which indicates that it is an element of the Absolute and consequently not able to be designated in time or space as we know it. The Self, however, does not consider itself to be of the Absolute Nature, neither does it consider itself to be of the Soul level of consciousness, for most of the time it is identified through the Soul Entity with the Personality, which in turn is often completely identified in its conscious attitude with the Physical Body Entity. This map shows clearly the nature of the problem confronting us if we wish to know ourselves and to understand the significance of the position we are in, for we not only have to correct our identification with the physical body and the ordinary psychological body which is called the personality, but we also have to aim eventually at detaching ourselves from the Soul body in order to identify ourselves properly with THAT, which is the Absolute Nature within us. This Nature is designated as THAT because the first sense of it gives the feeling that it is someone outside and beyond. In fact there may be at first a confusion between the True Nature and its activity, with God and with God's activity. Very often even the experience of the Soul Nature seems to be Divine and to be an experience of the presence of God and the end of all endeavours. Later this higher consciousness is found to be relative and to belong to one's own identity. This does not mean to say that the experience of the presence of other Beings is not possible but that often it can be the experience of our own Being.

Map 14 is an over-simplification, but what matters here is not that this map is incorrect in detail but that it may be correct in principle. If this

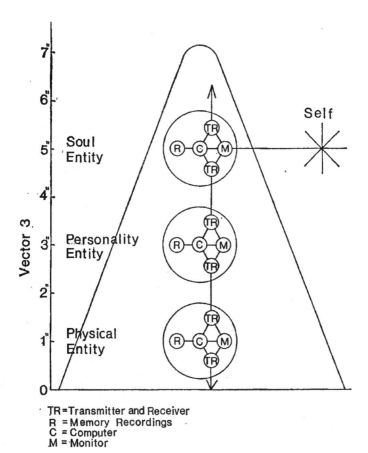

TR=Transmitter and Receiver
R = Memory Recordings
C = Computer
M = Monitor

MAP 14

principle is accepted it will create something to go by and something to commence work on if there is to be an endeavour to reorientate our attitudes. From previous discussion of groups and group functions it can be suggested that we ourselves are not only a part of a recognisable group system at the physical level, but that we are also a part of group systems at the psychological and spiritual level. This is the level of the Personality and the Soul. When we make some effort to evolve we are therefore bound to be involved with a hierarchy of groups and group effort at this intangible level. The difficulties of improving the level of consciousness are so many and great that it would be impossible to achieve this on our own. Yet the paradox here is that although help and guidance are necessary for progress, this help can only be given if we ourselves are prepared to use the maximum of our own initiative. For upon this Self-motivation depends our intrinsic identity and the ultimate quality of our Being. What seems to happen is that when we express the desire strongly enough to understand and enter into the deeper meanings of life, some agency puts us in touch with the efforts of the group most suitable. One may think that such contact is accidental and fortuitous, but this does not matter one way or the other. What matters is that the beginning of the next step is seen. The problem now is to take the step ourselves because any further help received will tend to usurp our innermost directive ability. If, however, the next step is taken with our own effort, then further passive help can be offered. At times active help is received but this is on the whole reserved for situations for which we are not fully responsible and for which we are not properly prepared. If any of us begin and continue to make real effort towards Self-knowledge we will perhaps never be alone or without supervision. But at the same time this supervision will allow us to burn our fingers if we have to learn something in this painful way. What happens when some progress is made is that the nature becomes stronger and shortcomings are thrown into strong relief. The ridiculous pride which we all suffer from is one of the obvious factors which will always require some sort of painful experience to reduce, for we are born into a world which pretends that the personality is the creator and governor of its fate so that we pick up and believe the notion that we are important and valuable as personalities. This is not the case. The personality is only valuable in so far as it can act as a channel of communication for the Divine Self. This aberration is now so common that it is accepted as a form of merit and encouraged as a means of helping one to get on in the world.

These groups which can be contacted are very likely to be unaware of each other directly and the members of a particular group may not even know one another. What is found is that the members of a group are engaged in work in the world which has the same quality of outlook about it. Some may be doing practical work in medicine, some in science, others in education, while others may be engaged in theoretical, philosophical or religious fields, creating works of art or writing books. They all function as a group, however, as they stimulate and inform one another in roundabout ways since they are expressing the same quality of consciousness through a number of different methods and forms. It must not be expected that a group meets once a week in someone's drawing room, although one must not rule out the possibility that part of the group may be conscious, with some sort of membership and organisation. On the whole, organisations are dangerous if it is wished to make strong and healthy progress, for they stimulate false personality and reduce the power of Self-direction. Added to which, the organisation invariably becomes more important than its purpose after a period of time. Since most of us are not strong to begin with, we have to accept compromise and limited help in an organised form. The obvious case is that of organised religion. This assists the focus of attention on to spiritual and unselfish ideals and emotions, but at the same time it restricts, at a certain stage of growth, by the fact that it takes away valuations and assessments of experience without which we cannot stand on our own feet in the world of pure Being. For this world of Ideal Consciousness is the kingdom of heaven which organised religion talks about but at the same time tends to put outside our reach. The fact that religious organisations do not really intend us to achieve the object of their existence is observable in the way they react to someone who says that he has found and entered into such experience, for they view such a claim with horror and suspicion. But to be cynical about such matters does not help and only shows that there is no understanding of the system of relativity which runs through every aspect of life, and without which much of the richness of experience would be lost, and upon which one of the highest values depends. This value is the sense of respect and appreciation for the struggle of living consciousness in all situations and under all conditions. This attitude is the result of realising that all these conditions stem from one Nature, which is our own Real Nature or Absolute Consciousness.

Before we can become remotely aware of the True Self, there must be freedom from many very powerful misconceptions, the most important of which are those based on the sense of identity with the physical level Personality. This Personality, which is indicated in Map 14, is meant to be nothing more than an agency which transfers communications to and from the physical level of existence for the benefit of the Soul Entity, and through this Entity to inform the real person, the Self, and to express its responses from the Awareness of the Absolute. By identifying carelessly with the physical Personality, the possibility of responding from the level of the Absolute is destroyed, and instead there is a response to events from various sources within the structure of the Personality which have nothing to do with the real identity. These sources of response are not only the reactive circuits which have been allowed to build up, but also the Personality Entity itself and various Entities associated with it. These entities are partly computers themselves and can repeat patterns of behaviour indefinitely with the best of intentions. Once that we have shown them a variety of behaviour patterns through the engagement of our real Self with life, the Entity can use these to go through the motions of living long after that Self has ceased to participate. This is something we can all observe. When we lose control of our Personality we do not lose it to one wrong centre but to many. This means that most of us are many people and that we have no stable identity to refer to or to act by. Until the stable and true identity is partially reclaimed, we are in no position to consider the real values and purposes of life and ways of making progress towards higher levels of consciousness. It is therefore no good expecting miracles to happen through the following of traditional and man-made organisations if we mean to achieve something in Self-knowledge. The intention to do more than dabble requires the whole intelligence and emotional nature to be in a condition of unity of purpose. Study and observation in every field of knowledge and experience, with the basic condition in mind of our own ability to motivate endeavour, is all important. Our own valuations and good sense must form the basis for our own building. Such things as knowing when to push ourselves a little and when to rest and reduce effort are necessary and will become clearer as the sense of balance becomes stronger. If there is no sense of inner balance and reasonableness then one had better not begin to initiate processes which will require such control; but at least these ideas can be given consideration without any necessity for further involvement.

CHAPTER SIX: Summary

Each of our main bodies of communication is also 'run' for us by an entity. The higher bodies are being built up by highly evolved entities all the time, and they endeavour to see that suitable experience for this building comes our way. Although help is available to be given to us at any time, help which constitutes the weakening of our own individual autonomy, endeavour and self-valuation is seen to be not real help at all and that is why it is often not forthcoming when it is asked for or expected. The only help we should expect to get is that which helps us to help ourselves and remain real and responsible individuals. The purpose of creation is not to evolve puppets, automatons or even servants but something much more difficult and more valuable—namely, friends. We thus find ourselves working in groups more and more as we evolve. These group members get closer and more concerned with one another as they build up their ability to further the purpose of higher life and bring help and guidance to the world. The members of such groups will most probably only be subconsciously aware of their connection with one another and the real relationship between them is at a high psychological level, but recognition is always immediate though wordless. Bringing our whole nature into line with a unity of purpose with life and a group of fellow humans is not an easy thing to do. Very high level Beings help it to come about and inspire the groups. The 'religion' of such groups is also very natural, unconditioned and wide.

CHAPTER SEVEN

Levels of Consciousness

It is now necessary to begin assessment of the levels of consciousness along the ideal vector, so that these levels can be more easily recognised. If the spacings along this line are numbered from zero to ten, the first half can be called the realm of the 'lower' mind and emotion and the second half the 'higher' mind and emotion. From the level 6 and 7 the world of ideal values is entered, and beyond this ideal world there are higher spheres which can be called Divine.

In Map 15 are seen the relationship these readings along vector 3 have with the type of outlook and interest associated with men in our society. What is called the field of cultural activity is seen together with certain other levels which may have special significance for us. The position of the intellect is of major importance and its similarity to what is described as the dead-centre position will be explained.

On the right hand side of Map 15 is a list of men which begins just above 2" with Lower Man. This must be thought of as the most primitive type of man in relatively uncivilised societies. Between 2" and 3" is found average man who can do a good job of work and who can manage a family together with all the complexities which are involved with this today. Above this level again is the man who is in charge of others and bearing more responsibility. This man also begins to feel a real need for culture and some of the niceties which make the relationship of man to man a graceful affair. This level of consciousness also enables the man or woman to stand apart more from other people to the extent that they form more individual judgements. This feeling of not having to conform in ideas and valuations makes possible the manipulation of forces, which at lower levels condition us, in such a way that we are able to condition the surroundings instead. It is a beginning of the reversal of the dominance of the surroundings and the society over the individual, so that the individual uses these processes in reverse to do the dominating himself. This factor makes him what can be called a creative individual. At the next level a continuation is met of the creative and more responsible man, but here there is an emphasis on learning which enables the individual to be aware of a wider variety of

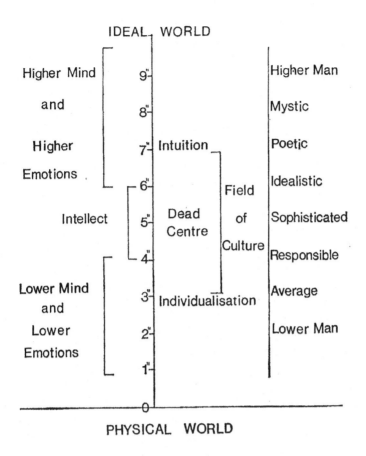

IDEAL WORLD

Higher Mind

and

Higher

Emotions

Intellect

Lower Mind
and
Lower
Emotions

9"

8"

7" Intuition

6"

5" Dead
Centre

4"

3" Individualisation

2"

1"

0

Field

of

Culture

Higher Man

Mystic

Poetic

Idealistic

Sophisticated

Responsible

Average

Lower Man

PHYSICAL WORLD

MAP 15

experience and of past cultures. The relativity of values is more clearly appreciated and the dichotomy between the demands of the physical world and the ideal world more keenly felt. Because of this balance or the two-way pull of these basic sets of values, the individual is apt to live his life comparing the two in a more and more delicate and subtle way. Thus he is often led to a position of cynicism whereby he endeavours to get the best of both worlds. This is the special realm of the intellect, and because the emotional pull of the higher and lower values are balanced, it can become an emotionless phase in which the brilliant analytical quality of mind is given full sway at the expense of the rest of the nature. In this condition man can create enormous structures of ideas and systems of thought which are perfect within their own terms of reference but which are cut off both from the practical experience of living in the world and from that higher world of ideals to which there is a striving to relate. The result is that such a person becomes divorced from both forms of reality and over-individualises in this intellectual world of his own, which appertains more and more to his own person and less and less to the rest of the creation and to other people. Such a position is very hard to get out of and very hard to move through. That is why it is designated the Dead-centre position. It is the position where there is danger of losing impetus although the consciousness may still be very active.

Above the level of the sophisticated man there is the type who begins to sense through the higher emotions and the higher aspect of mind those more universal qualities which are concerned with the good of the whole and the perfecting of the whole. These perceptions are sufficiently strong to enable the person to devote the greater part of his life energies to this task in one way or another. He is the idealistic social worker and the politician, the idealistic teacher, doctor, surgeon and artist. The next type of man is more difficult to define. He is that person who senses even more strongly the beauties of the ideals of consciousness, but he also senses them in a more collective or synthetised form whereby a whole series of higher values is perceived at once and together thus enabling the person to know an overall texture and quality which would otherwise be denied if the values were perceived separately. This sense and experience enables the person to know and describe to others through words, music and other art forms as well as by his general attitude and way of life those more sublime overtones, harmonies, attitudes and sympathies which emanate from the ideal levels and which make for optimism where there would otherwise be drudgery and endurance. While this level is called the poetic, one must remember that it describes the poetic spirit and attitude rather than the level at which most poets live and work.

The next level is the level of the Mystic. Here the individual has 'gone over to the other side' in the sense that he lives naturally in the world of values which belong to the ideal and he is more at home with these than with the values of civilised culture. This is the man who is able to take himself off into the wilderness and enjoy it because the loneliness leaves him free to commune with the ideal world. The mystic does not sense a loss when people and things are taken from him for he knows he can lose nothing and that he has already begun to enter his true estate where he owns and enjoys everything. The Higher Man is beyond ordinary understanding because he not only lives and works from the ideal level of values but he also works with ideal means which are not apparent since they consist more of the activities which occupy the highest levels of matter-consciousness and to most people would be too ephemeral. It may be supposed that such men are able to effect their purposes directly into the consciousness of other individuals thus avoiding the misconceptions and inefficiencies which arise when lower and more obvious levels of communication are used. These higher men may act as guardians in our midst, but we will never be aware of them or know who they are until we also are nearing their understanding and condition.

The true consciousness of the individual therefore resides within the absolute condition of awareness and being which is 'beyond' and 'previous to' the highest level of matter-consciousness. This means that it is in a dimension beyond anything described in Map 3, but it does not know this and consequently believes itself to be a variety of beings at a variety of levels within this field of experience. The basic level which the individual consciousness believes and feels it belongs to can be called its chronic level. This level changes, or should change, slowly to a higher and wider position and represents what is normally thought of as the condition of the Soul. Against this are all those fluctuations which take place every day, hour and minute which are the conditions of the outer nature or personality. As the personality is a partial and temporary extension of the consciousness of the Soul, so the Soul in its turn is a partial and temporary extension of the true consciousness or Self of the absolute. There is no reason to believe that the individuality of this Absolute Self is ever lost or ever becomes invalid, even though it must achieve a high degree of integration with other selves at its natural level of consciousness.

There are many schools of psychology, but the climate of thought which surrounds these schools at present is surprisingly 'concrete' and therefore sceptical about anything associated with the ideal or Divine level of consciousness. It does seem, if this theory is along the right lines, that there will be very many problems which will remain unsolved by these schools so long as problems stem from wrong identification with our system of entities and their associated bodies of communication. The solution to these problems can only be reached through re-education of the patient. Sedation and rest will never cure any but the mildest forms of misplaced identity. The basic identity pattern is the result of the patient's background, inheritance and social experience. All of these are generally directed away from such an attitude as has been described, even though the experience supplies the needs of the physical and personality entities. It is only the strong and well-formed Souls who enter into the field of true culture, and only the very determined who find their Self. Most of us are looking for our identity exactly where it is not and never will be. Because of this the process of seeking identity can become itself the cause of failure and the cause of maladjustment and illness. While evolution is at the primary stage, up to the level of the self-conscious personality, we do not seek our identity because we feel the physical body to be it. But as we become more sophisticated we refuse to accept identity with the physical body and so all these pseudo identities and facades are formed behind which we are still lost. The more desperate we become to identify ourselves the more likely we are to warp and destroy the work of our entities unless by some happy chance we begin to take a spiritual view of things. If we spiritualise our attitude we immediately lift the dangerous pressures off the entities who communicate and act for us so that they can continue their proper monitoring function. Needless to say, if the spiritual attitude we take up is itself the result of confused and distorted thinking and feeling, as it often is, then we shall be jumping from the frying pan into the fire, for these distortions will again upset the harmony of our intellectual, emotional and physical entities and we will not be free to experience the intuitive consciousness which is our saving grace. Clearly, even in our most respected forms of religion there are dogmas and attitudes which contradict and which are not in tune with our highest instincts. Such attitudes become positively lethal if we try to progress into the intuitive state of reality, even if they do not do much harm at the level of the lower intelligence and lower emotions.

It would be helpful to give a good reason why the Divine-Human evolution should be dependent upon other forms of evolution of the Divine-Entities and not be simply the same evolution. It can be put this way: The Divine-Entity evolution consists of these entities BEING their Divine Nature in the form in which it is given them. The Divine-Human evolution consists of the True individual UNDERSTANDING the significance of the Divine attitude and the Divine qualities. The first form of evolution, which is that of the Entities, is what can be called (so far as these words can describe such delicate and relative conditions) unselfconscious and instinctively perfect. The second form of evolution, which is the Human one, is self-conscious, considered (non-instinctive) and inevitably imperfect. It passes through the 'valley of death', the dead centre position, where it becomes detached from manifestation and completely self-centred. But it can develop beyond this stage of supreme imperfection to experience and KNOW the meaning and significance of manifestation simply because it can view it from the detached position it has learned and been forced to take up. Now the Entity evolution does not pass through this uncomfortable phase of detachment and it always remains in harmony with the processes and purposes of manifestation, but because of this it never gets OUTSIDE this process, however wonderful it may be, and is never in the position to know and value with detachment the ultimate

SIGNIFICANCE of all this experience. It is possible to simplify this statement by saying that the Divine-Human evolution digests its evaluations, while the Divine-Entity evolution enjoys its evaluations. The results of the two forms are in the end very different. The first has taken upon itself the pain and struggle of The Divine Aspiration. The second has manufactured the ground for this struggle and witnessed it, and enjoyed and delighted in the Aspiration, but it has not passed through the phase which enables it to view the Quality of the Aspiration objectively, and therefore will lack the basic valuation which the Divine-Human has obtained through knowledge of imperfection and the consequent suffering it has had to endure. We may think of the Divine-Entity evolution being that of the Elements, Elementals, Nature Spirits, Angels and Gods, in that order. But this gives a wrong impression very often because we confuse such names with myths and fairy tales which are very garbled versions of some of these functions. But most of our religions and mystical writings do recognise the possibility of such a different form of consciousness from our own. We make use of this knowledge when designing rituals, although we still remain rather sceptical in our minds.

This ritual can evolve when individuals are trying hard to keep their consciousness tuned to the intuitive and ideal levels of awareness in the face of low-level attitudes which are prevalent in the world about them. Ritualistic behaviour prevents attention of the individual wandering on to other things such as the hundred and one practical issues which arise in physical level existence. The physical action of the ritual enforces the desired focus upon high ideals and does not leave room for other physical perceptions to intrude. But the repetition of the ritual is also dangerous for the reason that it enables the computers to take over the process which lends itself perfectly to the task for which the computers were designed, namely, to do repetitive work. So while the adherent to ritual is closing his consciousness to outside interference he is also likely to numb it altogether since there will be nothing for it to do when the computers have once got hold of the ritual. This would all be fine if we belonged to the Entity form of evolution because entities are meant to enjoy such repetitive behaviour and no doubt this draws them to the ritual. But this is a complete disservice to the human evolution unless it is on a very small scale, for while it may enable something of the 'angelic' attitude and presence to be sensed, it does at the same time invalidate the main purpose which is to achieve Self-conscious understanding of Divine nature and Aspiration. A few sincerely felt moments of deep concern for this Divine Aspiration are therefore of far more value in the end than hours and years of partly felt and partly mechanical request for help, forgiveness, undeserved benefits and ultimate safety. Religious ritual often degenerates into a sort of Spiritual insurance scheme. Even worship, when it is not a high and natural form of love, we can see creates dichotomy. For how can we consider ourselves in our own Divine right when we are worshiping that right? The very basic of worship is to keep the object of our worship at a respectable distance in deference to its untouchable qualities. We cannot therefore be expected to enter into these qualities and at the same time worship them. We can only enter into them if we Self-consciously and simply love them.

Apart from the theoretical reason why one should expect the Entity form of evolution to exist, one is led to expect this by the recorded experience of all types of people who have at times witnessed the presence of the higher orders which are called Angels. Very little may be known about this evolution but the possibility must not be ruled out that after a certain critical level has been reached 'Angels' can enter the Human evolution for the sake of the experience it can give and also perhaps in order to assist evolution and alleviate some of the suffering it entails to humanity. And similarly we ourselves may eventually enter the Entity stream of development after our own critical point has been reached, which is the point where we have entered into and come out from the isolated and detached position of 'rebellious autonomy' which is our great and ugly 'sin' but which becomes in the end our most valuable experience and gives us that autonomy over manifestation which the Angelic evolution does not achieve.

There is one very good reason why these forms of evolution have to be different. Our right to and experience of autonomy is a very destructive and dangerous process in that it is paved with ugly and inharmonious desires and ideas. If the Entity and Angelic evolution was also open to this reactive phase the result would be total destruction and collapse of the necessary field of experience. So while we Humans make the great sacrifice of suffering and pain to achieve an Autonomous and Individual Divine nature, so the Angelic Evolution makes the great sacrifice which is to create and maintain the necessary ground for our Human Experience, the fields of matter-consciousness at all levels, and clean up the mess we make in the course of this experience; which work requires them to remain for ever in harmony with the Divine purpose and Aspiration and so does not properly allow them the experience of objective valuation which ultimate understanding requires. Such is the interpretation this theory would give to the Christian parable of the Prodigal Son. He is the Human who is bound to sin for a reason he does not understand which in the end gives him knowledge of very great value. His brother who does not sin and who does not venture off into the wilds of poverty and hunger does not experience the pain and misery of this hunger and does not value that which is hungered for in quite the same way. He is never lost and never has caused to be rejoiced over, for he never returns of his own accord with this priceless treasure and His Father in heaven never has anxiety about him.

CHAPTER SEVEN: Summary

The levels of our being and attitude are now described in more detail, and attention is drawn to the 'sitting on the fence' experience of the central intellect which views the higher and lower man with equal discernment but is unable to come down on the side of one or the other and therefore cannot move forward or backward. The highest men amongst us will not be recognisable to us unless we are already approaching their attitudes. These higher attitudes and higher abilities enable such leaders to work on us and with us through the direct means of the psyche. They are the proper teachers of mankind and do not necessarily require a physical body in order to do their work. Our real identity is of the nature of the Creator and is therefore of the Absolute, whatever that can mean for us. It resides 'all the time outside manifestation' but does not know this and is not meant to know this. The entity evolution helps to maintain the worlds for us to learn and play in, and Angels attend the religious services we employ to focus our attention on higher awareness. Ritual takes our mind off worldly concerns but ritual also endangers us since it opens us up to the automatic responses of our computers and this stops our real responses being actively engaged. For us, quality must take precedence. Ten seconds of whole hearted endeavour is better than ten hours of automatism. The entity evolution enjoys its experience, but we, through our painful sense of detachment, are able to digest the significance of it objectively. This learning, which requires us to make serious mistakes, means that we mess up the universe. The Angelic evolution repairs the damage we do. If they, too, were open to such mistakes then the systems of manifestation would be put at too much risk. The prodigal son must learn to be grateful to his non-prodigal brother for the suffering that he has been privileged to bear and profit by.

CHAPTER EIGHT

Relating Levels of Consciousness

There remains a very difficult part of the problem which is to suggest some method by which the 'material' of the ideal world is related to that of the physical world. To begin with there is less problem over the physical side of such a system for physicists have for many years now described to us just how little is known about what used to be comfortably taken as building bricks or atoms. Not only is very little known, but what is known points to the fact that atoms are largely space within which are very fast moving phenomena termed electrons and other particles. These particles could themselves never again be equated with the idea of solid particles, they are more nearly to be thought of as points of energy which possess distinctive properties. Or perhaps these are waves of energy of differing types which pass through one another and in so doing create resonances which become heightened temporary phenomena.

Map 16 is a diagram of an atomic sphere of influence. It has a boundary D which is the outermost effect and within which can be imagined the waves of differing sorts such as A and B. A point of interference or amplification due to resonance could be at the position C. These points, while being a very definite source of qualified energy are not really there as objects in their own right, they are induced. The most practical discovery that has been made about the use of electrical energy has been the discovery that when a current flows in a wire a cylinder-like field of force is created around it and along its length. By reversing this process a cylinder of force can induce a line of force along its axis. This process is not understood by anyone, but it is used in almost every piece of electrical machinery that is made.

In Map 17 a diagram illustrates the proposition whereby an energy following track AA induces around itself and along its length a screw-shaped track of energy BB. This track in its turn induces another smaller track around its length which is marked CC. This process can continue indefinitely and there exists no reason to limit either its largeness or its smallness since the hypothetical energy has no size.

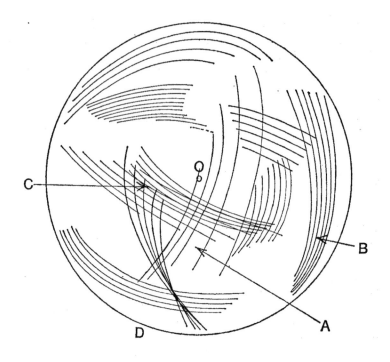

MAP 16

It can now be suggested that if an induced system of electricity-like energy was required to maintain a series of amplitudes such as that shown in Map 17, all that would be needed would be an energy charge to follow the line AA in a suitable medium; an unlimited number of related and reducing systems would follow as indicated. Similarly, if the smallest track such as CC were to be described in all its complexity, which is not shown in the diagram, then the larger tracks would be produced by an induction-like process. If this idea of series can be imagined then it can be taken as a tentative suggestion of the way that higher and lower levels of matter-consciousness are related.

Since the amplitudes and frequencies of this structure are related in a simple fashion, it is possible to talk about high frequency and low frequency levels of matter-consciousness. It can now be considered that only matter which pertains to a common wavelength or frequency can be explained as solid. As our physical bodies are constructed of the same type of matter as the world around us, so therefore do we get the experience of solidity in the world around us. If, however, our physical body were absent, then another frequency of matter would be sensed as solid to us. This

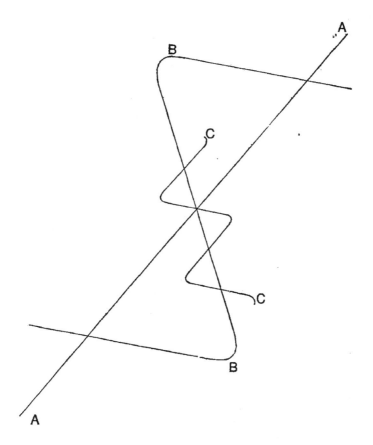

MAP 17

would be the plane of matter-consciousness of the next highest body of communication. The physical plane would then become ephemeral or even non-existent for us.

From this series an idea can be held which can begin to account for the various levels of manifestation being apparently discreet yet related to a unified system.

Together with this idea will be another possibility to consider and that is the fact that our actions and responses to events at the physical level are continually influencing higher levels and expressing themselves at higher levels. In this way, although we are unaware of the higher frequency levels of matter-consciousness, we are probably effecting these levels, the amount of this affect depending on the development of the individual and the responsiveness of the higher bodies of communication. The converse may also be true, which is that the higher levels of matter-consciousness will be influencing us at the physical level without us knowing it, thus creating moods in us which we cannot account for.

The third vector will now be seen as the vector describing this complex of inter-related but discreet conditions of matter which are associated with their own type of consciousness, and while the vector analysis implies that they are one above the other, it is most important to remember that this is not the case. More correctly these differing states must be realised as existing one within the other, or one through the other. So far as our real journey in the Universe is concerned, this means that the beginning and the end are both present here, and here is where we are at any instant. What we are looking for is not further from us but closer to us. We do not recognise who we really are.

To return to the range of induced energy tracks of Map 17, an interesting possibility must not be allowed to escape. This is that the creative act in such a system would be to know the shape of the smallest and most complex track. If this shape were then to be followed by a form of energy, this energy would induce all the other amplitudes of energy. Although no such energy or matrix is known, the principle of this fundamental complex pattern which contains the potentiality of all the others and which, in a sense, also contains the possibility of many dimensions, is a most interesting one and may give some insight into the meaning of such a term as the creative word or creative sound, for such a sound contains within its resonances, dissonances, desires and intentions manipulated and formed by Absolute Being.

It is possible to imagine the main levels of matter-consciousness as being such as the levels described on the third vector and each one corresponding to its own induced energy track. The plane of communication associated with each of these tracks can then be considered as a complex created out of modulations on this basic track, such as modulations on a carrier wave. In this way the atomic particle and atom and molecule may be formed in the same type of way at each level, but as each level rests on a carrier wave which is basically different, the results will be different also in the same degree. It is not a bad thing to remind ourselves that what we consider to be a very small atomic particle is just as likely to be an enormous particle, and a single living cell a gigantic cosmos. Our minds recoil from such ideas and yet still appreciate the fact that there is possibly a great deal of truth in the story of Gulliver and his experiences of giants and midgets. What we forget also is that the physical bodies we are associated with now are, within our own scientific knowledge, vast concourses of atoms organised to a fantastically small degree of tolerance and carrying within them energy forces which have enormous potential.

But again what strikes us when the physical situation is viewed objectively is that although the organisation of the physical body is a hardly believable miracle, it is still as nothing to the phenomenon of consciousness, which is indeed so miraculous that it escapes our attention altogether. What this theory is trying to do is not only to observe the physical situation more objectively, but to observe our various states of consciousness objectively also. In doing this there is an unavoidable sensation that behind all experience there is a calm, patient and undistortable observer; most of the time over-ridden and certainly only sensed consciously in moments of great stillness.

One may spend a great deal of energy pin-pointing the exact nature and composition of a drop of pure water and one may even know exactly what it is (which is something not known yet) but this knowledge may have no bearing at all on the experience of a rainstorm and the significance of being a physical being in a shower of rain among trees, flowers, grasses and shafts of sunlight. Knowledge of the factual make-up of the physical level of matter-consciousness is quite another thing from the experience of living as a wide awake observer and experiencer of that level of matter-consciousness. It is a little wonder that our increasing fascination for the factual side of the physical medium of communication leaves us in a state of morbid and pessimistic futility for it is exactly like dissecting a rose to find out what it is. A rose will tell us what it is, but only if we allow it to communicate in its own terms. It seems we must approach it on its own ground with a knowledge of how little we understand, only then may we be aware of what it is 'saying'. Unfortunately far more often all our effort and time is spent in chattering away at our background, telling it what it is. This is not audible chatter, but the chatter of recognition in the mind whereby every item that comes to our attention is labelled and pigeon-holed in the belief that this is 'experience' and 'living' but in the knowledge that it is only continual repetition of a few stock situations, and tedious and boring in the extreme.

Map 18 repeats the list of types of men which was first described in Map 15. It was brought in again here to indicate that recognition and understanding of one level of being by another level is limited to frequencies that are not too dissimilar. The range of understanding may only be two degrees above the chronic level, so that individualised man at 3" may be able to recognise and understand level 5" quite well, but level 6" hardly at all and level 7" not at all. Thus intuitive communications are a

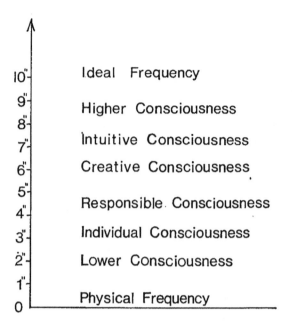

$10''$ — Ideal Frequency

$9''$ — Higher Consciousness

$8''$

$7''$ — Intuitive Consciousness

$6''$ — Creative Consciousness .

$5''$

$4''$ — Responsible. Consciousness

$3''$ — Individual Consciousness

$2''$ — Lower Consciousness

$1''$

0 — Physical Frequency

MAP 18

closed book to the man of level 3". Similarly, responsible man may be able to grasp a little of intuitive or poetic man but be unable to understand or accept him when he approaches mysticism and the higher consciousness. There are always exceptions to such ideas, but the principle in general appears to hold good.

The situation which human beings are in seems to suggest that there are major carrier waves of matter-consciousness connected with evolution which are the physical, the mental and the ideal. If these three main influences are shown to overlap as in Map 19, the boundaries of each circle describe points of specificity which can be equated with lower, responsible, intellectual, poetic, higher and ideal levels of consciousness. Entering into, fully experiencing and moving out of the influence of the mental plane at 5" seems to be the object of evolution for man as we know him as a human being. At point 3 in Map 19 the purely physical influence is overcome. At point 4 the dead-centre position is experienced. At point 5 the influence of the Ideal plane is entered and at point 6 the individual is freed from the limitations of the mental plane influence. These are reasonably well marked points of differentiation in human society. As a general principle it is also possible to notice here that the three main planes form what can be

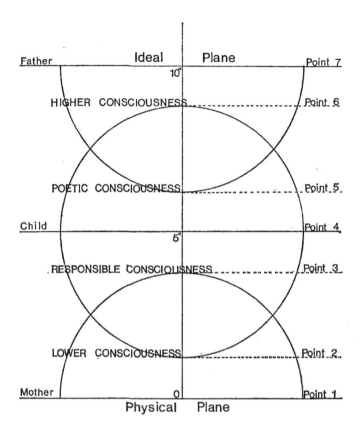

Father   Ideal   Plane   Point 7

10"

HIGHER CONSCIOUSNESS   Point 6

POETIC CONSCIOUSNESS   Point 5.

Child   Point 4

5"

RESPONSIBLE CONSCIOUSNESS   Point 3

LOWER CONSCIOUSNESS   Point 2.

Mother   0   Point 1

Physical   Plane

MAP 19

thought of as a Father, Mother, Child relationship with one another. This is a phase, the significance of which will move as the individual moves higher on the third vector. This central plane is called the mental plane, but this is only a label and does not imply that there is no emotional content. There is no stage at which the emotions are not present but the quality of the emotions alters a great deal between point 2 and point 6, and at point 6, the emotions are a much more integrated part of consciousness and are no longer separable as they were at lower frequency levels. As indicated in the first Maps, the emotions are the vital part of the sympathetic ability of consciousness which is very often the chief factor in the widening and heightening of attention and understanding. The difficulty with a verbal theory such as this is that there is always a danger

122

of forgetting the importance of the emotions since much of their meaning is lost in verbal discussion rather than person to person communication. It is not uncommon to find people studying esoteric life with their emotions set on one side or almost completely inhibited. It should be made very clear in consequence that the basis of this whole proposition is that the emotional understanding be considered as of equal importance to the intellectual understanding and the two phases of consciousness be kept in an harmonious working partnership. Needless to say, the emotions as well as mental concepts must be continually observed, controlled and refined but not inhibited, if consciousness is to be widened and deepened.

However, one of the most important parts of this theory is now to be proposed and it is one which has already been tentatively brought in. This is the major idea that the seat of consciousness is in the Absolute and not in what is ordinarily considered as manifestation at all. The proposition is that the function and purpose of manifestation is to create the ground for experience and the communication of experience. The experience itself is only valid when it is a part of this absolute consciousness which we ourselves are not normally in a position to be aware of and properly identify with. The manifested worlds are consequently no more than the 'stuff' of communication itself. To put the idea very simply, the whole of manifestation is a communication on the part of the creative cause. Manifestation with its many universes and planes is something which God wished to say. We are the individuals that God wishes to say it to. Thus the real significance of every instant is the response being made by us to events . . . not the events themselves. This suggests that the world we live in is the world of absolute consciousness and that the worlds we are identified with are statements, are communications of qualities and principles. When we look around us what we are really seeing is a prolonged lecture, but the language it is given in is not the one used in man-to-man communications but an infinitely more complete and efficient language. This language is the one of the rain and sunlight, trees and grasses, children, mountains, clouds, colours, scents, sounds, responsibilities, loves, dangers, mothers, fathers, wives, lovers, friends, facts and foods, happy times, sad times, beautiful times, absorbing times, boring times and futile times. To try and equate reality with the physical worlds of communication and to try and equate human consciousness with the human body, which are both very common attempts, is like trying to understand and identify the reality of a book by measuring its proportions and analysing the paper and the ink. Such an attitude could only arise if it was not realised that a book was meaningless as a physical phenomenon but meaningful as a communication. While the book is a real phenomenon and capable of physical analysis, the secret of understanding it is to realise that it is a continuing statement of qualities and attitudes of consciousness. To know what a book is one has to let it speak, and speak to one's real Self. If this is not done, the most searching analysis of the paper and the molecules and atoms and atomic particles and energies and proportions of the paper will completely fail to explain the reality of the book as a phenomenon. We may gather a very impressive knowledge of the way that the universe is built, but this will be as nothing to understanding what the book and the universe is saying. The stuff of the physical world we live in is thus no longer to be considered as 'mere stuff', if we ourselves are to be more than 'mere clever things'. If we are to discover ourselves as significant living consciousness, we must accept the world we live in as an important communication. A tree must not only be a potential source of timber and money. A tree must be one side of a conversation, the language of which we must take the trouble to learn and respond with.

The sort of statement that has just been made will not be understood by anyone unless they want to understand it. It is a statement from outside the accepted culture of our day and would be easily ridiculed by any person wishing to do so. Nevertheless it is intended to be a serious factual suggestion as to why so many people find so little meaning in life. The painful part of failure to observe and read the communications that are continually being made to us through natural phenomena is the experience of extreme boredom. If the theory is correct the boredom arises because the valid and most real part of the individual feels itself to be fulfilling no purpose, in fact it feels ignored and forgotten. It knows it is something of great value and potential, but for some reason it is unable to become responsive and alive except in a few minor ways. Without knowing it, the individual is creating this misery for himself because he is living in certain restricted categories with which he has classed earlier experiences and has long ago ceased to let events speak for themselves. The person lives in a world of labels of his own making, perhaps on the grounds that he thinks he will be unable to cope with real events themselves and perhaps be unable to make the significance of the events fit into his 'safe' but 'uncomfortable' philosophy of reality. Because of this situation such a person is extremely aware of the apparently concrete unalterability and stony-faced aspect of the world around him. He is very aware of matter seeming to be dead, heavy and dull and monotonously unalterable—in fact the walls of a prison. When, however, responsiveness is felt within his being, then immediately the situation alters. The boredom ceases, the unalterability is not noticed, the prison vanishes and time goes quickly. Meaning and purpose creep back into life and the question of what it is all about seems partly answered and, indeed, only an important question is thought of as 'what can be done in co-operating with life?'

This sense of being aware of matter as a prison, as the beginning and ending of something hopeless and meaningless is not uncommon, particularly among people who have grown beyond the first hectic and unconsidered flush of youth. The world of physical material becomes part of a 'solid' identification which, for the purposes of this argument, can simply be termed matter. This is not the matter of the physicist but matter as experience. Not the matter that is measured but the matter that is felt. Not analysed but identified with.

In this context the following statement can be suggested as a verbal equation:

'Awareness of matter is failure to communicate.'

Non-awareness of the materiality of matter is thus the result of success in communication. Matter as materiality only exists in the experience of human beings who have ceased to remain responsive. To the rest of nature materiality presents no problems. It is consciously or unconsciously accepted as a most interesting and absorbing communication of qualities related to survival at the lower end of the third vector or related to beauty and idealism at the upper end of the third vector.

Matter can also be thought of as space and time experience. In the imprisoned mood of materiality, time drags and assumes very obvious characteristics of its own. It intrudes. Together with this, the size and number of phenomena becomes over important. The daunted observer reflects on the littleness of his own body and the insignificance of his own single identity among so many thousands of his fellows. He looks from the world out into the universe and his senses are numbed at the thought of the vastness of the cosmic system and the distances that are involved on every side. The background of his whole existence becomes unmanageable by his consciousness. It does not even appear hostile, for what is worse is the fact that it appears indifferent, quite unaware of him.

Solidity of life as an experience, or matter as an experience, can now be related to a degree of responsiveness of the true Being. It can also be related to the level of consciousness of the individual Being. When matter in this sense obtrudes into our life, it indicates that we are not being our Self. When matter does not obtrude, whether we are at a chronic high level or low level of consciousness, we are being ourself as much as we can be, responding with all we have available. This healthy state also indicates that we have not allowed many false circuits to come between Self and events. A false personality has not been allowed to form and insinuate itself between our Self and the world of communication.

CHAPTER EIGHT : Summary

In order to relate the highest level of matter-consciousness to the lowest level, together with all the intermediate levels, a model is proposed which shows inductance forming another inductance in a chain of the 'stuff' of manifestation. This is a simplified idea but it contains the seed of a very subtle idea. In simple terms, a 'line' of the force of this 'stuff' creates a field 'around' it which in turn creates another field around itself and so on. How or why induction really works is still a mystery to us. But the subtle part is that the initial shape of the primary force conditions all the others. This shape could be complex indeed and this complexity could be passed on. It could be the initial creative 'sound' which serves the purpose of the Creator. We must therefore learn to observe what is being said to us through the many forms that this primary saying results in, stop chattering to our background and pay attention to what it is trying to say to us. The main inductions or transformations of this 'stuff' are the main carrier waves of manifestation and the main levels of our worlds of experience in matter-consciousness. There must be many minor ones as well. We feel we live in these worlds, but in fact our real self is all the time 'beyond' them and has to learn to become objective to them to witness them accurately. We must learn to read meaning and value in forms while not allowing ourselves to get hooked by the forms themselves. Awareness of matter as dead or empty forms is our failure to communicate and observe efficiently.

CHAPTER NINE

Relative Philosophy

If this theory is accepted, of the Prodigal Human relationship with our Divine Parents (this phrase assumes that if we have a Divine Creator He is not all Father, but Father and Mother in keeping with the Masculine and Feminine quality of manifestation), it allows for us to develop our individual nature in a psychologically detached way so that it is not dominated by the much more powerful Personality of our Creator which would detract from our true individuality and tend more to make us an extension of His personality. The basis of individuality is not merely that we grow without this over dominating presence, but we also grow into and out of a state of consciousness which is one of self-conscious analytical mind, which feels it belongs neither to the natural physical world nor to the natural ideal world, but to a world of its own making and of its own responsibility. This would seem to be the true and proper Humanist Philosophical position. It cannot give itself to nature or to God, but at the same time it respects the information which either stems from or points to these levels of reality. This is the true position of the Human Being proper, but while the 'Stoic' Humanist values his position and the honesty which causes him to take it up, the position is valued even more highly in the light of this theory which sees in this central position of human experience other and ultimately more valuable reasons for experiencing this state of consciousness.

The beginning of this phase thus generates the Logical Positivist attitude, it leads on from this into the Humanist outlook which later becomes an Evolutionary Humanist Philosophy. Beyond this again it steps out from the rather analytical attitudes of the above to the beginnings of what is classed as the Intuitive and Poetic state which can be called the Intellectual form of Existentialism. This is followed by a higher form of Existentialism which comes close to Zen Buddhism, in that it is neither philosophy nor religion but the beginning of true 'Beingness'. Now this true Beingness is what has been described elsewhere as the beginning of that order of consciousness which is based on our Self Nature which is a form of Divine consciousness and which gives us the ability to play upon our 'Harp'. In other words, to respond with our highest instinct and discover that awareness is symphonic and universal and relatively sublime. This Universal Symphonic response is the 'music' which we eventually find our True Self embedded in. It is the state of consciousness which, when it is achieved, makes sense out of the process of becoming wherein we 'string and tune' our nature. But this process of becoming is itself hard to understand and hard to live through and full of paradoxes so long as we are in it.

The philosophical implication of this theory of Evolution is slightly different to the ordinary theories of evolution in that it starts with the Divine Frame which is 'given'. In this way it recognises that the evolution is already conditioned and that any fortuitous behaviour or sense of freedom we find will only be in operation between given limits. We must even recognise the fact that although the 'music' eventually made will be unique and creative in the positive sense, it will have to be true to its own nature, part of which is already conditioned by the number and length of the harp strings. However, the order in which we discover these strings and learn to play them will be very much a part of our individual uniqueness and will no doubt reflect in the type and expression of the final music.

The reader will note that in order to express the spirit and philosophy of this theory of consciousness, very definite statements are made which are later qualified in an equally definite manner. This is bound to be irritating but it is due to the fact that one cannot express this theory without shifting the viewpoint of our general outlook and without using a common form of language to indicate views for which it is not fitted. It will also be found that the value of the theory should never be taken at the factual level when attempting to describe the workings of consciousness. The principles behind the facts are the only things which really matter for in every case the facts themselves will be found eventually to be wrong. For instance, a scale of awareness levels is described and compared with types of people. There is suggested the number of the main carrier waves of consciousness and the number of Entities involved in the average person's make-up of bodies. It must be realised that these 'facts' will be wrong even if, as is hoped, the principle behind the facts is approximately correct. As scientists are finding now, facts can be very misleading, however simple and concrete they may seem. Not only do strictly factual statements fail to express the conditions within which they are true, but they also fail to express the level of consciousness from which the facts are being viewed or stated. It is the old problem of learning anything. If we learn to drive a car, the instructor will no doubt tell us that we will only be able to drive well when we have forgotten everything he says. Or if we learn to play the piano, we will understand that all the theory and practice we plod through, as though it were very important, is as nothing to the sense of music we will reach, towards which sense the theory can only point. We know that a master of any of the arts consistently breaks all the rules of his subject. We know that all the factual knowledge absorbed to pass exams is relatively useless if we wish to become composers of music or pictures. The facts learned can positively get in the way if one attempts to understand what lies behind them. So it is with this theory and philosophy of consciousness. It must all be taken as mere tentative suggestion. It will be wrong. But behind it there may be a spirit of understanding which is correct enough to get us to a position from which things can be seen more clearly.

The theory talks of Angels, Elementals and Entities. Such things are ridiculous in a discussion which is meant to be taken seriously by intelligent people. It is felt one should apologise or recant if one does not wish to offend. And yet this aspect of the theory has not been arrived at through unreasonable speculation. One can arrive at this position by simply following through, without too much prejudice, the basis of thought concerning the two fields of experience, matter and consciousness. The theory will be seen to be neither Spiritual nor Materialistic in essence, for these two aspects of experience, which we can all verify for ourselves, are observed in such a way that matter does not have to be divorced from consciousness. The position is neither materialistic or spiritualistic or even religious in the general sense of the word. One has merely accepted the fact of our own consciousness and (limited) ability to observe and value and respond to events. Together with this one has accepted the fact that the awareness which we feel to be our own is only connected with events and never identical with them. However hard we may try we can never become identical with events, though we may 'consider' that we are. To consider that we are identified with events is to fool ourselves. Above all, one has accepted that the physical body and the psychological body and any other body which awareness is associated with, are all a part of the field of events and of matter, however responsive and aware this field is in its own right. This leaves us in the position of belonging essentially to an order of consciousness which is Absolute or Divine. One has accepted too, the fact that scientific law or physical mechanics neither explains nor accounts for the remarkable integrity of matter at all levels which shows a degree of responsiveness in extremely complex situations under continually changing conditions which reflects an efficiency level that can only be accounted for by some form of very high awareness, even if an extremely 'limited' one. It is said of this that it appears also to stem from the Absolute level of consciousness and 'knows', within the narrow limits of its function, all necessary things. So the fields of matter are called the combined name of matter-consciousness to remind us that no longer can these fields be considered 'dead' matter or 'merely' matter, but are a manifestation in relatively rigid form of life and awareness. In other words one has accepted, and gone a little way beyond, the thought and experimentation of contemporary scientists. This acceptance of the fact that there is consciousness associated with the Sub-atomic particle, Atom, Molecule and Compound, leads up more easily to the point where it can be accepted that the living cell has consciousness. This breaks down the artificial barriers set up between living things and non-living things. If the cell is accepted as a form of conscious life, then again this leads on to accepting more complex forms of cellular life as being associated with more capable forms of consciousness. This is a process of evolution of consciousness which, for understandable but obviously unfounded reasons, is considered to develop only into man, not parallel to man or beyond man. This head in the sand outlook forbids us to accept the possibility that life can evolve beyond the condition of consciousness we call humanity. It is bound to do this because it is the process of identification which is evolving to higher and higher forms; as the awareness only communicates through these forms it must belong to a level of consciousness which is 'beyond' or 'previous to' manifestation. This is called the Absolute or Divine consciousness. In this respect true consciousness is not becoming Divine, but realising that it IS Divine, even if still limited in the way it can express this divinity.

The theory has failed, as it should, to explain what Absolute consciousness is. It has not tried to know and explain the simplest factual thing in the field of events because it realises that there is present this Absolute form of consciousness, in however a limited and restricted way, in every event at every level. Instead of identifying events in terms of 'how we use them' and mistaking our knowledge of their *function* for a knowledge of their nature and *significance,* it faces the fact that we know nothing real about anything. We will not know what anything really IS until we know all things simultaneously. This is another way of realising the relativity of all valuation and manifestation, and perhaps the fact that the most relative thing we shall ever be aware of is the awareness and response which we identify vaguely as our Self, but an unknown Self, and a Self which can only be entered into if we recognise how little we know about it.

When we eventually come to understand the nature of 'events' instead of merely how 'events' are related in their function, the significance may very well be entirely connected with the communication content. 'Events' here signify all functions of all forms of life and include physical functions of matter and energy. At the present time we observe carefully that hydrogen combines with oxygen to form water. We understand and use this knowledge of the gases but we know nothing about what the gas is. We say it is composed of atoms and their atomic particles and we talk about the electrical forces and charges of these particles, their weight and mass and position. But we have still said nothing about what any of it is. We define the nature of force in terms of what it does. We define the nature of electrical charges in terms of what they do. We are unable to define anything in terms of what it is except consciousness itself, and consciousness is not *being* itself unless it is communicating. Unless it is active. The activity of consciousness can only be communication. A person may only be communicating to himself, sensing or feeling a part of his nature or memory or aspiration, but this is a vital form of consciousness just as much as communicating with other people. If the person is not communicating with himself or others, then he is completely dormant and only exists so far as he is a potential communicator. Communication in this sense includes the reception as well as the transmission of information, which transmission is the reality and purpose of the physical world about us and all forms of matter-consciousness. The degree in which we can receive and perceive this 'message' from matter conditions its significance. When we are not perceiving what matter is 'saying' to us it appears to be inert stuff and the space and time dimensions which it occupies appear to us to be its main aspects. When we are getting the message, our field of observation tends to unify and transmit to us a quality or series of qualities. The field of vision becomes a living theatre and we sense that we are not only enjoying the 'play' but also in some way responsible for it, both in creating it and maintaining it. And of course we are, for we only get the message when we begin to observe from our True Self, and this Self recognises the Divine nature in everything, both in the extremely limited forms of the elementary aspect of life, and also in the very developed forms of the highly evolved worlds of plant, animal and human life and landscape and background within which they are orchestrated.

The sort of message that matter is communicating depends upon its level and the order to which it belongs. Just as the significance of time and space alters almost beyond our understanding when we change from the human world to the world of the atom, so also the type of message being communicated will differ and belong to other orders of significance. Nevertheless however hard it is for us to grasp, it is the content of communication which must be looked for when we wish to understand the nature and responses of matter at any level.

This theory will have a very muddling effect upon some readers because this attitude towards the great mysteries of life is very different from the ones to which we have been accustomed. The objective has not been to complicate and confuse, but it is bound to seem so because it had to alter the position from which we usually view these phenomena. The purpose has really been to deal with the problem of identity, which is a pressing, very fundamental and often painful part of existence. It has tried to show a possible reason why this most fundamental essence of experience upon which our confidence and peace of mind is built is so often unsatisfactory. It has tried to understand why 'nature' has left such an important part of our awareness in the air. The theory explains that this is because we are still in a preliminary stage of development which is necessary before we can experience a unique and creative identity at this fundamental level of consciousness which is called the Absolute or Divine level. It is a shock to find the theory pointing to the fact that our true nature (what there is of it in a responsive state) is already Divine and that all the significance we attach to this level of consciousness we must also attach to ourself. It puts us in a position which is bound to be uncomfortable and even weird, for we are conditioned to believe in almost any form of identity but this particular one. We must stop thinking of the Divine as being something beyond and something other than our Self. We must learn to accept and enjoy it and not be in too much awe of it. We must learn that we are a part of the Absolute, but that we do not know what the Absolute is. We must experience it to know it and this is the only way we shall know anything. We are what we think of as *That* consciousness and *That* cause. And *That* is always here and now. The problem of identity is only solved when we cease to fear to let go . . . of the identity we have consciously or unconsciously decided to make do with. By losing ourself deliberately and without fear, we may sense and experience the True Self. Some cannot do it suddenly in this way and have to complete a gradual course of intellectual metamorphosis which must extend in time. But in the end, what is time? Neither long nor short and not of any consequence; only the result of one individualised aspect of this Absolute consciousness wishing to communicate with another. This desire resulted in time and also in space, in all their related forms which in the end cannot be compared to anything that might enable us to know if they are large or small, long or short. Logically speaking, even the qualities which remain in our experience when we have absorbed them from the quantitative aspect of events are themselves only aspects of one overall quality. This is 'The Quality' beyond comparison and is the ultimate standard of what is called the Absolute Consciousness. If an Ultimate God exists, this quality of attitude is what this God values most. Speaking poetically, however, it is the quality which we will all find enthralling, and perhaps unconsciously do already. It may also be thought of as the Aspiration or as the Beloved (depending on the attitude of the reader) of God. This theory is not concerned with the basic problem of most religious philosophy, which is the reality and nature of God. The problem does not really exist in this way, for one can go ahead now with the realisation of True Nature without having to decide for or against a Personal or Individual Parental Creator. One may use the system of consciousness and manifestation that *is*, and when this is used successfully, one will have learned to operate consciously and deliberately at many different levels of awareness and experience and be in a position to discover if this God exists and what He/She is like. And again if one has faith and instinctive knowledge of this Absolute God, nothing said denies this. The theory only suggests possible ways of accepting our closeness to such a Creator, and discovering ways in which we are preventing ourselves experiencing the 'Hearts Desire' and our Divine Parents' presence.

One thing is apparently certain, and that is the fact that the scheme of consciousness we are in has made ample provision for us to become and remain autonomous. And if we ourselves were such a Creator as this system requires, we can understand that the reason for this is that He prizes, as we do, the true and unique individual identity. God feels, as we do, that He can only have a limited and temporary friendship with a machine, a robot, a computer or a person who insists upon being a slave or a worshipper. There is a great difference between being enthralled by a quality and worshipping a quality. And yet with this freedom which individuality requires there are limitations which prevent us growing into the wrong species. But this is not a limitation in the last analysis. It is intended to 'guide' us into that species from which consciousness springs and in which it has the best chance of expression. So the limits set upon the initial stage of development are only a means whereby we can eventually become limitless. This is something we experience in bringing up our own children and is the expression of our desire that they should be free of things which we as more experienced people know would limit their chances of survival and balanced development.

When we become more detached from our bodies of communication and their informing consciousness or Entities, we are then able to view the situation and valuations from the Absolute level of consciousness, which level is free of fears or desires which might be inclined to warp our judgements. When we sense this innermost knowing which tells us what is better and what is best, it also enables us to take the pressure of fear and desire off our bodies and Entities so that they can work more accurately and efficiently. We have a series of garments to fit every level of manifestation, and we learn to put one on and another off as we wish. These garments or bodies are like beads on a string, and the string is our Individual consciousness and the powers which are inherent in it. Unless our attitude to these bodies is correct we do not stand a chance of relating them correctly or using them correctly. Now the only attitude which can achieve this harmony and co-operative response from the Entities is the one which in the Western World is known as the Christ Consciousness and which in the East is sometimes known as the Buddha Consciousness, or the consciousness of Universal Love and Concern. The reason is this: The Entities consist of the Divine Consciousness itself and this nature working within them recognises the 'Voice of the True Master' which is the True Self and rejects the voice of the False Master which is the make-do or false facade. The only way a false facade can keep the Entities working together is by taking their place and/or dominating their consciousness. But we make an awful mess of the work which the Entities do very well, so that the result of this wrong attitude is stress, numbing, and displacement of control leading to breakdown.

The Christ Consciousness we see now to be the result of the recognition and realisation of the unity of all things because, from the highest to the lowest, they all have their basis and purpose rooted in the Absolute or divine level of consciousness and are therefore a part of our own nature and a part of our well-being. We cannot have our own well-being without also having the well-being of our Entities and all those levels of matter-consciousness with which they are in touch. But it may be more than this. It may be that not only our well-being is related in this way but also our aspiration and enthrallment. In religious terms we might say that God's aspiration and love is represented as a quality of consciousness which is built into our nature as the frame of our harp. It is given and not within our ability to alter. Whatever or whoever formed the basis of the system of manifestation covering this part of the Universe in which we find ourselves, which is the Galaxy called the Milky Way, the expression of this aspect of consciousness may well be the key factor which gives purpose and integrity and unity to it. So that the understanding of this outlook and the acceptance of it is a condition of growth since Nature and the Entities we are involved with take this as their basic concern and identity because they have no choice. If this is so, then whether or not Christ lived as it is written in the gospels, the principles and the attitude and teaching given do, in fact, perfectly symbolise this prerequisite to growth and attainment of Self-realisation. Not only this, but if Christ exists as a particular Individual then He/She is also the embodiment and pattern of the Divine Aspiration through which Divinity becomes Creative and goes beyond

Itself. This Pattern in our midst, while it may not be absolutely copied by us, gives us the most valuable clue and insight into our own true nature, and therefore brings us to life as nothing else could do.

CHAPTER NINE : Summary

The relative nature of our philosophy can be seen in the nature of the Schools of Thought which range from logical ones to illogical ones. It is as though man rose from a level of primitive instinct through a process of deliberation and non-instinct which we call human culture, to a higher level of intuitive instinct. A process of immediacy with life, which becomes second-hand in our culture and sophistication, in order to reach immediacy again at a much higher level when man becomes mature. The whole field of manifestation is united to a developing purpose so that it is not necessary to call it materialistic or spiritual—to us it is all relative. Nothing can be shown to be totally without some form of consciousness. However much we think we know, we know very little, for the system of relative knowledge points to the fact that we shall only know what anything is when we know everything and understand everything. We should take up the humility of Socrates, then we might be told that we were becoming wise. We should try and understand events by trying to understand what the elements in them are 'saying'. Yet we must respect our self more highly without allowing it to breed conceit, for we are far more valuable than we think we are. We are of the nature of the Absolute, our Divine Parents. The Person of Christ is the Aspiration and Prototype for us and is thus also a catalyst since we can recognise instinctively in Him what we lack . . . if we are that interested. If we are not interested, the system waits for us.

CHAPTER TEN

Conditioning Factors

Our human nature and situation is not fortuitous and could not have come about without a certain design being present in the system of manifestation. This design stems from the level of Absolute consciousness which exhibits all the signs of being a very knowing and efficient state of awareness which is not limited in its abilities by the function of the communication systems which affect the lower orders of consciousness and which are, relatively speaking, more viscous, more of time and space. It suggests there is a motive behind things being what they are, behind the fact that human nature is such and such, and seeks to know and understand its loves and desires and longings. This motive comes from the Absolute and one can name the consciousness which conditions this Absolute by any label one likes, as long as it is remembered that one knows very little about it and does not jump to unnecessary conclusions. It can be said to be the Architect of the Universe, Allah, God, Our Divine Parents, The Ancient of Days, The Supreme Being, but it appears that one should be very wary of considering it as a mechanical function of consciousness like a giant computer. For either a thing is conscious or it is imitating consciousness. However complicated and clever the imitation is, it is limited in respect of consciousness as such, which in turn may be very poor and full of aberrations. There is a stream of consciousness in human culture which unknowingly describes the orientation of the whole species. It cannot be represented by one person and we can only observe it if we study the lives of many people. One aspect is represented in one individual and another in another. But the result of understanding all these together is more than the sum of the parts. It represents a striving towards another dimension of consciousness, and it is this which gives a clue to the design in which we grow and develop with less and less restraint as we cease to be in need of it. Like the rest of the phenomena we are able to study, the ability to choose depends upon a vast complex of conditioning and unconditioning factors which make the process a part of a relativistic system.

If we could combine the attitude and motive of the great artist, scientist, philosopher, mystic and political leader, we would begin to approach a vision of the idea towards which consciously and unconsciously we strive. But the sum of the parts of the vision do not give the true quality and purpose of the vision. This can only be obtained by the instinctive and unconventional experience of the intuitive state of consciousness. The problem of relating this intuitive vision to the normal 'rational' attitude is extremely great and it is the problem confronting this theory of consciousness.

Without some apprehension of this pattern of growth one is not in a position to tackle the problem of freedom of choice. This problem is sometimes referred to as the problem of 'free will'. But there is another function apart from the process of Self-motivation for which one should more properly reserve the term will-power. For those who have had the opportunity to study the direction in which the finest lives in our history are oriented, the overall drive seems to be an experience of an ideal state of consciousness, which signifies this more fundamental quality or attitude of which we are hardly aware, but from which the virtues of loving kindness, serenity, optimism, beauty, knowing and aspiration stem. However, the quality desired is the result of a state of living consciousness one 'dimension' beyond these attractive virtues, which virtues will never add up to this condition of consciousness itself, however hard they are manufactured and collected. This realisation is the cause of the passivity found in many religious teachings. In one system it may be explained as the doctrine of Grace, which is given and never deserved. In another system it may be considered as the philosophy of sudden attainment. In another system it is merely referred to as genius. In another system it is called insight or revelation. But in whatever way we have come to recognise this principle the general impression is that the process involved is not one which works according to the normal idea of cause and effect or which fits into the normal sense of what we are as human beings.

The disquieting thing about all great men and their work is that they themselves give the impression that the key factor in their creative function is always something which arrives in their consciousness ready-made as it were, and which thereupon enables them to motivate themselves to digest the significance of the new arrival and reorient their attitude about it. The key factor itself never seems to be within the field of what they consider to be their own command. It is not they, but we, who insinuate that the great men themselves give us the fruit of their lives. They would more generally say that their part in the work was one of interpretation and that the 'thing' which they found within their consciousness was what they tried to express. No man of this stature ever feels that he has adequately translated the full significance of his 'thing'. No man of this stature ever feels that his work has been to create the 'thing', he only feels his work to be the interpretation of it. Now if such an obvious source of motivation as this is considered by those closest to it to be given, then the Self-motivation of the man involved consists only of his acceptance and study of this 'thing'. It appears that in this way we do not have control over the source of inspiration, but only over our own acceptance of it. If we don't accept it someone else may very well do so. Therefore so far as the species is concerned, the race of man will receive and be conditioned by this new 'thing' because it will be received by one great man if not by another.

If this is correct, then every human being is conditioned by the type and quality of thought, attitude, sense of beauty and so forth which natural leaders feel comes to them and which they thereupon interpret and express to us. The greatness of these leaders is not so much in their vision, which is often 'given' them, but in their ability to communicate it. A great many people must have experienced valuable visions and insights, but we have never heard of them because they did not have the type of personality which could communicate. So there are two important points here, the one suggests that we are conditioned by the perceptions made available to us by natural leaders of thought and feeling and sense of beauty, but that these leaders are also in their turn conditioned by these perceptions which arrive in an unpredictable way within their consciousness. If this is not always correct, it is correct often enough to make us consider just how completely we are controlled in our experience of free choice by the material available for us to choose between. If, for instance, there are ten baskets of apples for us to choose between, the law of averages would suggest that out of a hundred people the number choosing from each basket would be approximately equal. But in practice we find that the situation is quite different for only one of the baskets has sweet apples in and the rest are sour. By tasting the apples and telling other people about the taste, we discover that what happens is that all the sweet apples are quickly chosen and eaten, and most of the sour apples are not touched. The point here is that if there is some informing consciousness beyond the level of our own awareness, which we think is very probable, then this consciousness can control the whole of our human existence by the type and quality of the perception it lets fall into the consciousness of the human race. If this informing consciousness has control over the nature of the 'things' which our leaders pick up and interpret to us, then it also has control over us. This is in fact how many people feel the situation is. They know they have the ability to choose, but they also know instinctively that they cannot choose just 'anything'. They are in fact conditioned as to what they choose by the quality of the things available from which to choose.

The second important point is that what we often admire our cultural leaders for is not truly their creative ability but is more accurately their ability to communicate. The value of such a person is in his ability to take to himself and to relate efficiently a number of communication bodies with their associated Entities who monitor them. Such an ability as this is certainly not within the conscious nature of the individual—he merely discovers that he has the ability to do such and such a thing better than other people can. The problem thus stated makes us wonder whether a Beethoven was the communicating personality or the informing consciousness or both. It is possible, according to our theory, to be both but it is also possible not to be either, in that the informing consciousness may deal directly with the Entities, and that the merit and value of the individual human being consists in bringing together and maintaining in an harmonious and responsive condition that series of bodies of communication which are necessary to transmit from the level of the informing consciousness to the level of the physical world or whatever level is suitable for its expression.

This way of looking at human events may help us to understand the many and differing factors involved in the lives of great men. It is found that very often the personality of an artist is hardly related to the value of his work. It explains the idea of the Muse who informs the poet, of the God, who informs the prophet, of the master who informs the disciple not only in religious fields but in all the cultural field as well. While this may be the case on occasions, very often the informing consciousness is the higher nature of the individual himself who has obtained the faculty of his true Divine Self, while at the same time 'descending' to lower and lower levels of communication and stringing together the appropriate bodies for this extended translation. In this process he may be cut off from the direct knowledge of his own Divine Self, and his work may be accomplished instinctively.

This informing consciousness we now see may be of many kinds and of many levels. It is obvious from the study of mediums that they have the ability as human beings to make their communication bodies and circuits available to an informing consciousness which they 'consciously' know nothing of. But we sense in the results of such activity that the informing may be done by a part of the medium's nature which he is not aware of, and that this part of the nature need not be a high level one even if its awareness can perceive things which seem uncanny. Also we are inclined to accept the fact that at times a medium may channel information from a relatively high level of consciousness, and while it may seem uncanny, its merit will be an integral part of the communication. The informer who uses the circuits which the medium is able to supply may also be another individual, a human being who has a physical body of communication or who does not possess one. The informer may be an Entity, whose proper job is to monitor the building and work of bodies. It may be an Entity that has evolved to a high level of consciousness, or it may be a Human or Entity who has reclaimed his Divinity and so become a 'God' in relation to us. In cases it may be He/She who dominates the Absolute level of consciousness, who is the God of Gods and who we think of as our Christian God. Or it may be such a person described as being the Embodiment or the Aspiration of God, who we call the Christ or The (particular) Son of God.

This is the complexity of the situation which may exist when one tries to determine whether or not one possesses the power of self-motivation. The simple answer is that it is impossible to be self-motivated. The best we can achieve is a relatively large amount of conscious motivation mixed with a number of unknown and unrealised motivations. There is probably a degree in which we are all 'mediumistic' and there is probably a larger degree in which we are controlled by one of the Entities with which we are associated. We are acting mediumistically when we channel our unconscious motives as well as when we channel our higher nature. We are also at the mercy of the 'things' which other people are receiving and translating into the world around us. To be independent and in command of all our motives in the face of all this would be a victory indeed. One thing seems fairly obvious however and that is the fact that we can only hope to cope with all these factors if we salvage the ability and awareness of our own individual Divine nature. For without this overall attitude of our highest consciousness, we are not even able to see what the problems are which beset us. So we have a certain amount of freedom of choice, but we are in a situation where we do not necessarily gain what we want by using this freedom. Rather do we profit best by sensing which are the sweet apples and which are the sour apples and accepting the fact that we have no control over what is in the baskets. At the moment our idea of freedom is the ability to make ourselves miserable and ill by eating all the apples in the first basket we choose. We don't like people to think we have made a mistake and we feel that to possess and to consume a larger number of apples than other people is a measure of our success and intrinsic worth. Freedom is far more subtle than that, for it involves the ability to choose that which is most fitting for the nature we possess and the situation in which we find ourselves. Since we hardly concern ourselves with what we are or what the significance of the Universe is, it is not surprising that our concept of freedom is nothing more than a tribulation to us and a mockery of our potential responsibility and aspiration.

So not only is it virtually impossible for us to have freedom of motivation, or as people call it, free will, but neither is there any particular point in possessing it since it will not bring us to what we really want but only bring us to what we think we want or what we think we should want. The little motivation we have should all be concentrated on the very light touch necessary to manipulate the helm of a ship. We must realise that our job here is to learn to sail our ship well, then and only then to make a journey in it. We do not control the wind or the water and it does little good to pretend to be a type of boat which we are not. We must take a good look at our ship and our sails for they are already there. We must study the wind and the sea and learn to use them to move about safely and efficiently. We must ask and seek to know what lands are at hand and we must decide which are most favourable to the capabilities of our craft, and the direction of the wind and state of the sea and visibility. We must reckon on how much food we can take and how well we can sail. By the time we have done this there will be no choice.

To make a journey in a craft which we cannot handle to a destination we are not in a position to reach, just for the sake of feeling we have made a free choice, is a form of insanity which we are all inclined to indulge in but which has no place in the scheme of things. The sooner we understand this the better, and it will save us the time and energy we waste in talking about freedom, for what we are really doing is trying to avoid the experience and understanding which is beyond the verbal level and beyond the level of prestige and self-satisfaction. This is the poetic and intuitive consciousness which enables us to begin to have a true knowledge of what is. From this time onwards the idea of freedom of choice or freedom of motivation no longer concerns us, for we will be too busy living our true nature.

What freedom of choice really means is the ability we must develop to sense the whole of the situation in which we are involved, both in our own nature and in the world around us, and then to take the best course available. Freedom is not in choosing, it is in seeing the irrelevance of choice.

CHAPTER TEN : Summary

Our Loves and Longings come to us from the conditioning which has been deliberately worked into the system. The Conditioner is not mechanical. He-She is a living reality and the best of our culture as a whole points to the values this Creator has in store for us. We cannot get what is offered if we try and snatch it for the wrong reason, for the reason is part of it. We should endeavour to make the most of what we already have, only then perhaps will we be given more. Our leaders and guides are those who are able to interpret to us the values our nature needs in order to truly become itself. Not any values are sufficient, only the ones which our nature is designed to employ. Wrong values must be rejected by our real self recognising that they are indigestible. How these higher values come to us through certain people can be very involved. Sometimes the process is conscious and sometimes unconscious or mediumistic, its 'highness' is also relative. To become free-will individuals in this involved world is much harder than we think. In fact freedom is not really what we want. What we are really in need of is more like fulfilment. Freedom of choice should not exist except in unimportant matters. Real freedom is freedom from the need to choose by being fully aware of what is best and correct.

CHAPTER ELEVEN

Sin

This theory suggests that we are only in a state of preparation for the experience of consciously becoming a Divine individual. We are at this time a potentiality which is slowly becoming actualised. A part of this potentiality is already given us in what is called the shape of our harp, but the music which this harp will eventually play can only be played by us, and in this respect we are uniquely creative. However, during the necessary long and tedious experience which we endure, life after life, in order to generate self-consciousness and to prepare the strings in our Divine Instrument, we do (and we are expected to) make repeated mistakes. Because we are bound to be wrong in our preliminary valuations and because the system we are in must expect this, then such mistakes cannot carry the serious implications which much of our theology would have us believe. If we did not make mistakes and were not prepared to continue to make more mistakes then the process of evolution would come to a halt. Since this evolution of the Divine Nature in each of us is what we have come to accept as the purpose of manifestation, then the refusal to make mistakes in this sense would be a refusal to take part in life and would be a negation of our purpose. As we use the word sin to represent the idea of resistance to Divine purpose, then the fear of making mistakes and the refusal to live life are themselves sins.

At this point it is necessary to differentiate between what we think of as sin and what we think of as evil. If sin is equivalent to bad, which is the necessary opposite of good, then it is no more and no less significant than the processes of trial and error which are used in the sciences and technologies, and in this sense it can carry no stigma or punishment other than the natural repercussion of making a mistake in any situation. Evil is in a slightly different class in that it is a deliberate making of what we know to be a wrong action in the knowledge of why it is wrong and the harm it may do. While this can be described as deliberate wickedness, here also there must be care not to judge the situation hastily, for what may be a position of conscious choice of wrong action to us may not be so to another person for the simple reason that the 'person' concerned may not be in control of the situation.

What was referred to as sin a hundred years ago can now be regarded as psychological illness, and clearly it is difficult to know where the responsibility for so called sin lies. In the sense that the true individual should be responsible for all the activities of his bodies of communication we have all failed to achieve this; and in the sense that what is not under our proper control will take its image of behaviour from the surroundings, we are all controlled to a large extent by the environment.

Since there is a very good reason why we should make mistakes and also a very good reason why we should force ourselves, through an honest and proper realisation of our autonomy, into the dead-centre position where we become the apotheosis of estrangement, we must not allow the concept of mistaken action and valuation with its accompanying suffering to deter us from following upon the evolutionary path. It seems, however, that all too often those who succeed in reaching this uncomfortable phase of conscious separateness from all things, fail to understand the significance of the pain involved and the efforts cease. Instead of continuing to the conclusion of the detachment, aloneness and lostness— from which position we are able to deliberately take up again the life we have rejected—we compromise to the extent that we put up on the surface of life a personality that is 'with it' and socially acceptable while remaining underneath empty and afraid of that emptiness.

This aspect of experience, which leads to a total divorcement from other individuals and from nature, is something which has not been dealt with in this way before, and yet in religious terms it may well be a significance of the symbol of crucifixion. People have, of course, dealt with suffering to the extent that we are all tired of the subject, yet to see it not as 'payment' of some kind, but as a positive and creative act of honest objective valuation makes of it a very different matter. Psychologists are already dealing with it along these lines, but the theory which lies behind the value of the dead-centre position is not a common one. The name dead-centre describes well the symptoms of this experience. If now is added to it a creative context which suggests the extreme value of this detached and objective view point, we will take much of the sting out of it and perhaps enable more people to live through it successfully. The context is simply this, that in gaining the sensation of being an island on our own, we feel the horror of too much conscious self-determinism and we at the same time appreciate the value of the group. We have emerged from the 'pack' with the thought that this was the objective of greatest value for us, but now we are made to understand that life cannot be lived alone, that like music and art it has no value in isolation. We therefore have to surrender our new found autonomy to a group, but in deliberately selecting those whom we wish to share with, we overcome the limitations of the pack and take on the responsibilities and pleasures of shared objectives with all the possibilities for communication of individual view points which this opens up. But this is not the only significance of this position of aloneness. By far the greatest one is beyond words to describe, for it is the sensation of being without the instinctive feeling that we are a part of 'something'. Which means we feel what it is like to be a part of 'nothing'. Verbally this may not mean very much to the reader, but in the philosophical sense in which it is given it does in fact signify a great deal. It does, above all, teach us a little humility, for the pain involved is of a very particular sort, for it is the pain of negation and not only does this tell us that we value consciousness above all else, but it teaches us as nothing else can the truth of the fact that consciousness is not only shared but that it is given. After this experience we will no longer neglect to put into life what we take out of it, for we will sense that consciousness and life are the same thing and that our own life is an integral part of this. Like breathing, we must immerse ourselves in the medium for which we were designed. Like a God to execute our highest intentions, but like a wise God to realise the limitations of those intentions.

One of the chief effects of the idea of original sin which the Christian churches teach is common experience to us all. It is to take away from us the source of initiative. While we must be wise in the estimation of our limitations so far as autonomy is concerned, without the desire to enter into life and gather its experiences we will undoubtedly fail to actualise our potentiality through the course of evolution. But with the idea of original sin the mainspring of life is broken, for we associate with this idea the fact that there is something rotten at the core of nature, and of course it is from the core of our nature that we must draw if we are to enter fully into life. Therefore the suspicion insinuated into us regarding our essential nature not only destroys, to our instinctive intelligence, the value of our nature and ability, but it also destroys in our instinctive understanding the value of any god who can take over where our own ability has been invalidated. For who can value a god who has created us rotten at heart and who thereupon makes great play out of saving us from this wretched condition?

It would seem that the whole conception we have of sin and punishment comes to us from the pre-christian era, and while we have had ample opportunity to change our views on this we have unfortunately failed to do so. It is only recently in the atmosphere of modern society where the religious view of life has been partly lost and forgotten that men have once again begun to take life at its face value, and while this is sometimes a shallow affair it at least has the merit of being an honest affair. The old idea of sin is based on superstition surrounding high frequency teachings that higher men bring to the world from time to time. These high frequency teachings tell people not to do certain things because the teacher understands that such actions will cause one part of nature to war with another part and thus cause suffering. This leads to the assumption that certain actions cause suffering and thus in superstitious terms invite punishment. Now it is a short step from this to the idea that if God uses punishment we should use it also, in fact that we might please this God by doing the punishing for him or even by doing it when it is not deserved. We come to the conclusion that this God enjoys punishment and is largely concerned with dealing it out to us. In fact better still, he creates us full of sin in order that he can punish us all the time. He only stops punishing us when we have given up all right to life, to enjoyment, to initiative and to individuality. He only stops punishing us then because we are no longer present as a valid person and so God would be punishing himself.

Now it is a long step between this sort of conception of life and of God to the conception that God sends us teachers from time to time, not to punish or judge us, but to explain to us (so far as we are capable of receiving it) that certain actions and attitudes destroy the harmony in our living parts and cause one of our entities or natures to interfere with and upset another. The teaching of purity and simplicity, as it implies directness, is essential from the point of view of this theory. For this allows us to feed directly on the innermost understanding of our being which is our Divine Nature and which we cannot reach if the channels of communication are cluttered up, diverted or short circuited. Until we act and value from the level of this Divine part of our nature, we are not able to make sense of life or intuitively feel our purpose in it. Without this basic knowledge we are lost. Whatever we build or value will be arbitrary and unsatisfactory. The teaching of purity and simplicity is therefore not an attempt to narrow down our life and experience, it is not a type of punishment, it does not invalidate our individuality neither does it bring special dispensations with it from God. It is nothing more or less than what is understood in scientific terms as a law of condition of nature which we must accept and work with because it is not within our ability to change. To be pure is not to be in fear of making mistakes which will make God angry with us and thus punish us. It is rather to eradicate from our attitudes the hesitations and suspicions which prevent us acting and experiencing with intensity and conviction. For true intensity only comes from the level of high voltage or potentiality which is the highest frequency level of the Divine Self.

The nearest thing we possess to original sin is the heritage of wrong attitudes in the society into which we are born. This is a very real obstacle to us in that it upsets the balance between the higher nature and the lower nature since our society is biased to observe and value life from the low frequency position. This acts on us like the teaching of original sin and causes us to believe that there must be some truth in it, but we can now think of this as being nothing more than the habit of centuries which one generation passes on to another in the very atmosphere of its consciousness.

Sins are all those habits we grow into from our childhood which we pick up from our parents and our surroundings which put first things last and last things first. In that we only truly live, whether we wish to or not, from our inner consciousness we learn either to shut off this consciousness with its instinctive knowledge of what is right and wrong for us, or we go to sleep inwardly and go through the motions of life only on the surface of our consciousness. What we have to learn to do is to reassess the values of society for ourselves and hinge them on what we feel to be the qualities of deepest and most enduring value which we experience for ourselves or which we find in ourselves. We have to accept that we cannot experience everything and that we must learn to gather and judge some experience through the communications of other people. But this is all a part of the function of the proper group with which we choose to associate when we have got beyond the stage of wishing either to be a part of a pack or an independent island. This is the dead-centre experience. But we must not expect this to stand out as clear cut experience on its own, for this is not the way life seems to work. What we find is that many aspects of experience are jumbled together and come and go at different parts in our life. We may have a few days of the dead-centre position which does not occur again, but which causes us to reassess many other experiences that we have had. On the other hand we may experience the sensation of this detached position at intervals throughout our life.

Apart from the wrong habits we pick up from our environment, there are all those wrong assessments we make which we have now come to think of in terms of psychological illness. These also are often interpreted in terms of sin when they are no more than the result of unfortunate circumstances, or the wrong valuation in the process of trial and error through which we are bound to go. These wrong and often destructive reactions we build into our nature are also capable of being considered as overladen and fear-ridden circuits which run around and cut across the proper and healthy circuits which we should normally possess. The result to the casual observer is often deliberate wrong doing which should be rewarded with punishment. The result is often the apotheosis of sin so far as we can judge the situation. But we are not in a position to judge the situation properly and so the use of the term sin and the punishment we would give are both meaningless. It would appear that the only corrective punishment that works is the punishment that is given by a loving parent to a loving child. When this condition is not present, then the value of punishment decreases rapidly in proportion to which the ideal relationship is lacking. Real punishment is always an act of love. The rest is revenge.

In the analogy of the harp which represents the building in and sounding of the various responses of our true Divine Nature, the strings that are missing represent potential weakness in our make-up. If we are born into an environment where the characteristics of this weakness are required, we will be at a disadvantage and inclined to misbehave. In this sense, so far as it refers to the slow and relatively timeless awakening of the Divine Nature, the blank areas in our harp represent areas of potential sin and can be considered in certain ways as original sin because we are born into the world with them. However, this weakness through lack of experience on the part of the Divine Self, is not a planting of actual sins in our nature which would be a positive act, but it is simply the lack of actual knowledge of how to behave which is a negative factor. This negative factor is necessary if we are to be given that most valuable right to develop as unique and real individuals. If the system did not allow for this the whole process would be mechanical and nothing we represented or expressed would have any value and the idea of evolution would be pointless.

Another factor when trying to understand the nature of what we call sin is that a certain time is necessary when the process of physical death occurs and the physical body of communication is vacated, for the other higher frequency bodies to be 'shuffled off' also. These bodies require a certain time to de-activate and return to the matrix from which they were composed. If the time required to decompose is not allowed, then they will still be in some state of composition when the True Self takes up another physical life and all the bodies that are associated with it. This means that instead of starting with a clean sheet of paper to work on, the unfortunate individual is liable to pick up where he left off and find he has attracted to himself some previous body or bodies of communication with all the old circuits still active. He is really up against it in this circumstance because he finds he is doing things without any knowledge of the reason behind them. In this sense there is some truth in the concept of original sin, but again it is not the doing of any other but the person involved. The only safeguard against this vicious circle of pointless birth and death which tends to repeat old lives and mistakes over and over again, is to turn our attention to high frequency considerations and experiences, for after death these act as a draw to our true nature and enable us to spend sufficient time at the higher levels of consciousness between lives for the lower bodies of communication to neutralise and return to the common condition from which they arose. This may be the teaching of the Buddha regarding the wheel of birth and death from which we must learn to free ourselves. It is also more loosely implied in the teaching of Christ in terms of 'losing our Soul', for if this process of picking up old and mistaken responses from one life into the next continues, the lower nature does indeed become incapable of communicating with the higher and truer nature. The lower nature may be very clever on earth and very rich also, but it may lose the whole point of existence which is to relate experience to the Divine Sense which is the only way to overcome that deep and grief laden fear that, in spite of everything, life is nothing but a part of some odd dream or nightmare.

There may be some truth behind the idea of original sin, but it is not the sort of truth that we have been used to. Similarly, there is some truth behind the teaching of salvation in the sense that 'waiting for Grace' to accomplish the transformation to the higher nature for us puts us into a passive state of consciousness. This not only prevents our lower nature reactivating too many false circuits in our bodies but it also tends to put us into that condition of quiet in which we can sense something of our own higher nature. This was present all the time but overlaid with the noise and confusion of a too active lower nature. While it is not suggested that there is no Divine intervention on the part of God or on the part of our Divine Brothers, it is possible that in dealing with these matters we do in fact accomplish far more than we think by the working of our own nature. It is this true and proper working of our nature, at all its levels and in complete harmony, which is the crux of our training and preparation. This is why so many religious teachings, which are half truths, fail us. They fail because they consider only one part of the process and by taking it out of context they make the process unnatural. What is suggested here is that there is a natural religion woven into the nature of things which alone can succeed where the man-made religions are bound to fail. That the purpose of religion is in no way a repayment to a God or the worship of a God, but that it is primarily the discovery of our own worth and ability. If we envisage a creator he would be very 'small minded' if our worship and service were all that interested in Him. The truth may very well be that He/She enjoys bringing up independent individuals who can delight in the many experiences which are available. In other words, the relationship is much the same as with good parents on earth. They wish to give their children a good healthy start which will enable them to mould themselves according to their nature and not simply as copies of their parents. Parents enjoy the fact that the children are enjoying themselves, but at the same time they have to indicate to the children that there are right ways and wrong ways of doing everything. The idea of over-devotional worship would be as wrong between us and God as it would be between us and our children. What one wishes to arrive at with one's children is ultimately a spontaneous friendship when they come of age.

In religious terms, mistaken attitudes are not the same as deliberate evil and what we think of as sin has no basis in reality and therefore does not require forgiveness. If we accept the existence of Divine Parents or God then we must accept that this God expects us to make mistakes because this is a necessary part of our intrinsic value. This is the value of an independent and autonomous individual who chooses to live a more and more creative and beautiful life as he understands the significance of timeless and unchanging values within the framework of his Divine 'Harp', which is given him and not chosen.

There is a natural way to the discovery and enjoyment of our True Divine Nature and this way is built into the very structure of the universes since it is the creative purpose behind the whole project. While it may be necessary to indulge in man-made concepts of religion at an early stage of development because our climate of thought has wandered too far from the high frequency tone, this man-made religious structure will become a positive barrier to later understanding since it tends to cut out all those natural processes and responses which are inherent within us and which are there for this very purpose. The lower order idea of what man is and how he relates to the structure of nature is far from the true one and we can see this for ourselves if we study the findings of contemporary science. Unfortunately, most of us do not study these findings or relate them to our systems of ideas or philosophies.

This theory is not trying to discount the concept of Divine help and intervention, but would lay it down very clearly that when this help comes, its nature will be to enable us to help ourselves and not to take the initiative from us. It will not be in the nature of a 'joy ride to heaven'. It would be a farce if our Creator designed us in such a way that He lived our lives for us, but this is the very thing which many of his devoted servants wish for. They do not realise that in taking up this attitude of wrongly interpreted faith they are in fact serving their God the most cutting and hurtful insult. For they are implying that creation is a cunning swindle in which God creates them only in order to take away that Individuality of consciousness of which He gives them a taste. Any help received from the

Divine Nature will more likely be teaching which we can absorb to enable us to get out of a hopeless rut of repeated lives. We are trapped in this process of rebirth, because our aspiration is not strong enough to free us from the patterns of our old attitudes between physical lives. However, so long as it is not appreciated that we can return to one life after another we will not take this seriously. But at the same time we will not take our Divine possibilities very seriously either if we feel we have only one Life in which to generate them. We can believe that we do this in some after life, but the degree of this later development may well be in direct proportion to the amount achieved in this physical world.

The teaching of sin is therefore likely to be one of the most destructive religious forces at the present time, as the way that it is interpreted to us is that we are rotten at heart. This idea invalidates the main spring of our nature and destroys our image of God and our conception of our purpose and possibilities. It is unlikely that we will turn to the source of our salvation, which is our inner nature, if we are taught that it is here that God has planted weeds and caused them to flourish.

CHAPTER ELEVEN : Summary

While there is in us the feeling that we should not sin and also the preference for feeling virtuous, the fear of making mistakes is one which is against life. For life depends upon us making mistakes and correcting them. We would not grow if we did not do this. We consider evil to be a deliberate sin aimed at making other people miserable. But even evil may have a partly justifiable cause and the evil doer may not be sufficiently in charge of his nature to prevent it. While society must make rules to protect the rights of the majority, and while it must inhibit those who break the rules, it cannot be in a position to know how far any individual is to blame for his actions. The conditioning of parents, social background, education and all the complex pressures brought to bear on children cause them to grow into people who cannot cope. We are then apt to punish these non-copers. We should also be wary of being too virtuous if it prevents us 'living'. Not trying to live is the worst thing we can do. Purity is not goodness, it is having clear and undistorted communication with all our levels of experience. The idea of original sin is crippling, since it sets something rotten in the heart of our being where in fact our Divine Parents have set the best of our nature. Original sin is what we get when we catch the sickness of wrong living from the society we are born into. Between death and rebirth we should reach up high enough in our being to throw off the bad responses of the previous life. If we do not aspire to a sufficiently high level of consciousness, then we come back quickly into the world with our bad habits still clinging to our lower psychic bodies, with which we again become associated, becoming imprisoned by them. This is why Saviours try to help us by teaching us to aspire to higher values. There is a natural way of religion built into the nature of all things. Man-made religions fail us so long as they lose sight of this. Everyone is engaged in the religious life no matter who or what he is.

CHAPTER TWELVE

Justice

Another subject to be studied in the light of this theory is one of justice. This is not the sort of justice which is insinuated in our systems of law. It is that idea and sense of justice which we relate to ourselves in the circumstances we are born into and the fortune and luck we experience in our lives. Because the theory indicates that we are already individuals before birth, this individual nature is not sown at random into any situation on earth. It is not fortuitous the way some are born to good parents and others to bad parents and this is not some Divine blank spot. We must clarify our ideas concerning the nature of the working of justice as it affects the structure of our lives and the experiences that come our way. It must be decided if we are in a purely mechanical system of reciprocal effect, or whether we are in a system of conscious intelligent effect or whether we are in a system which combines both.

The superstitious attitude assumes that there is some cunning and perverted consciousness presiding over all our acts and, if we fail to keep to the special and secret rules, this presiding entity causes unpleasant things to happen to us and to our loved ones. This sort of thing concerns touching wood, sitting thirteen people at a table, spilling salt, breaking mirrors, putting up umbrellas in the house, wearing certain colours at a wedding and many, many other peculiar activities. These are at first harmless and childish thoughts but they do become more serious when they enter the field of religion. The examples one can give in this context are many. They start with offerings and supplications and they finish up with the idea that dispensation can be bought from God for hard cash. There is no doubt that the teaching of the fear of the Lord has much to do with this, but there is still a great deal of pagan and demoniac thinking behind a lot of outwardly religious observances and ceremonies. This type of attitude leads into the one which considers that God is not only capable of knowing and judging our smallest act and thought, but that He considers each one important enough to merit separate and distinct response in the form of applause or rebuke. Then there is the attitude which considers that if our acts are secret enough they will not come within the realm of any sort of judgement either from man or God. There is also the attitude of science which sees everything as 'mechanical' cause and effect. Lastly, there is that vague frame of mind which many of us are in which accepts that we have runs of good and bad luck.

Most of us oscillate between the idea of luck and the idea that somewhere along the line we get what we deserve, but we have no picture in our minds of how these processes can work. We must, if we are going to attempt to understand seriously our position in the scheme of nature, try to construct some system of reciprocal effect which is neither purely mechanical nor dependent upon the constant personal attention of God.

This structure of ideas which concerns the Divine Individual, matter-consciousness, bodies of communication and Entities, does in fact resolve itself into a reasonable system of response which goes a long way to satisfy the needs of a philosophy of justice. While many of the hypothetical processes will seem too weird and peculiar for serious consideration, they not only fit into the picture of the world which science is giving us, but they also fit into the experience we have of our own psychic nature and the instinctive knowledge which this nature seems to possess.

The basis of this theory of justice must rest upon our attitude to life. This attitude, which is our position on the vectors and which also represents the volume of experience we are in touch with, causes us to value events in a particular way and also to experience events in a particular way. While the position of development described by the three vectors is one of the factors involved in our attitude, the other is the nature of the Individual Self which we are not fully aware of and which has not as yet fully actualised. So that all the events are conditioned in some way by what we consider our self to be and unconsciously by what is in fact our self. Because the conscious image of what we are changes from time to time and because we are also changing more slowly at the essential but unrealised level of being we must therefore be in a constant state of change in relation to the happenings which occur around us and those which we ourselves initiate. If our sense of justice depends upon our attitude and this attitude is not static, then natural justice will seem also to be in a state of change. The condition of justice cannot by its definition change if it exists at all, therefore what is changing is our own valuation of events. If this is the case one cannot expect to find any system of justice in being which is capable of being understood until we have more nearly reached the end of evolution and are able to value occurrences from the highest frequency level, which is the level of consciousness least likely to fluctuate. While, however, it is impossible to understand true justice, it is possible to consider some of the principles that this universal justice might be governed by, for in the light of this theory it would seem very unlikely for such a thing as luck to exist.

Perhaps the simplest and most important single factor to realise in trying to understand why we are sometimes surrounded by pleasant happenings and at other times by unpleasant happenings is that the matrix from which all these happenings arise is not mechanical but is consciousness in some form or another. This is not taking the literal considerations of pure physics or mechanics to task, but treating of the broad issues of consciousness itself. What is being defined is the 'attitude' which the rest of creation seems to have towards us and which makes us seem either lucky or unlucky. In superstitious terms or even religious terms, one sometimes considers that one is going through a phase of losing or winning, in that things seem to be going wrong or going right. This is put down to the fact that we have either been behaving well or behaving badly and are getting our 'just' deserts. However, instead of thinking that these conditions have been created by ourselves, it is thought that someone is weighing up our good and bad points and creating the conditions for us. This, of course, is where God is brought in again. He is the one that is giving us heaven or hell. A more accurate picture of these 'just' deserts is that the thoughts and emotions we generate are continually radiating out from our bodies, at all their various levels of matter-consciousness, and impinging upon other lives or units of consciousness. If these radiations are of an irritating nature then we are creating unpleasant conditions for these other forms of consciousness in our proximity and in our own bodies of communication. These other entities and forms of life, like ourselves, resist influences which upset their functioning, they therefore tend to act in concert to remove or neutralise that influence which is irritating them. This influence is our own consciousness, in particular our attitude, and this attitude feels that the world is becoming hostile to it. This is so, but not a bit the way we think it is so. There is no one above working our punishments for us to suffer, but only friends and neighbours in the form of teeming millions of different units of life and consciousness (all the entities we are associated with) giving us a bit of our own medicine. Not because they wish to punish us but in order to indicate to us that we are putting them under pressure and interfering with their proper work which in any case is largely on our behalf.

Our own life, at all levels, exists in a matrix of other lives. We can only upset these other lives at our peril. These other lives are not only human acquaintances but also the entities we are associated with and all those minute forms of life which these entities govern and control for us. While many of these are at the physical and near physical level, others are at the level of the psyche in its higher and lower forms. What it adds up to is the fact that living experience comes to us as the result of an enormous group effort. If we wish to live with this group we must be aware of its needs as well as our own. The group is not only the human one which we communicate consciously with, but is also that which we label the world of nature, the elements and the psyche. Normally one thinks of these areas as being a neutral and a mechanical background to our activities. It is perhaps time that they were considered more carefully to see if they are in fact either neutral or mechanical. If they are not, they themselves will create the sort of conditions which we associate with our fortune and our luck. The matrix of existence is a living composition of millions of lives which, while they are different from our own, are still in some way conscious and responsive. If we upset their consciousness then we must expect their responses to upset us, and this is what seems to happen. The concept is the saying 'do as you would be done by'. While this saying is true of the human relationships, it has not been considered true of the whole natural background of our lives, particularly in the realm of consciousness. There is nothing mechanical in nature unless we ourselves have made it so. What appears to be mechanical in the function of the universe is the computer aspect of the individual units of consciousness. These computer functions work in our own world of experience and identification as well as in the rest of creation. While we consider our own computer activity to be consciousness, we deny this to our background because this conscious activity is one which we do not recognise as similar to our own. There have been many assumptions of this sort which have been discovered to be wrong. There seems every reason to think that this one is wrong also.

A very simple example is that it is accepted that if we cut off the leg of a live bird, the bird feels pain and distress. But if we cut off the branch of a living tree, the tree neither feels anything nor is aware of anything. While it is accepted that the tree is a living 'thing', it is not considered a living 'creature'. This is because the tree cannot communicate its distress to us. But the fact may be that we are simply incapable of receiving the tree's communications. This may seem a frivolous example, but it indicates quite clearly the sort of assumptions which are being made. It is not unreasonable to suppose that out of the thousands of these assumptions made about our natural background, many will be quite wrong and a lot more partly wrong. Whereas the activity of the tree is limited in the way it can affect our consciousness, the activity of the entities which live and work on the hyper-physical levels are far more able to communicate their distress to us. Not only can one expect them to communicate their distress, but like all forms of consciousness they will also tend to communicate their pleasure. We have denied real intelligence to most of the animal world, but species like the dolphin are found capable of a high degree of intelligence, playfulness and co-operation with man. This has not been recognised before because we have not tried hard enough to develop communications with the dolphin. It was too readily assumed that lack of communication implied lack of consciousness; but never in ourselves, always in what we failed to communicate with. While it is not suggested that we can talk to stones, there is some sort of communication which links us with everything. This 'talk' is not the conventional way of communicating which is only a very partial and inefficient form. If the structure of nature is conscious of us, even if we are not properly conscious of it, this structure will express its friendship or hostility which will be based upon our own attitude to it. This expression will not be anything obvious because we are in the habit of taking all background phenomena as being insignificant. The beauty of a lovely day in natural surroundings is assumed to be accidental and not intended. It never occurs to us that it is a definite communication in another language. Because we do not get the messages from the background the onus is not put on ourselves. We are not the ones who are failing to communicate. The background is failing to communicate and must therefore be without intelligence and consciousness. When we suffer from savage storms, the savagery does not originate from ourselves. Superstitiously some God is angry with us. One does not consider the more reasonable possibility that we ourselves have upset the structure of the natural background of which we are an integral part through the more intangible aspect of our personalities. If one did consider such a possibility, one might at first be inclined to think of it as pagan or as another form of superstition. But the teaching of Christ suggested that the lilies of the field and the birds of the air are a concern of God, as we are.

The burden of all this is that a great deal of our 'luck' may be caused by the reaction of our background to the quality or attitude of our own consciousness. As this is a collective phenomenon in most instances, we may find ourselves conditioned by unpleasant effects which are not the result of our wrong attitudes but of the attitudes of our fellow men. This sort of luck or background conditioning falls equally upon the deserving and the undeserving.

This sort of luck is not luck at all, it is the result of our collective behaviour. To put it into a few words, it is a rational proposition to say that if we lived more harmoniously with one another as well as with our background of 'natural phenomena', then this background would become more harmonious to us. This would not be caused by the intervention of

God, but as a direct result of the unconscious effect our attitudes are creating in the structures on which they impinge.

It is easy to see at this point how we have come to possess the fable of the fairy godmother and the semi-fable of the guardian angel. This system would place the fairy godparents and the guardian angel together at the level of our higher bodies of communication at the reading 5" or higher. In this case these beings would be the entities in charge of the function and building of these higher bodies. Being comparatively highly evolved in their own line of evolution, they will have attained some comparatively high degree of identity, understanding of reality and values, and sense of responsibility. Their intelligence will be acute and their work, which they will delight in, will be in direct line with the purpose of creation at whichever level they are 'at home' in. Those associated with us will very likely see their work as being not only to build finer bodies of communication for our present and future use, but also to guide us in situations which they can foresee and understand and which we cannot. This is not simply in order to save our personal selves from injury or pain, although this may be a side product, but it is to guide us into situations which will provide them with the material they consider they need for their building activity. In a nutshell, they must influence us to obtain 'better' experience if they are to build for us 'better' bodies. Our reactions to experience provide them with the 'stuff' with which these bodies are built. It is important to emphasize here that like most things in nature, the bodies of communication which these entities are building are fulfilling many functions and are not only there for our own service and convenience. They are no doubt providing some qualitative and structural service at higher levels of matter-consciousness than we are aware of, as well as being a focus for creative experience on the part of the entity evolution. Our 'fairy godparents' and 'guardian angels' love us as expressions of God's qualitative expression through humanity. They help and guard us as centres of this Divine activity, but they are not the slightest bit interested in our personality, which is the concept of ourselves we have come to give all our attention to and which is often so dreary and pointless in its way of life.

Another aspect of natural justice which is hard to understand in the present climate of thought, is the one which conditions who we are born to, when and where. This time and place aspect of parentage is as important as the quality of those parents, for while parents give us the vital security and lift into life experience, the time and place condition the type of experience which is available. None of this comes under the heading of chance or luck or even Divine intervention but the cause may be the nature of our own development and the nature of that group of humans with which we have come to develop.

To understand the argument it is necessary to return to the part of the theory which concerned the nature of our function after the process of physical death. We gravitated at this transition to a level of consciousness which was dependent on the level of chronic awareness. If this awareness showed a degree of aspiration towards the ideal, then the strength of this would enable us to reach and enjoy higher worlds of matter-consciousness. However, until a critical point is reached in development we will have to return again. We will wish to return again to the physical world in order to build in basic experience which is also used in the construction of higher bodies and of the 'strings' in the Divine Nature. Gradually one integrates in this way with a group of other humans who have interests in common. This will not only be family and friends but also people who have work in line with us which they wish to accomplish. The quality of this group conditions the environment we are born into in each physical life. If the quality is high we will have a good start to life and consider we are lucky. If the quality of the group is poor we will have a poor start to life and consider that we are unlucky. It goes without saying that the value of such a group is not measured in terms of its financial wealth or aristocratic connections but is measured in terms of the love, interest and understanding they have one for another. To be a part of a group who consistently ill-treat one another is to be in a position of one's own making and subject to one's own correction. This correction only comes as a result of acute discomfort of some sort. One does not necessarily help such a group by giving them better conditions unless at the same time one can improve their attitude. But there is often a direct link between physical conditions and attitude. One can also be in a small group which is high tone within a larger group which is low tone. In such an instance, the lower will tend to destroy the value of the higher. But again, one cannot measure the tone of a group by the outward success of its technical civilisation for this is likely to be as misleading and arbitrary as the personality itself. In fact, history shows that the best of a civilisation comes at the commencement of its growth. It then deteriorates although outwardly it may become more powerful, complicated and florid. For the vital part of any growth of this sort, such as the Greek or Roman civilization, is the initial high frequency impulse which is relatively pure, aspirational and unpredictable. It implies that it has been deliberately organised from a higher level of matter-consciousness. The potentiality of this higher level impulse is then worked out in time with the original spirit being lost in the trappings of its own expression.

There are very many instances of the working of this aspect of this theory. But all that concerns us now is the idea that we are the ones who condition our own future by the type of people we gravitate towards, and by the attitude that this group has towards one another. We follow this grouping beyond the metamorphosis called physical death, through the experiences of living in higher worlds of more ethereal matter-consciousness and then back to this physical world again. We continue this until there is no further need of the physical experience. However, after a certain level of expansion there may be the desire to achieve some definite work in the world which requires the assistance of a group of people. This group is within the natural group of evolution, and one plans with them, perhaps together with some higher level person who has developed well beyond average vision, to be born in some particular time and place to some particular parents in order that group efforts can link up on the physical plane. Such links, like the after-death experiences, are forgotten on return to earth. But they are still valid at the unconscious level and achieve something if not all of this purpose.

Ideas such as this are accepted and considered more easily in the Eastern half of the world. But because attention in the West has become focused upon physical techniques and because Christian interpreters leave no place for them these ideas seem at first very peculiar and suspect. But since they fit so accurately into this picture of reality, and since they allow for an understanding of many facts which otherwise have no explanation, it would seem wise to give this metaphysical structure some thought.

Apart from the bearing this concept has upon the sense of justice and the reason for birth into particular circumstances, it also helps to explain the fact that many are born into faculties already developed and with definite leanings towards certain professions long before these could logically be formed if we began in a condition of neutrality. There is also the case of the prodigy who performs superhuman tasks at the infant state. While certain of these might be put down to accumulated heredity, such as the prodigious memory, the artistically creative appear to be outside this category and there is no explanation available other than that of an act of God. The theory prefers to put it down to an act of an individual within the whole creative act of God. Without this individual autonomy the value of individual nature to the essential consciousness of reality would seem to be lost.

It is hoped that this argument will help to assess the function of natural justice and luck in our lives in terms of our own behaviour and effort. This is necessary if civilisation is to come of age and take its place in the universe as a centre of constructive behaviour and not as a confounded nuisance. For so long as it is considered that fortune is created by God or by 'simple' chance there will be no reason to expect that aspiration and effort will alter things. There is nothing purely mechanical or purely fortuitous in the universe unless we ourselves have made it so. Men and women play bingo and roulette when their lives have become purposeless. Nature never plays such games because it never becomes purposeless.

CHAPTER TWELVE : Summary

As well as the justice we make for ourselves in society, there is a deeper justice we are aware of in the field of what we more often think of as good and bad luck. The situation we are born into, how the world reacts to us, how our schemes work out, how other people behave towards us and the nature of the opportunities afforded us. This justice we find very difficult to understand. But if we recognise that all nature and all things are made up of countless lives which also think or feel to some extent then we can begin to account for this deeper and more far-reaching justice that comes to us. If we learn to value and use the rest of life rightly then we will find it trying to help us along on all sides. If we value all these lives wrongly they will become hostile to us on all sides. This situation affects our bodies as health and outside us it affects us as well-being and satisfying fulfilment. The higher entities associated with us try to steer us into better ways of living for our sake and for theirs. The group of humans we become associated with in our lives punish us or help us to the extent we punish or help them. God has already forgiven us before we make any mistake, but the other lives are not in a position to forgive us if we continue to impinge on them in the wrong way. There is thus a natural justice built into the structure of manifestation.

CHAPTER THIRTEEN

Education

With education there are three recognisable divisions in our attitude. The first is to consider that education is a training to fit the person for living in society as it is. The second is to fit the person for society as we think it should be. The third is to fit the person, not to society but to the nature of his or her own consciousness.

The first is the commonest and the easiest form of education. Here we accept society in an uncritical way and simply adapt ourselves to its techniques and tricks, to ensure the ability to get on well and enjoy a good return. However idealistic, nearly all of us are forced to compromise with this aspect of existence. While many agree that it is not the sort of education we should be teaching, the available staff, space, money and talent make even this an extremely difficult project, and we admire the teaching staffs who are fighting a gallant battle on our behalf.

The second form of education is basically like the first. It has its feet on the ground but it does have the time and disposition to look carefully at this ground to see if it is as good as it might be. Instead of accepting in a relatively uncritical way the society as it is, this attitude to education sees its method as being a means of altering the future society by altering the outlook of the people who will be living in it. The image of the future society which this form of education models itself on will differ at different times and in different places, and may still be an arbitrary construction in relation to reality. It may be called idealistic but at the same time it can be an ideal of the personality level of consciousness and not possess any intrinsically valuable qualities.

The third form of education is from this point of view the only proper one. Unfortunately it hardly exists at the present time, and even those schools which attempt it are criticised in terms of success in the world, which would only apply to the first two forms of training. This attitude of the third approach to education seeks to resolve the problems of teaching around the reasonable belief that each child is an individual with a unique potential which is a product of universal reality or nature. Not only does such an education as this seek to understand and draw out those unique qualities from each individual but it also seeks to understand the nature of this reality, from which we all arise and into which we venture. It can help the individual to relate those qualities which are drawn out to what in fact IS, rather than what society happens to think IS. This is not only hard on the teachers, it is also hard on the pupils, not only in their time at school but also in their life after school. For if the education they get succeeds, they must carry about with them the burden and sadness which comes with the knowledge of how far we have wandered from the potential joy and value of living. In this sense they will have become carriers of that key which opens up the possibilities of the real identity and the Divine Self. Such children will carry with them the attitude which is the key to evolution. They will be saviours or, as one might put it in scientific terms, catalysts. But who is going to say that their children should be trained for such a purpose with all the difficulties which it must involve? The answer may be that such children would deliberately involve themselves with a group who wish to accomplish such work. This group would form and plan its time and place of birth for this purpose as described in the previous chapter. In this case the parents would possess some urge to send their children to such a school which would be stronger than the rational arguments which prevent us sending ours. While such a process of education could succeed, in many cases it would fail. But here there is no difference to other forms of education except that a failure of this sort would be more obvious. Those who succeed must of necessity take upon themselves a sensitivity and pain which other children are largely immune from; on the other hand, an ability to integrate with reality brings with it a strength of its own and rewards of its own.

The third type of education will seem far too idealistic to be practical and it presupposes that the teachers of such schools have themselves succeeded in integrating themselves with the Divine frequency of consciousness. This is difficult enough with the help of some sort of schooling but it is even more so in the present situation when the individual has to do everything on his own. The nearest thing to this now are those groups of adults who come together for the sake of their common interests in such things. But here it is often too late to do more than discuss possibilities, for the habits and assumptions unwittingly absorbed in growth to adulthood are too strong to alter even if we so wish. The assets in such matters of being able to begin at an early age the process of valuation from the highest frequency consciousness would be tremendous. At present, valuations are all thrust upon us by people who have no reason to question them or to relate them to any underlying reality for, sad to say, such a reality often escapes them even as a possibility.

And yet, idealistic though it may be, this type of education must come one day if the human evolution is to progress into its fullest estate, and while one must not be hot headed in the desire to bring this estate nearer, there should be at the back of the mind some structure of reality and purpose, and some system of education which will help to assume it.

This ideal education will differ from the present methods. One of the chief factors is that the present systems tend to invalidate the deeper instincts of knowledge, quality and identity. They do this because they force facts upon the minds of their pupils which they cannot properly explain and which therefore do not hang together in any way which the higher and instinctive intelligence can grasp. Because the findings of the child are so often at variance with the findings of the teachers, even if the child is not consciously aware of it, this higher nature is gradually destroyed or thrown out of communication. Whereas this deep instinctive ability is not patently evident, (and in some cases may not be available) in a large proportion it is latent and reachable and the most valuable part of the child's make-up. If there is any truth behind this theory, this level of consciousness is that which composes the Soul level and which is one of the three main transformer systems. The others being the Divine Self and the personality. Because this Soul identity is relatively permanent and gathers values from all personality experience, it carries with it into the life of the child that unconscious understanding which at this stage can only be described as a deep instinct. This instinct not only possesses the fruits of very many personality level experiences, but it will also have some awareness of much higher levels of reality nearer that of the Ideal world. To fail to suppose that this consciousness exists somewhere within the reach of the child's psyche is to force lesser valuations upon it. This is indeed a great disservice to that child and to the society it is in. Unless the society is as it should be this deeper instinct which many children bring into the world with them is the one factor which not only can change society but change it in the right direction.

The practical difficulty here is that every child possesses lower instincts which are those of the personality and physical body. All children are lazy, destructive and insolent if they are allowed to be. To simply give them too much freedom with the idea that this will develop their innate higher consciousness will be wasting our time. It must be remembered that the lower bodies of communication all have lower order entities overseeing them. The subduing and training of these entities to see to their own work is part of any educational programme, although it is not recognised in this way. If these entities are not treated with firmness and understanding they will take over the life of the individual. Although one cannot differentiate too accurately, a lot of the high spirited foolery that children indulge in is influenced by these entities but, of course, also a lot of the natural beauty. Only gradually does the individual sort himself out from these entities; some never do.

Therefore whatever the attitude to education, it must begin with the task of teaching discipline and as far as possible, self-discipline. It accepts that most children will be little terrors if allowed to be, even if at a higher level they are well developed. It is over the actual substance of teaching in class and the teacher's attitude to his subject that it is necessary to deviate from the accepted methods. To begin with, there must be a way of behaving with more humility towards knowledge without losing the respect of the children. Not only must there be a way of hanging all knowledge upon a single unified structure but also of teaching how much is not known as an equally important part of what is known. This has hardly occurred yet. But it is this completed and all-round attitude that not only makes for greater interest but also for greater truth and that type of understanding which reaches towards the higher intelligence of the child and generates respect as no other way can. This is all a far cry from examinations which are only concerned with enforcing ideas and systems of thought upon children even at a stage when those ideas are proven wrong. When Society gleefully exchanges memory for ability and cleverness for intelligence and sends its pupils out into the world licking wounds in their nature from which most of them 'die', they spend what should be the fruitful part of their lives simply as clever and fact-filled computers, not as living expressions of their True Self.

However, to know what should be done is one thing and to succeed in doing it is quite another. When one takes into account all the entrenched opinions that exist without and within the school system one knows that even the most clear-sighted and ardent teacher of the ideal education will stand little or no chance until the climate of thought changes.

While there is as yet no unified system of knowledge which can relate science and religion to philosophy and sociology, neither is there any method available of taking the consciousness of the individual out of the situation in which it is identified with time and space. The nearest it is possible to come to this would be in the pure thought of mathematics, comparative study of history or art. But as these subjects are taken in the context of the contemporary attitude, the value and opportunity of seeing the significance of this state of consciousness for what it is, is lost. It would be tremendously healthy and True-Self-orientating to realise at an early age that consciousness was able to be dissociated from life in the world and life in conformity to rules and habits and opinions. This process of lessening the tight hold which the physical world has would give one the opportunity of strengthening the channels of communication to the higher levels of matter-consciousness which hold enormous areas of potential being and identity. This would enable the student to observe the world and the general situation more accurately. This detachment and unhindered judgement which encouragement, practice and patience can enable the student to obtain, gives him a fulcrum on which he can act not only to observe more accurately what is, but also to change what is to what should be. Detachment from the compulsions which are a part of believing to be time and space creatures does not imply becoming less efficient in the world. On the contrary, it would imply becoming more efficient. This comes about by virtue of the fact that the higher frequency view and sensing of occurrences enables one to be aware of higher level sources of their motivation. It is at the higher levels of motivation that the potential power in events lies. To put it simply, at this more detached level of consciousness one may be able to achieve results which gunpowder and brute force, or propaganda and superstition can never achieve. We may be able to speak or write in peace and achieve what all the king's horses and all the king's men can never achieve in turmoil by manipulating the much finer causes of psychological activity which control events at lower levels of consciousness, but of which the lower level is not aware. Detachment enables the individual not only to get at the root of his own nature but also at the root of the rest of nature. He is able to understand and manipulate events from the level of their most fundamental beginnings. This not only enables him to act more efficiently to achieve results but it also enables him to act with the existing situation at its most fundamental level and therefore to act in a way which is not only efficient but also correct from the point of view of evolution. At present it is assumed that free society is something in which one should be able to achieve power and ability to do just as one liked. This is not the truth of the situation. For what we really like is conditioned by what we really are, and what we can really do is conditioned by what our natural background is doing. We must develop a healthier respect for nature since, in its overall aspect, nature has a definite purpose which it respects very highly and which we will find is an immovable barrier to our philosophy of 'anything goes'.

This would seem to be one of the attitudes taught in ideal schools. Viewing history, art, philosophy and science, not as external accidents but as symptoms of an internal reality and purpose. This might help to achieve a unified structure of reference and at the same time a way of bringing the whole nature of the individual to birth in the physical world situation instead of some minute part of it which is all that present education can hope to do. And yet at the same time how can this education be changed when the first necessity is obviously to learn what is required to earn enough money to keep ourselves and our family? Perhaps this possibility will come nearer in the future. It may then be possible to treat survival as a thing of secondary importance to living, understanding and enjoying the significance of life.

Another aspect of education which at present is not clearly defined is that of moral standards, ethics and so on. As these cut into the boundaries of both the laws and habits of society as well as religion they are obviously very important. But since they have largely lost the religious basis of their function and as the legal and social aspects do not remain constant and are never very noble, there is a large area of vital human activity which is neither understood nor properly valued. This is a well known and difficult situation. Society fails to remedy it because it has lost any base to remedy it from. It will be helpful therefore if a new position can be found to view this problem from and to supply some reasonable arguments of a more universal nature. The chief reasoning could be based on the theory that people are in the process of building their individual Being through the experience of an evolutionary system which functions in a finely graded matrix of formalised consciousness which is called matter-consciousness to which they are connected by discreet communication systems which are partly under the control of another evolution which is called the entity evolution. Conscious experience is therefore only a minute proportion of the actual experience they are capable of and only a proportion of the experience which is taking place in their nature at any given moment. Conscious experience of physical plane life is very valuable because it indicates to conscious nature what the less obvious part of the being is. It is here that the injunction 'to be true to your Self' avails. For morality must be based on this situation and seen as a part of the means we have of knowing this hidden aspect of nature and not as a means of exhibiting to other people what it is we would like them to think. In the most practical terms morality is the result of the Being of any individual maintaining a high pitch of valuation. This implies not only its ability to keep clean and efficient channels of communication between itself and the events it is experiencing, but also the ability to believe in the responses and valuation it sets upon experience. Which means that in terms of the Absolute it is ethically more valuable to be honestly bad than dishonestly good. It would seem that behaviour easily degenerates to the level where it is glad to achieve a good front to its activities. People do not realise it is their own Self that they are cheating. They think it is others they are scoring off and also that any God who lets them get away with it, as He does, deserves to be cheated. This is because it does not occur to them that God and the natural background are in the process of giving them absolute values. They judge the situation in a small-minded way and consider that the 'pay-off' is coming and that they had better enjoy some short-term fruits before it comes and snatches away their treasure. It does not occur to them that the 'pay-off' never comes, but exists continually in the attitude they have towards their own Self. Without knowing it, we are largely our own judge, court of appeal, sentencer and executioner. We are also our own valuer and God-maker. No one can realise our own divinity for us, and similarly no one can take it away from us. We cannot be truly moral unless we act with the knowledge, attitude and conviction of our own True Self. This is the Self which is all the while Divine but does not realise this fact. Morality which does not stem from the natural response of this Self is not worthy of the name and is nothing more than convention. It may be a good convention, but its goodness is as nothing to its honesty. It seems one should aim at honest living if one wishes to achieve the sort of goodness which religious feelings require, otherwise it is like putting the cart before the horse and letting goodness get in the way of 'livingness'. This is sin, the narrowing down and inhibition of the full encounter. Full encounter is not achieved by living the free and bohemian life, but is achieved by that free and natural release of the innermost spirit together with the quality and attitude of that spirit which, from all previous arguments, will be understood to possess that respect for, care of and love towards all other forms of life which are alone true morality and ethics.

It is essential to stop teaching morality in terms which can be mistaken for the philosophy of external and obvious valuation; of valuation which concedes that behaviour must be good if it is not 'found out' to be bad. Rather must it be said that unless the inner aspect of one's attitude is healthy, the result of any behaviour will be psychological unrest and discontent. One may succeed in the world and gain the adulation of many people, but if this is to fail to remain true to innermost nature it will mean failure in our own judgement of ourself and in the relating of our many parts to our whole nature. Since this is the root cause of unhappiness it is also where real success and failure lies and where one reaps and enjoys the real treasures of existence. The essence of real religious and moral aspiration is not between ourselves and God but between ourselves and our Self. At the same time the monitoring activity of God and His many Divine Assistants is necessary, not as a substitute for Self-confrontation, but rather to ensure that this condition comes about. Aspirations towards God are therefore of the utmost value, not as a means of becoming a slave or servant of God, but in order that they can be directed towards their true goal which is the valuation of our True Self. As we direct the love our children have for us in such a way that it enlarges their own nature and not in order to make them more devoted and servile, so our Divine Parents divert our love in such a way that it reflects back into our own essential nature again. Love is therefore valued by God, not as something he wishes to possess, but as a positive expression of our highest attitude which He can receive in the spirit in which it is offered and then use for His creative work. This is the bringing of our individual nature to a condition of Divine Self-consciousness.

CHAPTER THIRTEEN : Summary

Education exists for us at many levels. The outer form is to learn the tricks of our man-made culture, the innermost or highest form is to bring through from our highest being to our physical personality the responses and understanding of the Divine nature which is given us to exercise. In so far as the higher form of education is avoided, we do a great disservice to those we educate. In so far as we try to employ the highest motives in education we help to achieve the greatest fulfilment in those we educate and it becomes no different to what we term religion. The child recognises in a wordless and instinctive way the efforts we make to help him really understand himself and his situation in the universe. He is equally upset when he recognises the fact that we are despoiling him and his chances of coming through into the world properly. Most teachers do not believe in the possibility of this real education or they do not have the time or conditions in which it can be attempted. A great many factors weigh against such endeavour but it must be attempted if we are to bring our culture to a higher stage of maturity. What we do not know or understand is as important in this form of teaching as the things that we do know. Most of our problems will remain unsolvable until we do succeed in achieving this real education and the children we teach in this way will be in a position to save the world from itself. It is very hard to know where to start, for the teachers themselves must be in a position from which they can help. They themselves will have to be evolved people. The ethical side of education is most important. But ethics are not things that man can write down for himself, they are only derived through proper response from the real self to each situation. There is no rule of thumb and every situation is different.

CHAPTER FOURTEEN

Religion

The last chapter discussed what might be called the essence of religion in terms of education. This one will try to understand education in terms of religion, for the more one goes into the real significance of these subjects the more they appear to become one and the same thing.

Most people understand organised religion as being the observance of group ritual and group prayer, some of which is sung and some spoken. This is a reminder of our spiritual beginnings and our spiritual heritage. But it is realised that there are many reasons beside this why some take part in these semi-public ceremonies. Apart from the reasons already given why the teachings mostly fail to validate the spiritual nature and realise the Divine heritage, those who take part in organised religion are often unable to discuss the significance of what they are doing and, in fact, are loath to try. While one respects the fact that this is a very delicate subject and therefore not to be discussed lightly, one is bound to suspect that in fact the followers of such religion do not really understand what it signifies in terms of their own identity, daily experience and sense of purpose, for if they did, it would be natural for them to wish to communicate more freely to one another. This is only one of the many indications that religion, as we know it, fails in its primary purpose in today's climate, that of education. But today's climate is meant the fact that our western world is altering from what has been an emotional approach to life for the mass of people, to one which is more of the mind. Our religious organisations and institutions are still functioning on a level of consciousness which was suitable for its purpose some hundreds and even thousands of years ago. This level was primarily an emotional one and attempted to raise the awareness of the individual directly from the level called the lower emotions to a level called the higher emotions. This is roughly from the position 3" to position 7" on the map. In this way the mind itself was short-circuited, and this was a highly desirable and effective operation. But today the minds of people are being brought to bear more and more upon every aspect of life. Consequently the religious systems which used to work no longer do so, simply because there is a large gap left where the mind has to gain a footing if it is to be included in the general ascent of consciousness. This central area of the mind is the 'dead-centre' position which can become a real obstacle to progress. However, if the mind is actively functioning one cannot avoid this area and so one must learn to use it to advantage. This can only be done by understanding the quality and nature of the mind at the higher level of its functioning where it enters the realm of the higher emotions and is able to gain the flavour of the ideal world. If the lower aspect of mental activity is called the concrete mind, the middle aspect the intellectual mind, then this higher aspect can be called the time and space-free mind or abstract part of the mind which verges on the intuition. So whereas religion used to aim at the sensing of the emotion of Divine Love, today it must add to this the faculty of insight or Divine Wisdom. Present civilisation, it seems, may not be able to proceed without this higher intelligent understanding and is finding that an emotional approach to religion is no longer enough.

This is saying that the only hope in religious activity today is to face up to the fact that people have a mind and must use it. It is realised that the central portion of the mind may become entrenched between the higher and lower aspects of its nature and can lose its bearings in relation to any underlying reality. But it is also expected that the higher aspect of the mind can be studied, exercised and strengthened in such a way that it can overcome the pull of its lower concrete nature and free itself to absorb those emotive and delicate perceptions which emanate from the unified and idealised field of very high frequency matter-consciousness. This, of course, is the source of that unified structure of knowledge which is so important, not only to religion but also to any proper form of education. It is necessary to overcome our suspicion of metaphysics and to cease to call it by that highly coloured name. It is necessary to learn to use the imaginative, detached and synthesising intelligence to gain an overall basis for identity and experience. This can not be done by simply applying ourselves to those subjects which happen to be established as academically polite. It is most unfortunate that the very field which could today be most profitable in the search for a unified structure of knowledge has been poisoned for us by the suspicions which surround all occult matters. While this is a field open to a charlatan, it must also be pointed out that the slightly lower field of the intellectual philosopher is no less open to misuse even if the terms of such misuse are high sounding and respectable.

It is not easy to identify this higher aspect of the mind, for it is not simply the intelligence which is capable of the higher forms of mathematics—this would seem to be a more specialised part of the middle or intellectual mind. The higher mind one might say is not only capable of highly intricate and abstract reasoning but it also has a leaning to universalisation. This would seem to be the difference most easily understood, for the intellectual mind can be abortive in a situation where the higher mind is more successful on account of its closer proximity to the unifying aspect of higher consciousness generally. The true higher mental faculty tends therefore to slip across the boundaries of any subject it is dealing with and endeavours naturally to relate it to all other findings and all other experience. This is the healthy aspect of mind which can be lost in the middle or dead-centre position. But also the higher mind will begin to fuse with the higher emotions which, again, not only tend towards universal understanding and a universal attitude, but also the universal respect and responsibility which the higher consciousness has towards all other forms of life. This is not the result of a wish to do the right thing, but the result of positive experience of common underlying purpose and value in all fields of manifestation. After all, one's brother or sister is not sensed as having a special relationship because one is fond of them, but because of the unconscious realisation that they are a part of a particular group function in nature. When one feels that all manifestation is a part of one's group function, the true sense of respect and affection results.

And this is where one can arrive at the position of the emotional type of religion. One does it through what might be called insight or infeeling of the higher intelligence, whereas it used to be done only through ardent emotional anticipation. This new position can now proceed to enter into and enjoy the higher emotions of Divine love and care, but it no longer feels that it is leaving a gigantic gap behind which it is intellectually dishonest to ignore.

Since the sense of consciousness depends upon processes of communication, even if these are ruminative and internal, any improvement brought to the religious life will not only depend upon being able to exercise the ability to communicate generally. This means not only in conversation and writing but also by all the other methods which are available. One of the chief barriers to communication is the one caused by the fears which surround systems of 'beliefs'. These beliefs are working hypotheses which are expected to be wrong and which are fundamentally doubted, as are our own identities. These are no ordinary hypotheses, for in most cases they are a tangle of unrelated conclusions, enforcements and superstitions and are a positive menace to their owner and to all that they come in contact with. People cling to an hypothesis because they substitute it for an identity, so that if they lose it or have to change it, they have the feeling that they are losing their self . . . so they are, but not their True Self. They are enabling themselves to gain more of that True Self. But this is no comfort or reason for them in a climate of society which has lost its sense of, and faith in, the True Self. Obviously, if one feels a change of view to be a change of identity then one will abhor any form of communication which will precipitate a situation in which this can take place. This is exactly what is found. We are not only inept at communicating real feelings and ideas, but are positively afraid of doing so because we suspect that they are wrong. Now any useful form of religion has got to take this pressure off us in some way and open the channels that can not only reveal our misconceptions but also replace them in what we feel to be a safe and comfortable manner. If we have to replace our original beliefs with no-belief then this is the situation we must face. It would seem to be better to possess a clean and empty cupboard capable of being stocked rather than to possess a cupboard full of decaying goods which leave no room for new provisions. One feels that some forms of religion are anxious to stock us up with anything so long as we feel full and are not inclined to search for ourselves.

This raises another point, that of the position of those men who are in charge of organised religions and who consequently exercise some traditional control over the highest and most valuable part of our nature. No one is able to say whether these men are a reflection of their religion or whether their religion is a reflection of them, but either way the position is not a very healthy one and a great strain must be involved, if they are sincere, in maintaining a common outlook and understanding. When one considers the system of training which the clergy are put through in theological colleges, one cannot ignore the fact that it seems wrong for them to live and study in a climate which is committed to definite and particular attitudes, which attitudes are incumbent on them for the rest of their professional career and which carry the financial security of their families. It may be said that it is most unfortunate that their highest perceptions are connected to a system which relates to their paid career and which supports their welfare. Knowing how difficult it is to be aware of true motivations, one cannot be blind to the fact that paid clergymen are a contradiction in terms and in function. This is in no way intended as a criticism of the clergy themselves, it is intended as a criticism of the situation which has been allowed to arise. Not to put too fine a point on it, it would be hard for any of us to be quite sure about the honesty of our motivations in more concrete aspects of life in our business affairs and in our social life. But our highest and most ethereal attitudes are less open to judgement than our business affairs, and if on top of this they are liable to be influenced, not only consciously but more importantly, unconsciously, by the fact that our bread and butter depends on them, experience tells us that these attitudes may very well become subject to discretion. If this factor only affected the lives of the clergy themselves it would not matter, in that it would be their own private affair. But unfortunately they put themselves in a position where their own lives are not only exhibited to the public but are designed to influence the public. It can be said that these men look after our spiritual welfare for us because we are not prepared to take the trouble and make the effort ourselves. By paying them to do this job we deliberately open them to all those overt influences which tend to make dishonest people of us all. We hopefully expect, in this way, to have the best of both worlds. The uncompromising situation is that these highest and deepest convictions, attitudes and faiths must be honest, true and valid for our own experience. If not, they will poison ourselves and our environment and it will do us no good to blame the clergy for this, for they are acting largely as we condition them to act. It can only be suggested that if it is wished to improve the situation, a way of attracting men of the highest frequency levels to this task must be found. But their status must be an amateur one in the proper meaning of the term. Which means that they must perform their task entirely for love and not for money. This is not intended to be a reflection upon them, but only a reflection upon the human condition. Those who have had the opportunity of revealing discussions about the nature of their own identity and the nature of reality will most probably have found that such discussions have been with laymen and that attempts at such discussions with clergymen have been very limited. It does seem that now and in the future, such discussion between man and woman with no pressure upon them, combined with self-study and general reading, will become one of the foundations of our religious structure. There will remain for a long time however a great number of people who wish to feel associated with some religious observance but who have no desire to enter the religious life proper or to probe too deeply into their own religious motives. For such people a bad religion is as good as a good religion simply because they will use it for their own purpose in any case, and that purpose is not strictly a religious one.

A principle behind higher knowledge can be called the principle of diffusion. One can appreciate that one does not gain true knowledge and understanding of the whole of life experience from the study of religion only, but from the study of everything else besides religion. The knowledge that results from this widest of studies can be called religious knowledge proper. What one gets from studying religion on its own is often a hybrid knowledge which is a hotch-potch of human superstition, social customs and behaviours, men's hopes and fears. What one must aim at is a synthesis of knowledge from all aspects of life and experience which has the backing of careful and unbiased observation. To study religion for its own sake is putting the cart before the horse. Religion is the observance and understanding of the whole of life experience, it cannot be a subject on its own. On its own it simply does not exist. What exists is the purpose of the natural background and the Divine Nature. The study of this one may have to call by some other name than religion since it entails all the sciences, psychology, history, art, music, poetry, literature—in fact every possible facet of experience. One may call it conscious evolution, for the purposes behind religious activity are fulfilled through evolution. Religion is the fulfilment of life—how can one therefore treat it as though it were something to be undertaken on its own? One must, it seems, learn to live without religion if it is wished to fulfil the urge which has led to the construction of religion. This seems a paradox indeed, but it explains the fact that one must learn to think of spiritual growth as a far more natural process, whose ways and means are built into our individual essence natures, and whose purpose can only be achieved through the innermost initiative. To think of religion as a narrow corridor which will lead to eternal life is to see the problem in the wrong way. The narrow corridor is the result of passing through the vast background of possible experience, but the narrowness is an indication of the ability to look for and sense innermost honesty, for this gives direction and drive. Without this there is no corridor at all but only a static market place which gets wider and wider, more and more confused. Human shortcomings continually bring us back to suspecting that the universe is a vast practical joke or even a psychological torture chamber. The art of reaching heaven has become like the art of outwitting the fiendish constructions of the very God one thinks one is trying to approach. No wonder people hesitate to fully engage in this art.

The art of reaching heaven must eventually be understood to be the art of living. This art has no need to be called religion. People who achieve it love one another and, in fact, love everything which it is possible to love, which would include God and Nature and all form of life of which they become aware. What religion can achieve this?

However, this problem has another aspect which must also be considered. If the natural background to people's lives remained constantly at the same level of matter-consciousness, then the situation would be as in the previous paragraph. But if, as may be expected, the matter-consciousness system which people are related to is evolving, this will continually alter the nature of the problem. This would seem to be a permanent change for the better and in their favour. One might take it as an indication that time is on their side, and this might help one to accept the fact that the whole of manifestation is also on their side even if it seems to be opposed on many occasions. But what one has to do before sensing this and so learning to avoid all the clashes and discords which are created, is to stop thinking as though one is separate and accidental. If it is considered that we are an intentional part of all schemes in the universes, we shall surely look for and find reliable indications as to how and what we should do written into the very stuff of the background matrix. This, of course, does not mean reading the signs in the entrails of a sacrificial chicken; it means reading the signs in the field of biology and higher psychology where experience can be stronger than the conditioning of the rational mind.

The main drives in civilisation are to conquer and subdue and exterminate in order, it seems, to replace whatever exists with our own humanity. We can never hope to enjoy a harmonious and creative relationship with matter-consciousness in this way, any more than we would expect to have human friends if we treated them thus. The basis of all friendship and productive relationship is a profound respect for the other partner. We have little or no respect for anything for the simple reason that we have lost respect for ourselves. The sense of Human Rights must improve to a sense of Divine Rights before the collective image of humanity can be anything more than a poor one. Until this is done our background will cause us discomfort and suffering. This is not only the physical matrix, but the psychological one also; and of the two, the psychological one seems to be the most important. Unless we learn to sense and respect the 'movement' of the levels of matter-consciousness at reading 2", 3", 4", and 5" our chances of successful, happy and peaceful living will have vanished before we can reach them. In other words, if we do not make a serious effort to harmonise with the psychic qualities which are caused to fluctuate by the movement of the various levels of matter-consciousness in their climb towards the ideal, we shall always be out of phase with the most helpful influences as they come along. In this way we shall continue to think that everything is against us and that we must fight to survive.

It has never occurred to us that there was anything with which to be in phase. But once it is realised that development is an intentional part of universal design and function, we will accept that perhaps there is a syllabus to be read and acted upon. If the syllabus is there and we are continually going to the wrong class at the wrong time, all the trouble of building the college, training the staff and making equipment is completely wasted. We will end up with a vast number of unrelated facts and technical tricks which have lost their bearing on the purpose of the educational programme. The universes can be sending us just the right atmosphere at just the right time in order to facilitate the perception of our causes and purposes, but if we are resisting and obstructing all our deeper instincts, then what should be in step with our efforts will be just out of step and may very well double the load we have to bear. The timetable of the universe cannot be altered once it is set going since time itself is the very function of this table as it relates to all levels in all places. We must stop crying because the universe is out of step with us and perhaps change step ourselves.

CHAPTER FOURTEEN : Summary

The chief method by which religion has reached a higher consciousness has been to raise the level of the emotions from the ordinary lower level to that approaching the ideal level. To achieve this the intermediate levels of the mind and higher intellectual understanding were left out. Now we feel we should fill the gap and the movement away from religion 'as a habit' is the result. Our understanding will now have to face up to our doubts and not hide them away behind the curtain called 'lack of faith'. We will have to overcome our mental lethargy and emotional fears in this battle which will enable us to arrive at a new degree of honesty in relation to God. We will raise the steam in our effort when we allow ourselves to marvel at the wonderful structure and working of all things in the universe, when we take enough time off to observe the whole thing with a clear and straight consciousness. This new movement in psychology is discovering that healthy specimens of humanity are already oriented in this way. They are already motivated by higher understanding and higher values even if they do not use special terminology to express them. Rather than depend on prayer and worship which often requires very little of us, we should do more in the field of person to person communication to exercise our own muscles in our higher nature and to clarify our concepts of God's ways of communicating these concepts instead of being afraid of their inadequacy. We should enable our priests to lose their 'professional' status which inhibits their attitude towards us because of established custom. We must make them amateurs who work for love of their work alone. Religion is the 'keying in' of our whole nature with the nature of God on a basis of absolute friendship and love. We have to live life fully to do this. We have to try to understand and experience all things in order to sense the bigness of the Divine Nature. Therefore the education which aims at full confrontation with the universe is also religion. There is no difference between religion and education or fully being alive, they are all one and the same thing. Thus our living must, in becoming fuller, also become more reverent, and more perceptive of the background matrix of natural phenomena.

CHAPTER FIFTEEN

Astrology

It would be desirable to avoid the subject that has now arisen, namely that of astrology. However, it need not be tackled in terms of the Sunday newspaper or woman's magazine; what can be done instead is to try to observe what may be the underlying reality of this subject in terms of this theory. To those who study astronomy, the term astrology is like a slap in the face, so one must avoid treating the subject in such a way that it would remind them of the vulgar side of astrology.

Fortunately, there is already a reason for believing that a true science of astrology may be a thing of the future and may have been a thing of the distant past. The reason for this is based on the proposition that our common manifest universe is composed of an ordered and interpenetrating series of life formations which have some degree of consciousness in specific energy complexes. These inter-related groupings form response fields of life activity which have been called the fields of matter-consciousness and which have been described in terms of the three vectors.

Previously it was not indicated that these fields of matter-consciousness were themselves evolving, but it was suggested that every group in manifestation at all frequency levels was monitored by a group consciousness called, for want of a better word, an entity. These entities are now expected to be evolving parallel to ourselves, but although we are all the time closely associated with them, we do not at present recognise them. While the primary stage of this evolution is very limited to the degree that it is mistaken for a machine-like activity at the level of the atom, molecule and so on, the higher stages must pass through a similar level to our own and continue far beyond any development we have been able as yet to imagine.

The levels which compose the matrix of psychological activity from say, reading 2" to 5", form a sea or network at each critical level of frequency. This network is not an inert background any more than physical nature is an inert background. It continually expresses moods of differing psychological colour. The terms of these moods may be long or short and they will no doubt have small cycles of change within larger cycles of change. Since these cyclic activities are taking place on all the basic inter-related levels, such as 2" and 5", the whole forms a complex influence very like that of a kaleidoscope which is all the time affecting our thoughts and emotions by virtue of the fact that it composes the 'stuff' in which these thoughts and emotions are formed and transmitted. It must be pointed out here that the consciousness of an emotion or a thought is not the emotion or thought itself but, as at the physical level, a coded message which bears the content of the emotion or thought. It is important to visualise this fact and be detached from the process in order to observe it clearly. What appears to be an instantaneous perception of thought and emotion is not so but only relatively so. In relation to time intervals at sub-physical levels, the transmission of thought and emotion requires lengthy processes. Now not only is one affected in this way by tides and eddies in the matter-consciousness matrix, but the entities which control the formation and function of the various bodies of communication are also affected. They will tend to make one sort of body under one influence and another under another. Together with the factors of heredity these combine to give the characteristics of personality which are again continually influenced by the quality of the Soul and Divine nature. The resultant is a very involved situation which only sorts itself out by virtue of the fact that all the influences resolve themselves continually at any instant. If they do not resolve themselves then we get the situations developing which eventually lead to psychological stress and malfunction. This was already discussed elsewhere. Also the value of harmonising the various entities we are concerned with, and maintaining their natural function in line with our individuality, since what they do is not only on our behalf, but much better done than we could do in a great many cases. If collective attitudes in society are unsympathetic to the fluctuations in the psychological matrix, then the whole of that society will continually be out of phase with its natural background. Individually it is necessary to add to this the phases which concern us in particular which one may be in tune with or not.

This continuous fluctuation of mood in the mental, emotional and higher fields of consciousness is not just an unfortunate by-product of the scheme of manifestation, it is a very vital part of the scheme. It is because these fluctuations continually force us to see the same situation in a different psychological light that nature prevents us becoming more hidebound and habit-ridden than we are already, for it is a way in which nature ensures that one day is never like another even if we do everything within our power to make it so. One knows only too well that many of us would make it so if we could. This would be a terrible thing for us and for the evolutionary scheme. In fact, because the background to physical existence changes all the time, one gathers many thousandfold more experiences than if the psychological atmosphere remained static.

The endeavour to know and to harmonise with the psychological changes which are being rung in the universes about us is the proper science of astrology. One cannot make this a science yet because one cannot observe the factors involved in this function. But since all levels of matter are related in some way, and since they may all be based on a single underlying motive, it is possible that the movement of astronomical bodies are an indication of the movement of these tides and seasons. There may very well be a connection here that will not only be of great interest to the physicist, psychologist and astronomer, but to the historian, theologian, sociologist and philosopher also.

The scheme of evolution does not merely rely on ordinary individual ability to sense and harmonise with these psychic tides. For in the system of re-birth those who are monitoring the larger group functions are able to link a race or a culture to the movement of the psychic atmosphere by causing special men or women to be born into the world at particular times. These people bring a strong and highly-developed knowledge of a certain sort with them which they interpret to us and in so doing guide our attention and consequently our direction in thoughts and emotions. Such men are the outstanding characters of our history like a Bach, Giorgione, Da Vinci, Newton, Shakespeare, Einstein, Buddha, Socrates, Goethe, Christ, Paul, Galileo, Blake and so on. Such men, while they do not exactly alter the course of civilisation, tune us in to psychological factors which are active and which do indeed alter our ways and opinions. There are many such men who have existed but who remain unknown to us. They act like catalysts and enable us to react more quickly to the changing situations in our background which are not open to normal observation. Whereas such a theory as this is not exactly necessary to the main thesis, it does suggest the sort of way that patterns of life are organised without our knowing it, and it does give us good reason to be on the lookout for such men and to expect them to be different and even difficult people to understand at first. It also gives us a reason to believe that the die-hard sort of conservatism found in society, while trying to protect valuable ways and customs, can have a very destructive effect in slowing down adjustment to changing conditions and thus throwing us out of phase with the intangible situation in force at any given time. One must perhaps look at this problem together with the ideas concerning freedom of choice, and consider whether or not the freedom to choose is one of the illusions we must overcome if we are to get the best out of the opportunities which life is continually offering to us. One may very well find that the field of choice varies inversely with the value and importance of the choice, so that one should only feel to be choosing in situations which carry no responsibilities. What one often fails to do in situations which involve choice, is to survey the field widely enough or accurately enough. If one took more trouble to observe the whole situation one would no doubt find that the outer and inner sense of fitness would indicate that there existed only one proper course of action. Problems do not arise because we do not know how to choose, but because we do not know how to observe.

It is realised more and more that harmony and well-being in industrial societies is going to depend in the future on the ability to discover at an early age the leanings, tendencies and abilities of each separate individual in order that not only their education but also their work is suitable and as far as possible fulfilling. One person can be tremendously different from another although brought up in the same situation. The pleasurable function of society depends upon accepting this and catering for it. It is accepted now that fitting the right man to the right job not only makes for happiness at his work but also in his home. In the distant future the difference between work and leisure will have lost its present meaning, but one must be careful that the meaning arrived at implies that we use knowledge for our fullest purpose and not that knowledge has enslaved us. It becomes obvious that knowledge gained in the right way can free us from all those labours which at the present time are necessary to survival and are often no better than drudgery. By making the minimum number of machines supply the common needs we may free ourselves from many useless and repetitive activities and enable (or even force) ourselves to get on with the vital business of bringing all our attention and abilities to bear on a full confrontation with life. This cannot be done except by bringing the world of the Soul and the Divine Self into the physical world situation. This not only fulfils and quickens the evolutionary process in ourselves but also in all the other fields of matter-consciousness which we touch upon. The bringing of the Ideal world to birth in the physical situation is not only a desirable and pleasant idea, it is also the underlying purpose of matter-consciousness and so forms a basis for increased co-operation and respect in these fields.

The proper science of astro-psychology, when it comes, will not only assist greatly in understanding the individual's innate character and ability, but it will also help in understanding something of the underlying activity in the matter-consciousness fields with which we are all the time in touch and which have a purpose which we must learn to appreciate and with which we co-ordinate our civilisations. A study of this sort, by whatever name one calls it, may very well lead to tremendous benefits and to the solution of problems from which at the present time one feels we will always have to suffer.

The theory of consciousness has resulted in a reversal of nearly all attitudes and concepts. Life itself has become religion and what used to be religious activity has lost its significance. People can no longer take refuge in a material or spiritual life for, in either case, they have lost a great deal of potential value. The correct attitude is one which integrates the highest with the lowest, the distant with the near, the universal with the particular, the time-full with the timeless and so forth. The full confrontation with all facets of existence is the only way and therefore the only religion. This religion is not so much a way to God but a way to our Self. We may expect God to hide Himself from us until we have become strong enough in our own reality to withstand the power of His personality. We must seek not to concern ourselves with God so much as to concern ourselves with what concerns God. This is the coming of age which we have to enter into if we are to take up our position of responsibility and delight in universal existence. We must stop supposing either that we are an accident within an accident or wholly a cause within a cause. It will assist us to consider the significance of the family unit as we experience it for ourselves, and to reflect that it may hold within it the secret of the underlying pattern and purpose of the whole of the manifested universes. We may expect that a few moments of sincere and wholehearted adaptation to life experience will be of more value to us and to God than a life spent in worship or supplication. There is a knowledge to be gained from living as a true and distinct individual which produces an understanding of the underlying quality in existence to which all are probably attracted. The realisation of this quality of consciousness for ourselves would seem to be the objective of manifestation. By approaching reality in this way we will not only further all the purposes of our Creator but we may find that if by some chance we should encounter God Him/Her Self that it will not be an encounter of embarrassment implying unworthiness on our part, but it may be an encounter of two people engaged in creating and enjoying the same supreme attitudes and experiences which will give them a great deal to communicate about. With our present attitude to religion we would shrink from any confrontation with God. If it came about we would be nothing better than a lot of simpering fools begging for forgiveness or adulation. What a worthless and destructive meeting it would be. We may never recover our Selves from it. It is not that one is advocating an arrogant attitude for this would be absurd. It is simply that one is advocating an attitude which leaves room for supreme respect for the Creator's motives in bringing us to a condition of Self-conscious existence. If our own respect for our Selves cannot be up to this value it implies that our God has not given us of His utmost, but something less than His utmost.

This has now described what we should do but has not said how we should do it. It is because we have got to find our own way for ourselves. To try and describe a method of attainment would immediately defeat the purpose since it would substitute the means for the end and in any case imply that we knew what the end was. All one can do is to say that the proper attitude to life experience creates a condition of consciousness in which the end and the means are continually brought together in a relatively more and more complete way. If this attitude is discovered, then life for us is not something which we are waiting to enter into, but something which we can enter into now to the fullness of our capability. As the capability grows the relationship between what we are, and what we feel we are entering into, remains comparatively constant in degree, so that the actual life experience, which is one of vital growth, is a continuing and fulfilling experience of the Universal motive. What one can say however is that our attitudes have become so biased away from the highest frequency levels that we have lost the sense that we are creatures of the highest possibility and we allow ourselves to be defeated by the lethargy of the physical body and the ill-considered desires and activities of the physical personality. To entertain the experiences of the higher fields of consciousness is the first task in order to balance up this conditioning bias, when the sense of balance has been reached, one will be able to discover the next step for oneself.

CHAPTER FIFTEEN : Summary

There is now a reasonable cause for us to look for a science of astro-psychology or astrology. For if we accept that all things are living and form a structure of entities, then the larger aspects of manifestation such as planets and solar systems and galaxies are also entities. If this is so then all the entities have psychological colour of some sort, and since they also move, the colours that come together by the influence of one upon another are continually changing. Our planet is thus travelling through ever changing psychic atmospheres of a sort which we have not yet learned to recognise but which nevertheless affect those of our bodies of communication which belong to these psychic or more ethereal levels of existence. Our background, in which our conscious nature resides, is always changing but this is not something which merely adds to life's difficulties for us, it is also a way of adding a tremendous amount to the possibility of experience for us. Without this changing background, we would be able to make one day just like another, and this is something many of us would like to do. But if we could, we would be in a position to reduce life to a trickle and thus destroy its long term beneficent purpose for us. It is possible that the 'chord' of the first bar in the music of our life conditions that life on earth. This enables the real essence self to experience many chords and colourings through different physical lives. In order to make better sense of any life, the knowledge of these chords and colours could give us very helpful guidance.

CHAPTER SIXTEEN

The Will

This chapter deals with that faculty of our nature which we commonly refer to as Will Power. While it is agreed that there is such a power in our true nature, it is necessary to describe this ability in such a way that it is differentiated from what is normally referred to under this heading.

People generally use the term will when they imply that the intellect or emotions have fastened on to a desired objective to be attained. They also imply that the strength of the will is dependent on the tenacity and intensity of the desire for the objective. This process produces, quite understandably, a direction and a force in their lives which very likely can and does achieve that which it requires. We can call this mind power or desire power and agree that it is a way of obtaining what we want by directing all our effort and attention to this purpose. The objective or desired result in this case is a focus for the whole nature which would otherwise be more diffused and less concentrated. But this is still self-direction, self-motivation or self-control and need not be given a special name as though it were a special and distinct faculty.

It is possible to suggest however a function of the Self which is a special and distinct faculty but which is one never thought of or imagined. This function can be referred to as the Will but one must be extremely careful to fully understand the significance of it and the way it functions. What is suggested in this theory is very subtle but, if it is at all approximating to the truth, a very important and far reaching factor.

The understanding of this theory rests upon the previous argument that the True Individual Nature of each one of us belongs to the nature and substance of the Absolute. We are thus in touch with the underlying power, strength and purpose of this Absolute from the time of our first glimmerings of pure and non-reactive consciousness. But what we have to visualise and remember is that we are entirely unconscious of this level of awareness until we have evolved a considerable degree and have become Self-conscious at the Spiritual or Soul level of awareness at reading 5" and above. The 'life' or 'livingness' of our True Nature grows and intensifies as we rise in the level of awareness along vector 3, but our Absolute Self is functioning to some extent long before we become remotely aware of its nature and significance. The essential function of this highest aspect of consciousness is so to say, sounding or singing its nature. In other words to express what there is of itself in terms of a murmur which later becomes a song, which is the chord of notes (as far as words can be used) which expresses exactly what it is in terms of qualities of Absolute Consciousness or Being.

Now this Absolute Self, in becoming a resonating body at the highest level of manifestation, unconsciously manipulates the matter-consciousness at that level which is the level of cause as far as the Universal Nature and structure of manifestation is concerned. So that from the first activity generated in its nature each Self commences to be a cause not only at the physical level of creation but at the fundamental level also. This activity in Absolute awareness causes all the lower levels of matter-consciousness to conform to its 'sound' in a relatively stronger and more complete way as the 'life' in the Self becomes stronger and more fully actualised. When we become spiritually Self-conscious we can begin to learn how to actualise the life in our Self directly and thus become able to generate this formative power more consciously. But what we cannot do, and this is the point of extreme importance, is to *use* this power. What we find is that we are faced with the fact that we *are* this power and that we can no more use it than we can 'lift ourselves up with our own braces'. What we find is that this Will Power is a spontaneous and unconscious faculty and expression of the Absolute Nature which we have been given to exercise and actualise. The power of this faculty is to reproduce in all the other frequency levels of matter-consciousness the image of its own Self. By this we mean that the 'sound' of its 'name' is causing this 'name' to be reproduced at all the other levels of life in terms of form and quality of consciousness. All the untold millions of casual sounds are therefore mingling together and producing modulations upon the basic and strongest amplitudes in manifestation which are the creative songs of God. All our real formative powers are thus knitting together at the very highest frequency where friction is almost non-existent and efficiency is very high. A harmony is made at this very high level of manifestation which at a lower level would be impossible due to the resistance of matter and the inefficiency of means of total communication between the many individual sources. This total harmony is thus affecting the world around us all the time and is causing events to arise in line with the various images represented in our innermost Being. The so-called will power, which we use at the personality level and which is desire and mind power, tends to interfere with the true Will to the extent that the personality is divorced from the nature and purposes of the

Self. What our Will is doing to us all is to reproduce in our physical and psychological surroundings an image which represents the nature and quality of our True Self at the unconscious level of the Absolute. Most of us will not be conscious of this Self for a long time yet, and until we are we will continually wonder why so many of our personal best-laid schemes come to nothing, and what agency is causing our superficial pleasures to be snatched away from us or prove so unsatisfactory. The answer in many cases will be the action of our own highest nature which is quite possibly directly opposed to the activities and desires of our personal nature.

The fact which emerges from this theory is that it acts as a safety measure in the scheme of manifestation. The power which is a part of the True Being of our nature is a very real power, but we can suggest that matters have been arranged by the Designer of the scheme of manifestation in such a way that we do not have access to this power directly. The power is a result of the intensity of our life at the Absolute level. This intensity amplifies the qualities of our True Being and transmits them to all the other levels of existence in terms of command, quality of consciousness and quality of form. This real power in the Universe is therefore conditioned by what can exist and be represented at the highest level of our Being. Negative and destructive and uncooperative attitudes have no means of expression in this highest type of matter-consciousness for the reason that their quality is not of a frequency which exists or can mean anything at such a level. The purpose of our Creator may be taken to be our education in the significance of the QUALITIES of Absolute being and not the QUANTITIES or the POWER aspects of such Being. The Power of the Absolute has therefore been reserved automatically until we have become fully conversant with the essential Quality of real existence. This quality is not one which we have any say over for it is the one which our Creator values most highly and also wishes us to value. This is Divine Love or Universal Love, of which our human personal love is only an incomplete expression.

If we seek power for its own sake it seems that we may well expect to be continually disappointed with the fruits of our own efforts for the whole of creation is weighted against us for the reason that such success would be a negative factor in our education and simply destroy the potential of our real consciousness. So in the same way that we keep dangerous and powerful abilities out of the range of our children's grasp, so God has arranged for the real power in the Universe to be kept out of our grasp. Power exists for us in direct ratio to the extent that we succeed in bringing our Absolute Nature to a condition of resonant life. This power then works for us quite spontaneously to reproduce in all our surroundings a DRAMA which represents the significance of our Being. In this way our nature is caused to be portrayed for us externally in order that we shall know it as an objective experience as well as an inner sensibility. Our Will Power causes people and situations to come together in our environment so that they may live out for one another the whole significance of the Quality of their True Being. This does, of course, take a long time at the physical level. But those aspects which can be or can only be expressed at higher frequency levels are obviously not under the same restrictive and viscous conditioning and can very likely be experienced in great quantities and at great speed. Unconsciously therefore we are all engaged in bringing the expression of the Absolute Consciousness into the condition of greatest condensation or crystallisation at the physical level of matter-consciousness. One aspect of God has therefore been laid out and conditioned as 'ground' in order that another aspect of God can use this ground to educate offspring. The conditions of this educational programme are arranged in such a way that the offspring shall learn what God sees fit for them to learn in the light of infinitely greater experience. Our experience of freedom and fulfilment therefore consists, as has been said, in recognising that so much of our condition has already been fixed for us for our own good. We are in a situation which is going to force us to pay attention to Qualities rather than Quantities and which is going to make us keep and use our individual Nature even if we would try to shed it. We are in a situation where power operates spontaneously in direct ratio to the degree that we pay attention to and bring to a resonant condition the Quality of innermost love.

We can imagine from this that if God gave birth to His very highest aspiration in the form of his First Born Son, this Son has as His Being the attitude of finest Absolute Quality. This also signifies that this Son also represents in the very nature of His Being all the power that resides in the creative scheme. If this Individual lives in the scheme as a model and inspiration for it, we see that His purpose is to cause an unconscious recognition in us of the Divine Nature which gradually increases to a conscious condition. In this respect He causes us to sense our innermost sensibility which causes our innermost nature to burn more brightly and thus to cause our Will to increase its function. This function enables us to experience more fully this highest nature and as a physical drama learn more about it, which in turn causes our fires to increase again. This aspiration of God is thus the supreme factor in bringing our natures to life. This Son of God is thus the Supreme Catalyst and without Him we would not germinate and grow. He has command of all power which he exercises in order to show us that we must not use it or concern ourselves with it. The symbol of the crucifixion represents a man who has all power living out the drama of refraining from its use in order to express a condition of absolute affection and concern for the Quality of our consciousness.

At the personal level we use what we consider to be the faculty of will as a tool which bludgeons its way towards its objective, slaying all who oppose it on the way. We consider it to be a show of strength and of virility in our psychological nature. Real Will however is completely contrary to all this. It achieves its purpose as far as is Divinely possible (which is very far) in harmony with every other Will and Real Individual purpose. Working from the Absolute level it recognises the value of everything so that it is, as far as is possible, harmless towards every form of life. It is extremely efficient, so it works quietly and patiently to bring the correct factors together in the correct place at the correct time. When, for instance, we notice that a strong and able person appears in our political life at a very critical time we say that the time produces the man. We can now also say that this may be true up to a point, but the man may be present just at that time because the crisis and his own Being were inseparably connected by his will. The ability of his True Nature was able to foresee the confrontation of the forces which created the crisis. The Will of the Individual designed itself to be present as an Individual in order to be able to take part in the situation which represented a dramatic and physically expressive theatre for it to witness its own highest nature and significance through. Winston Churchill is a typical case which comes to mind. Other natures witness themselves through other aspects of experience such as the arts, the fields of learning of science and medicine and so on. What matters from the point of view of the Soul and the Absolute Self is that it is present on an occasion in which its faculties will be used and expressed to the full and which will then enable the Self to grow and become stronger in recognition and faith in its own abilities and values. Some of the most unpleasant events in our lives can produce for us the experiences of most value, and we can see that by trying to make people psychologically and physically comfortable we can often be doing them what amounts to a great disservice. In this respect kindness and goodness have to be seen to be an extension of wisdom and understanding before we can be sure that they are in fact what they seem to be.

If we wish for real power in life it seems it may be a fact that we shall only acquire this when we have genuinely ceased to be interested in power. This means that as far as Nature and Reality is concerned power is the power to bring consciousness to life. Force, which we admire as an expression of power is of very secondary significance for nature can so easily amplify any individual expression of a true and valuable quality but cannot manufacture the spontaneous quality itself, only we can do that.

This is almost an exact analogy of our radio systems. The problem is to write and perform good scripts.

The amplification of these small noises in the studio into noises in other people's houses all over the face of the Earth is a comparatively straightforward mechanical process. It means giving more energy and amplitude to an already present pattern. The pattern is the thing. If we can create the correct patterns in life for the creative purpose of the Universe to further itself, then the Universe itself will concern itself to pour energy into those patterns. If you are a Churchill you make a few small noises into a microphone and you set forces in motion in people's natures which make all the difference between a degraded society overcoming the World, and the preservation of ideals which are the basis for any further spiritual growth and evolution of the Earth's people.

CHAPTER SIXTEEN : Summary

The consciousness of our real self is largely beyond the understanding of our more familiar personality self. At its most fundamental level, its nature is Divine and at this level its own purpose mixes perfectly with the purposes of all the other divine beings. The real will is the manifesting of this already harmonised purpose throughout the lower levels of creation right down to the physical level. Thus our Self witnesses itself as it becomes more fully mature and at the same time helps to perfect the purposes of others. The real will has this power in it as part of our divine heritage. All nature responds to its proper command. But the will does not command 'willfully'—it achieves command by being more fully what it is. Thus the 'sound' of the quality of its individual being mingles more loudly with the creative power of God. What we usually call 'will' is more like desire power and idea power, through which our lower self focuses on things it feels it wants or needs. But what we feel as a need in the deepest sense is not something we can make a decision about, we just pretend that it is a decision. Our real will has decided and is something we can only be true to or untrue to, it is not something we are in a position to use. Since it contains within its nature the real power of the universe it is just as well we are not in a position to use it. It is not in the interest of our real self to desire this power for itself. What should concern us is the qualitative content of consciousness. The quantitative aspect of our life should always be subservient—the natural by-product of our concern with quality.

CHAPTER SEVENTEEN

Beauty

It would be possible to discuss the concept of beauty at great length since the relativity of the sensation of beauty is one of the most generally understood relativistic systems. Most people expect their own idea to be different from that of other peoples and they are not surprised when this is shown to be the case. If the concept of beauty is viewed in terms of the theory of this philosophy, however, not only does the relative nature of the concept become a natural by-product but it can also be used to validate and describe the various levels of consciousness.

In ordinary use the word beauty has many different meanings such as pretty, emotionally exciting, intellectually exciting, clever, intricate and so on. It is used like the term marvellous which means we are temporarily inclined to be surprised. Or it can be used instead of the word lovely which implies that we find something easy to love or love compelling. But for this theory the term beauty can be represented as something reasonably specific.

In Map 3 there is a balanced vector of growth of the evolving consciousness of an individual. This is the line OZ which begins at a point of no self-consciousness and increases in an equal way along all three vectors. The balancing of these vectors is said to be a natural process and essential to the elimination of stress. No one will follow a direct path and some will wander about more than others. Every individual will in fact create a slightly different path of progression and at any instant be in a slightly different position to any other individual.

The experience of beauty can thus be described as an experience of qualities towards which this wandering vector of growth is moving at any time. Beauty to the individual is thus a representation of that towards which he is consciously or unconsciously moving. This need not be a form of ideal aspiration, for the wandering vector may have turned around completely and be heading back in the direction from which it came. If the individual is degenerating then his idea of beauty will be degenerate also, but it still represents something which, wisely or not, he considers that he wants to identify with. Beauty is thus both a representation of sympathetic and feminine qualities and also executive and masculine qualities combined with a tendency towards the Self or away from the Self. Since the personality is in general inclined towards its True Self, this other reversed direction can be an indication that a false personality has been allowed to arise. The idea of beauty which tends to restrict and hide consciousness instead of liberating it is consequently still beauty to the individual concerned, with the attributes of fascination and attraction like all forms of beauty. But this beauty is leading to further and further restriction, and consequently to an increase in oppression and the misery which this entails.

This idea of beauty recognises that the subjective desires of the individual compose it, but it also recognises that beauty is an objective reality for us so long as we are a part of this scheme of manifestation and experience. This objective beauty is therefore an expression of the Absolute Quality. This is a more real and unchanging beauty, for it only changes as the Absolute changes, and for us the Absolute is relatively unchanging. To say that the Absolute never changes would be unwise since this theory is inclined to the concept that God is also aspiring, but these terms are meaningless unless they are very carefully qualified. God is manifest and unmanifest. These two aspects would aspire in different ways. The manifested aspiration is focussed on a smaller gain than is possibly the unmanifest.

The individual lives in his own universe and this has its own orientation towards the desired qualities of beauty. But the Universe within which we are now communicating has a specific and objective quality of beauty in its expression. This is God's universe and the quality of beauty contained in it is something definite and something which He/She wishes to say to us. There is consequently something to be gained by a discipline which observes nature and combines these observations with the inclinations of the individual. The expression of the personal concept of beauty without reference to objective beauty is more than likely to be a limited and negative factor in human culture.

These remarks apply particularly to the visual arts. When the art of music is considered, however, the position is more difficult, for who can observe the objective music in nature? As in all forms of art there are three basic approaches on the part of the artist. The one is the ideal and inspired approach which can be called true intuition. The other is an intellectual concept based on the knowledge of how the great composers and artists worked so that well-tried forms are shuffled and recomposed. The last is the approach of the commercially-minded or 'hack' artist who is concerned with creating something which is in immediate demand but which does not represent any form of sincere valuation or commitment on his part. In music the last two types can be understood and fitted into the scheme of things. But the first or intuitive type must be credited with a faculty which is extra sensory, for many people would agree that great composers do, in fact, reproduce a type of beauty in sound which is relatively objective and beyond the personal or the observable. No doubt this is true of the visual arts also but it is a less obvious phenomenon in this case. This unobservable beauty must be described as an objective beauty which is expressed at levels higher than the physical but to which certain artists are sensitive. Great artists are consequently either men who have clarified their bodies of communication and channels of communication or men who are able to sort out the rational and conditioned part of their personality where most of the circuits become distorted.

To keep in line with the main trend of this philosophy, it must be said that art should be aspiring towards the Ideal plane and through this to the Divine. This is not something that can be chosen, this is something that is a fact in the scheme of nature of which we are a part. It is obvious also that art is a very important part of this evolutionary impulse since it represents for us an experience of that towards which we are moving but which we have not yet attained. When the culture of a civilisation becomes degenerate it represents a most unfavourable comment. In fact, when a culture becomes indifferent to the concept of beauty as it has today to some extent, this is also a significant sign of hesitation in the orientation of the whole civilisation. A virile desire for beauty as an aspiration is, conversely, a most healthy quality for a culture to possess, for it allows entrance from higher levels of consciousness of a great number of qualities which assist the development of many facets of life such as religion, philosophy, social behaviour, architecture and design and all forms of learning. This is so because beauty represents for us a most important position of reference and balance. It helps to set into proper perspective nearly all the activities of our daily life as well as the activities of our psychic nature.

Everyone knows the strength and importance of the quality of beauty in personal relationships, for it is this quality which we find lovable and the basis of marriage in the opposite sex. This is an indication that beauty is an objective reality which we see reflected in those we love, and it is also an indication that beauty is ultimately the expression of Divine Love which is God's aspiration for us. Beauty should therefore be loveliness above all else and if we can bear this in mind, it may help us to make more use of our culture and find the arts a more valuable and necessary part of our lives.

The idea of beauty has led to a discussion of sex since for most people physical beauty is the strongest experience of beauty and here can be applied all the statements about beauty which have just been made. It is clear that each person sees a different quality of attractiveness in the opposite sex and it can be said that this is due to the orientation of their wandering vector of development. The person we are attracted to most and for longest is the person who represents qualities towards which we are consciously or unconsciously moving. Some of these qualities can be retrograde if a retrograde direction has developed in our progress. It is this factor which makes it so difficult to understand the general process of personal attraction. The fact that attraction exists on every level of our nature goes without saying. The most valuable form of attraction is thus not only an ideally oriented one, but one which has value and positive orientation for each level of our consciousness as well.

If the theory of the Will is taken into account here, as it has been previously described, this will account for the possibility that the right partner for us, sexually and otherwise, will one day arrive in our vicinity. This is not an accident but the result of the working of that power which is causing us to know ourselves through the acting out of our qualities externally to our Self, as it were. The right partner to live with in physical and psychic life is obviously a most important factor in this process, for the right partner is the finest possible means of communication we can have of our unconscious or unrealised nature. And if the theory of reincarnation is taken into account it can be said that such partners are so important that they move together through life after life as different personalities but with the same two essence natures. The physical aspect of sex can be seen here as the physical aspect of real Will working out at all levels. The emotions, desires and aspirations associated with sex are therefore extremely complex and far-reaching, since they represent purposes and desires about which the conscious personality knows nothing or very little. The power of sex is also seen to be the power of the Will. When properly expressed it is thus a function of the physical nature which represents all those qualities which have been already listed as belonging to this true Will. One of the chief factors is that it is not under our control in the final analysis. We are not in a position to be able to decide to fall in love if it is true love. The sensation of love is not a thing we can make decisions about, we can only decide whether or not to live truly by it or not. But this is a part of the decision to live truly by everything or not. To be true to our Self or not.

Since it seems that the family unit is a very big part of the experience that God wishes us to have, it is also very necessary that the value and importance of sex is understood, since sex forms the basis of family life and our own fullest expression as an individual. The attitude towards sex expresses for us the attitude we have towards our Self. If our sex life is indiscriminate this means that our true identity has not developed. If we are afraid of sex we are extremely uncertain of our Self. If we are aggressive we think too highly of our Self. If we are timid we think too little of our Self. If we respond to love with love and it is sweet and gentle, considerate and patient then we are in a good relationship with our Self.

The consummation of the physical and psychological aspect of sex is a reflection of the consummation of will and consequently it represents very deep and valuable aspirations which are either enhanced by a truthful approach to sex or devalued by a dishonest and casual approach. The attitude to sex is bound to be involved with the working of entities and with the distortions we create in the work of these entities. Our frustrations and angers will be expressed; our guilt and anxiety will be expressed. Too much hunger for affection (or the punishment of this hunger) will be expressed. The involvements are endless, for it expresses every facet of our consciousness and our motivation.

One thing is clear, and that is the fact that we inhibit the expression of sex at our peril. This is not to say that we should not control the physical consummation of sex, this should be a natural outcome of our Self respect and honesty. But the affections and interests which are related to the opposite sex are of the utmost importance and must never be allowed to be thought of as unhealthy or wicked as they have been in the past. To suppress these affections and responses is to suppress the finest and strongest channel of communication between the personality and the real individual Self. What is needed is not suppression but a greater variety of means of exercise so that the physical act does not suddenly become the only possibility of communication. Such means of communication are bound up with all the other forms of communication, and it is with the exercise of these forms that education should be concerned since they are so essential to spiritual and social intercourse, as well as physical and sexual intercourse. If we do not learn to talk effectively to one another we are destroying the meaning and enjoyment of life. If education were more concerned with this and less concerned with the learning of technical tricks, it would fill society with happier and more purposeful individuals.

CHAPTER SEVENTEEN : Summary

We recognise that each individual's idea of beauty varies a great deal. There are three main degrees of beauty, the ideal and aspirational, the intellectually satisfying and emotionally acceptable, and thirdly the utility and commercial level. The highest type concerns us here since this is based on the objective quality of beauty which manifestation intends us to learn to appreciate. This is the quality behind the Divine Motivation and we may call it the quality of 'loveliness'. Each of us is aware of the attractive nature of higher beauty. It is the immediate response of our striving when it senses traces of that towards which it tries to move. Art should interpret these traces for the society it inhabits. If this vital function of aspiration and interpretation on the part of the artist is not achieved, then a vital organ is lost to the body of society, vital enough to kill that society as far as living, growing existence is concerned. Beauty is the direction towards which the 'wandering vector' is moving in Map 3. It represents the unique path of growth of each individual. If the path of this wandering vector loses its way it may turn around and retrace its direction as regression; in this case the sense of beauty will be regressive also. Beauty is a value we sense also in those we love. We often do not know if it is them that we love or the beauty in them that we love. We would expect it to be both, for the loving relationship is also a doorway through which we meet the Divine quality. Sex plays a very big part in these relationships and the confrontation of the whole of one's nature with that of another's means that it is also an opportunity for the true will of each person to show and express itself. If the relationship is not a truly loving one, this opportunity is not available, for the wholes of the two parts are inhibited. The more the expression of sex is limited by the inadequacy of our ability to communicate with one another, the more the expression is limited to the physical sex act. It would seem that the proper function of this act can only be achieved if the context for it is a 'whole life' one. This expression means the intention of being committed wholly to the loved person. Casual and insincere sexual behaviour is therefore a danger to the individual for it may raise factors which prevent the wholeness of the will ever being able to come through into that particular life.

CHAPTER EIGHTEEN

The Atomic Field

If the problem of matter is to be tackled in terms of the scientific theories of our day then it may be helpful to look at it in the light of the concept of the three vector system that has been expressed in this geography and the concept of matter-consciousness that goes with it.

First of all it must be stated that the science of nuclear mechanics is still in a very tentative condition. And while a tremendous amount has been observed and theoretically understood, a lot remains to be done. This remainder may very well alter the appearance of what has gone before.

Atomic physics has arrived at a more formal condition where there is agreement that the wave and the quantum descriptions of the propagation of energy particles are equally valid and not exclusive of one another. The photon has become the main unit of transmission of light and possibly all forms of matter. As there are a great many different types of particle and particle behaviour found in atomic physics, there is a hope that these will eventually resolve themselves into a manifestation of a single underlying substratum reality. This substratum would then exhibit different qualities and quantities under different conditions at the atomic and nuclear level, but would itself belong to a super-nuclear condition.

It is this particular condition that we would be looking for if we were to try and link the theory of this book to the experimental sciences.

It is agreed that the atom itself is a unit which has a distinct sphere of activity and influence. It is composed of an outer field of electronic space and an inner core which is the nuclear space. The nucleus is itself beginning to take on the aspect of a discreet space on its own with perhaps again an innermost core and an inner electronic space. As previously suggested, the fact that we think that the atom is small and the nucleus even smaller is no indication that these spaces are small in reality. If our theory is correct, these spaces are still relatively very large indeed, however difficult it is for us to grasp this fact with our imaginations.

From the point of view of this geography, we shall expect to find the following expressions of reality amongst the findings of the scientist:

A. The three vector qualities.

1. The feminine evolutionary influence, which draws towards the centre and attracts.

2. The masculine involutionary influence which ventures forth and which separates out.

3. The partly grown individual, ambivalent and changeable. The product of the Father And Mother aspect of The Creator.

B. The purpose of The Creator as a continuing communication or education.

C. A living, mutable basis for all events however mechanical their appearance.

D. A reservation of power in favour of quality and the purpose of manifestation.

E. The main and minor transformations of matter-consciousness as described in the scale of the third vector. These showing a higher potential of energy as they rise in the scale.

F. Paradox.

While it was attempted to describe the creative process and the link in the chain of levels of matter-consciousness in terms of the induction of wave upon wave, with the fundamental wave having the 'shape' of all the potential waves to come, this must now be thought of as a model which is only an indication of a phenomenon which is also pulsating. Thus it would be wise to consider the frequencies of matter-consciousness as possessing a quantum-like property which resolves itself into a wave form through the vast number of events of which it is composed. Thus the wave mechanics will continue to give a good approximation to the reality of the condition except in very particular instances.

If there is in this system a process which transforms the higher levels of manifestation into lower and more viscous levels, then we consider this physical system to be the lowest end of the scale and at the lowest potential so far as energy is concerned. But if we look for paradox, then we might expect that this lowest level in the above respects is the highest level in some other respects. The ones that come to mind are the masculine ones of detachment and individualisation. This makes sense when we consider that the Creator's purpose is likely to be the birth of real individual children of consciousness who are not to be overwhelmed by the too close proximity of His/Her own Personality.

If we allow ourselves to consider the minute aspects of the atomic level in terms of consciousness as well as physics then we can at least propose very slight traces of the expressions listed above, which up to now have never been considered to have any remote connection with the function or interests of physics. However absurd this may seem at first, it ceases to be absurd if there is any truth behind any spiritual philosophy within the history of man on earth.

If we are more than an accident (likely to be destroyed through some other accident), which most thinking people are inclined to believe but not explain, then we can look for the purpose of our existence here at every turn. We can also expect that the paradoxical element of our dilemma will be expressed in our surroundings. As has been previously said, the great paradox is that we can only develop the real individuality in our potential consciousness if we grow in a real situation where we have to take the consequences of our actions and are not allowed to become spoiled and artificial. So the Great Love of our Creator is withheld out of Great Love. We are only helped in the minimal sense. We are taught the values of love, bliss and responsibility through suffering as with joy.

To mix such philosophy directly with atomic physics is thus a reasonable absurdity, especially if it enables us to look at the problem from a completely different point of view which may give it that basis of simplification which it so badly needs.

Paradox there is in plenty in the whole of atomic physics. The highest frequencies which have the smallest wavelength hold the highest potential of energy. Particles which affect their surroundings and transmit energy have in some cases little or no mass. If they were not moving, many of the particles would have no mass. Some particles appear to have no actual presence. The size of an electron is considered to be a point of no dimension.

So what are we in fact observing? Certainly a manifestation of energy. Certainly a process which achieves a very great deal at a very high level of organisation, planning and effectiveness. A process which produces spiritual awareness, beautiful qualities which are known and judged to be beautiful. A process which also produces hate, fear and the sense of futility. This we would expect. At the atomic level there must be traces of these elements. Even if these are only traces, like the other elements of atomic physics, they can make all the difference.

It can be suggested therefore that between every level of matter-consciousness there is a threshold at which energy needs to be applied in a particular way to unlock the doorway through. The type and form of this energy is therefore an actual key to be used as required. The requirement is assessed by the element of consciousness present. Each element of consciousness is thus in possession of certain keys and fields of assessment. It has a particular job to do, which we must assume it 'wants' to do. An atom is thus a family unit. As our Solar system is a family unit and as we are a part of a family unit.

The major process we might look for is the mixing of the evolutionary energies with the involutionary energies to produce other individual energies, some of which will last longer than others. To suggest a form which the involutionary and evolutionary energies take up, let us take the idea of seed growth. This is an accelerating curve from a vortex to the boundary of its influence. If we can picture such a volute form of energy radiating out from a vortex to a boundary, together with a similar but opposite curve radiating in from a boundary to a vortex centre, it produces an interesting picture. These volute curves are waves of energy which are also pulsing. For the sake of simplicity let the pulse be thought of as the heart beat of the system, and the outgoing and incoming waves the blood system carrying energy and not blood. Now the waves give a spinning look to the model. But the spin is in fact two opposed but harmonised vortex movements of energy. Energy can thus be considered as the desire of these two opposite influences to create. Energy is desire which has two faces, one 'determination' or power, the other fitness for and 'respect' for that which is desired. At the cruder levels of energy that are available for us to use and experiment with, these subtle aspects are not evident, but at the higher levels of manifestation we should expect them to exhibit themselves more and more clearly. Desire can be understood by us, but energy itself is sure to remain a secret of the prime cause as is also space and their product time.

Now where the two pulsing volute waves cross one another in the atomic field there will be created a minor vortex which has no permanent existence or place but which will act as a minor key to unlock a minor amount of energy from the underlying field of higher potential as described on the third vector. This minor vortex which is a child of the two opposite major volutes will remain at a definite distance from the major vortice centre if the two volute waves are balanced in their valency and timing which they are sure to be. The Map 20 will show this in a diagrammatic way.

In the map the two pulsing waves are shown as Wi for the Involutionary masculine outgoing effect and We for the Evolutionary incoming effect which is feminine. The extremity of the wave movement is marked as B for the boundary and N for the central vortex or nucleus. Where the two waves intersect at Es and Ep will be two minor vortices

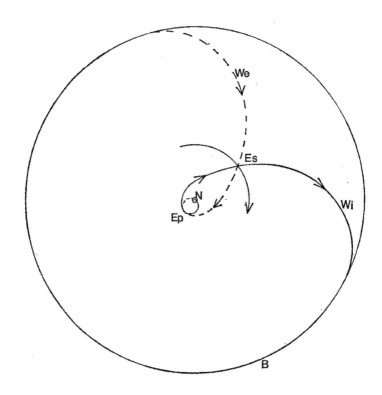

MAP 20

caused by the twisting interaction and this will act as a key which will serve to induce energy to enter in from a higher level. The path of Es and Ep will remain circular round the nucleus so long as the waves We and Wi are in balance and in phase in opposite senses. As these two waves tend to differ in phase, so will the circular path of the minor vortices tend to become elliptical round the nucleus. The Waves will have two axes each and also be able to rotate, which will give them three dimensions of direction in relation to one another. Thus the resultant minor vortices may have a very delicate and intricate path. The minor vortices would represent the electron cloud.

This system described for the electronic field can continue on into the nucleus where the same principles will hold good but where the energies and masses are very much higher. Thus our term matter-consciousness is equally valid as mass-consciousness and therefore also energy-consciousness. From the philosophical point of view this gives an interesting conclusion.

As was suggested above, it might be supposed that energy is a manifestation of desire on the part of the system. This includes purpose to the highest level. At this level the desire is termed Divine Love or Divine Purpose and the respect at such a level, for the end purpose, will surely affect the means. Manifestation is the means. This Divine attitude should very well be present in this most fundamental activity of the means of bringing about the Divine Purpose.

Let it be proposed therefore that as energy is the fundamental reality of mass and matter . . .

$$\text{Mass} \neq \text{Energy} \neq \text{Desire}$$

Where the sign $\neq$ means related to

Also . . .

$$\text{Desire} \neq \text{Determination (Power)} \neq \text{Respect (Aptness)}$$

Or

$$\text{Divine Love} \neq \text{Power} + \text{Wisdom}$$

Thus . . .

$$\text{Mass} \neq \text{Power} + \text{Wisdom}$$

The power we find in terms of energy, but we have not even thought of looking for the Wisdom. The sum of the two seems to be the Reality we are in.

Apart from the philosophical substance of this theory, which forces us on to a knife edge between profound meaning and meaninglessness, the mechanics of the theory are suggested in order to satisfy the experimental findings. The most important aspect of this is to find a method of resolving the difficulty of accounting for 'particles' which have been observed to carry energy and yet appear and disappear, amalgamate and also bounce, have mass in some cases and none in others, have both electrical polarities and two directions of spin, and in some cases become neutral in charge but potent in other ways.

The vortex is suggested to incorporate the fundamentals of philosophy with the fundamentals of physics. The vortex will readily amalgamate or bounce depending on spin, charge velocity etc. It accounts for spin itself. It accounts for a semblance of reality which does not really exist in the way which it appears to exist. It accounts for the type of adaptability and variability which is required. It can exist for a fraction of a millionth of a second only or it can exist for hours or days or years. It suggests a method of induction between levels of matter-consciousness. It is the sort of thing one would expect to find in nature.

If we take the proposition to the very limits of discussion it can account for the presence of mass and no-mass through the presence of power without wisdom or power with wisdom.

To return to the main theme of this philosophy of consciousness, it can be summarised as follows . . .

The created Universes are primarily a form of communication, a continuing lecture, a college through which we as valuable individuals pass and from which we graduate as mature or fully realised potentialities. This is evolution of consciousness and it is the main purpose behind the design of the whole system. Our individual reality, which seems so frail and impotent against the power and strength of the systems of nature, is designed to discover itself to be more important, more powerful and more potent but in much deeper and subtler ways. Consciousness is suggested as being related to a scheme of creation, the related levels of matter-consciousness, whose prime purpose is to enlighten us. In terms of science, light may be expected to be a central and favoured factor in this scheme. What do we find? We find that the photons of light are the essence of elementary particle exchange. They are the elements of communication for physical events as well as for our human eyesight. It may be more than a chance coincidence that the photon of light is also especially catered for in the system. The photon has no rest mass. This implies that it has a special ability to commute, or that all commuting is built round the commuting of 'enlightenment'.

The photon of light is that which finds this system of matter-consciousness least viscous. As elements of the system develop mass, so they find the system more viscous. This points to an implication that mass enters into the system in inverse ratio to the central purpose of the system. In other words . . .

$$\frac{I}{Mass} = \text{Power} + \text{Wisdom or Determination} + \text{Respect}$$

From this philosophical view it can be suggested that gravity and mass are resistant to the fundamental purpose of the system while being necessary to it. We feel the viscosity of this system to be a heavy drag upon our inner spirit. But this viscosity brings out the strength and definition in our nature which could not be achieved without resistance.

Because the photon is central to the purpose of the system and because the system is designed outwards from it, the photon is observed to 'float' in the system.

If this geography is correct, our physical system of matter-consciousness is related to minor levels within itself, but also to major levels above and below it in terms of ethereality or viscosity. It may now be suggested that each major level of manifestation has its own light system and that this light system is not only the central structure and purpose of the major levels but that it is through the central light aspects of each major system that the major systems link up.

It can be suggested that as in Map 21 the three major systems of matter-consciousness are based on the three light bands A, B, and C and that these three systems resonate in some way to unite the whole. It would be reasonable to expect that this resonance of the 'Skeleton Light' of each system would be observable in the structure of elementary events as a bifurcation of the event. It is this bifurcation which is observed in nuclear mechanics as a paradox. This paradox is expressed as the Particle/Quantum situation, whereby an elementary event is only describable in terms of particles of continuous existence and quanta of discontinuous existence, the whole being expressible in terms of wave mathematics.

The fact that the elementary particle can be assumed for all our practical purposes while being an unreal particle in our deepest theoretical purposes speaks for itself. It implies the unreal status of our physical system, which appears most real to our conscious experience of it so long as that reality or that group of lectures is required by our consciousness. When it ceases to be required we reject it and move on to other 'realities' and other class rooms.

As the system A is based on system B and so forth, the relative 'reality' of each system depends on that of the higher frequency and lesser viscosity. The bifurcation of the photon events is thus the result of the inner substance of the photon system A which is the photon system B (which is in turn founded on system C). The 'reality' of the event of the system A can only be understood in terms of system B.

Another proposition which springs from the foregoing arguments is that the 'interior' workings of the atom belong to and are a key to the next higher order of matter-consciouness. While the atomic activity is partly in our physical world it is also partly in the hyper-physical world. Thus we may suggest that the particles ejected from atoms are not necessarily the same after leaving the atomic aura as they were while they were still within it. We can imagine that the system of vortices already described are an activity belonging to the hyper-physical world and that they take on the

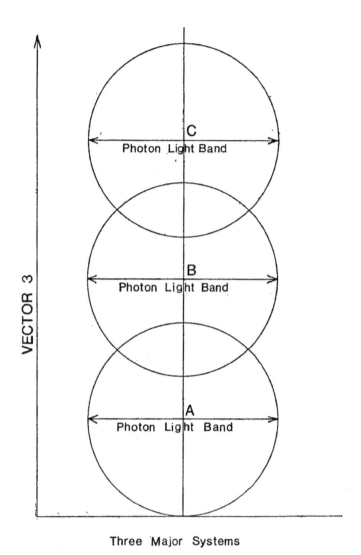

Three Major Systems

MAP 21

nature of a particle of our physical system only when they are externalised. The particles are thus 'reproductions' in our order of matter-consciousness of an activity which belongs to the next higher order. Our whole nature is however, actively engaged in and already a part of these higher orders, but our physical observations are restricted to this physical system which we have a strong tendency to identify with. When we observe the activity of particles we observe their traces only. We cannot observe the particle itself because the wavelength of light does not permit it. The light of the next higher order of photon spectrum would enable us to see these particles, but we are not equipped for the use of that order of perception. The system of photon bands shown in Map 21 is a literal 'Christmas Tree' and it gives a certain poetic turn to our thinking and supplies an association of ideas which is deeply longed for and it is sometimes wise to associate these 'given' parts of our nature with the purposes and problems we tangle with.

CHAPTER EIGHTEEN : Summary

The structure of the most fundamental particles of matter-consciousness should exhibit the fundamentals of the creative source. These can be seen as the father-mother-child relationships which produce the creative possibility in manifestation. The 'gardening' of children is the most creative situation we can ever be involved in. It is on a higher level than repair and maintenance. If we look for a proposition which will help to describe the structure and function of the atomic and sub-atomic units of matter-consciousness, the masculine outgoing and the feminine gathering-in motions can be made to knit together to form particles of another order, or children. The vortex created by these centripetal and centrifugal forces in the proposed model of the atom represents, in this sense, a child. The idea and 'feeling' of the vortex proposition fits in with the induction chain of Map 17. A vortex is a fluid focus of motions in the process of change, of acceleration and deceleration. It is in this sort of situation that we might expect to find the keys to the transformation process which link the higher frequencies and powers to the lower frequencies and powers in this chain of levels of manifestation in Map 15. If we remember to look for attributes of consciousness at these levels, we can add to the idea of purposeful and organised energy the concept of desire and even aptness or wisdom. Gravity then appears as a most necessary part of the wisdom, for it is the fundamental resistance which strengthens as it teaches. The opposite effect is the work of the carrier of conditioned energies, the photon. For the photon 'floats' in the system and provides the counteraction to mass and inertia. Thus it is light, and poetically 'enlightenment', which is most at home in the system. It is from the proposed photon band at each major level of manifestation that the 'muscles' and the 'flesh' of creation emanate. So that the structure of the photon system, which goes beyond the level of the photon of the physical sciences right through to the Absolute, is the skeleton of manifestation and the primary product of the 'Word' of the Creator.

Conclusion

I am sorry if this book has left some readers with a sense of bewilderment and dismay. My intention has not been to complicate affairs, but it seems to me that the valuable simplicities that we arrive at through experience cannot be arrived at any other way than by ways which seem to be complicated while we are as yet still in them. I would like to try and give my considered views on the whole subject of approach to God, Truth and Reality as it relates to Eastern ways and to Western ways and not to be too long-winded about it.

My own individual feeling is that Eastern peoples and Western peoples do not yet realise how much their attitudes differ from one another and how much they have to offer one another in this respect and what valuable results will come out of the joining of the two streams. On the one hand we have the ancient knowledge and disciplines of the schools of Yoga, whose sources go back and back and whose attitudes influence all Eastern religion and philosophy. On the other hand there is the teaching of Christ which has influenced the Western world more particularly and has a precise source. In between there are the Greek and Egyptian influences which are less complete or discreet.

Christian endeavour has resulted in many of the powers and special effects obtained by Eastern methods, but obtained them more as an accidental by-product. Eastern endeavour has been lead to a deep respect for the sayings of Christ through their special disciplines and the special powers arising from them. When a Yogi achieves his ends he becomes Christlike and ceases all the practices that we would associate with any special discipline. When the Christian in the West achieves his ends his attitudes are hardly any different to that of an Easterner and again, his disciplines become unimportant.

There is an unresolved situation that still exists in both cases however, and that is one which is not easy to describe without danger of misunderstanding. While the Christian and the Yogi are both trying to achieve union with God, I feel there is a possibility that we have not troubled to understand what union with God signifies. My own view is that God, like ourselves, is both 'personal' and 'Impersonal' in His/Her Being.

Many people will think I am splitting hairs on this factor which are best left unsplit, but I will try to explain why I do so.

I find it in myself to expect that the motivation behind God's action in manifesting the Visible and Invisible Universes is that they should be training ground for us, His children. Furthermore while we are as yet children, it is God's deepest wish that we should choose to mature into individuals of 'The Stuff of His Stuff' and who also choose Him as a friend. Therefore as the *choice left to us* is of the utmost importance there must be at least one other way for us to retain our 'perpetuity'. To me at least one other way is open for us if we choose to unite the impersonal aspect of our Being with the impersonal aspect of God's Being. In both cases the ground for union is mutual love of the same quality or qualities which results in the same Will and in the same desires.

I also think it is possible for our individual or personal Being to unite with God's Impersonal Being and that there is no limit to the sort of relationship we can take up with God. It must be understood that I am using the word Personal in a very deep sense which only the reader who wishes to understand will do so. I am not referring to the personality on its own or to the enlightened personal aspect of the ordinary individual. I am referring to the Divine difference in each of us which at the same time is fully aware of the Divine harmony and unity of our loves. The Divine Individual that each of us is in God's eyes.

I would further try the reader's patience by saying that I truly believe that God is a sadder God if we do not realise the basis of His deepest motivation, which is not that He should ingest our Individuality into the Blissful nature of His Being, but that we should, out of the simplest recognition in our Heart of Hearts, realise the unspoken longing and non-willing that lies behind the blissful aspect of Divine Love. This is to me such a subtle thing that I hesitate to go on, but in my blundering way I will do so. I believe that behind the Bliss of Divine Union resides a relationship which is deeper than Bliss and that is the attitude which upholds and, if you like, protects the Bliss. This is the attitude which has known that the Blissful Qualities are 'good', and in a creative sense can be made even better. This sounds like a sort of spiritual heresy but it is exactly what I find in myself to say.

Now if we choose to become a friend and companion of God, then we can also sense something of this underlying creative attitude towards the nature of Highest Being itself, and by standing apart from God while being perfectly in tune with Him we can in fact take part in a creative process which is endeavouring to improve on what to us seems the perfect and unimprovable. I am sure I have offended many sincere and highly spiritual people by my remarks on these lines for they feel it is conceited of me to begin to define or explore the motive behind what is referred to as The Absolute, and not only conceited but simply impossible. But if the 'personal' motive is felt, as I have felt it, then the problem dissolves immediately.

I would like to say a word about special methods used to raise and condition the activity of our bodies of communication which the Yogi uses. While I feel it correct to use all good means to spiritualise awareness and while I realise that the control and direction of the mental, emotional and physical bodies by the breath and posture are good, I would say that the Love of God and the Love of That which God loves produces the Yogic processes in such a way that first things are kept first and there is no likelihood of the deepest perspective being lost, for the greatest treasures are only a hiding place for the great treasure, and as I say I believe 'That Treasure' to underlie the Bliss of Union itself.

Similarly perhaps the Western mind has not delighted in the possibility of blissful attainment enough and is likely to lose hope of the beauty of intention behind their existence. It finds relief in righteousness and goodness, which is not good enough or thorough enough. I feel that in bringing the East and West together we should arrive at the thorough penetration of the East together with the thorough application of the West, and so find ourselves truly with feet firmly on the ground and heads firmly in the clouds and hearts firmly beside God's Heart, or within God's Heart.

I find it difficult to accept that God allowed the situation of our world to become what it is without a reason. While God would not deliberately push us into a condition in the world where we forget the higher part of our nature and so commit behaviour which is not good, it is possible that He deliberately allowed us to wander in that direction, of our own accord, for a very definite reason. This being to increase our ties with earth and increase our resistance to heaven so that we would eventually become more completely centred in the *midst* of His creation rather than at the top end of it. While we must know the heights of Divine Heaven as well as the depths of the earth we must also remember that God is 'outside' both heaven and earth. In this way it may be said that the Treasure He seeks that we, His children, should find lies in the centre or heart of manifestation and really is signified by the expression of a personal aspect of our nature. Perhaps the Divine power and glory of the enlightened soul is made to understand a further dimension in the uncomfortable and limited restriction of the earthly personality. Perhaps the value that God seeks in us is not our perfect unalloyed Divine Being Bliss, but the humble and imperfect yearnings and sentiments that our soul feels in the crippling form of the human situation. The compression and pain breeds a simple love that does not feed on pleasure, even Divine pleasure. It feeds on a 'craggy' determination, often beyond the hope of any reward in the form of happiness or joy, to improve the lot of those it loves. To my understanding this creates a love between persons, and the souls of those persons, which teaches them something about the nature of the heart of love which is not learned in the experience of liberated divine bliss or devotion to 'perfection' as we understand it. The highest teachings we have ever received on earth seem to me to say, 'do not take any notice of miracles and powers, God can make these happen at any time. Seek to understand the nature of the love that brought you forth. This is not interested in power or glory or even perfect behaviour, but has something to do with the response that only you can make, because there is none other like you.'

Behind the God who is upon the Throne of Glory and Power, is the vulnerable, sweet, gentle, humble, beautiful love which is naturally more protected, secret and hidden. When we discover the depths of our own Being we may also discover that there are greater depths revealed, and that there is no limitation to our nature or to the relationships that are able to spring from it.

Once upon a time there was a wonderful God sitting upon His throne amidst a great light whose expression was of magnificent beauty, glory and power. Around the throne were countless people enjoying His presence and worshipping Him with songs and praise. But one of that number noticed that every now and again God gave him a wink. At first he thought it must be an illusion but it happened again and again. Finally one day the crowd moved and drifted about in such a way that he came very close to God. Then again he saw the wink and the look straight at him, just him amongst all those others, and he heard a whisper. 'Hey, come around the back after the last show, if you can spare the time.' Well of course he did go. So after the last performance that night, round the back there was this God waiting. 'Hallo,' He said. 'Come up here to my little hill overlooking the sea, I would like you to come and sit with me on my lawn and daisy patch. We can have a cup of tea together and a pipe to look at the view together. I love to take my costume off at the end of a day and relax. Although I have all that worship and praise there are times when I like to get away from it all and be quiet. I like to come here and look at the sea on a lovely day, with the mountains beyond and the feeling of this little garden up here on the hill. For although I have so many beautiful children to look after and enjoy and although they say such nice things about me and serve me in every sort of way, I get so lonely. You see, I don't have many friends. No one recognises me after the show when my make-up is off. I have to be like you saw me, for they all expect it of me, but I am more delighted than you can imagine that you have come here with me so that we can sit together and I can show you this small garden and the view from my heart.'

APPENDIX

Letter From A Father

This is a simplified and direct interpretation of the understanding I have of reality and it is written as a letter in order to emphasise the qualities which are most important in life and most easily lost in formal literature.

My Dear Child,

In the beginning before time was, your mother and I had a longing in our heart to share our values and the substance of our being with others who could rejoice and be glad about them as we are glad about them. So we considered how we could do this. We realised that to make living beings directly and ready formed was one way, and to make the seeds of this, and plant them in a situation which would cause them to grow in their own way, as a gradual process, was another.

There were two things we had to bear in mind. We had to decide how important to us it was that these children were real and not remotely controlled puppets. And we had to decide how we could guide and teach them what we knew they would have to learn without them losing the position of judgement for themselves over the values which we already knew to be good.

We had to think of a system in which we could sow these potentialities of our own being as individual units so that they would grow and realise their potentialities as actual abilities. In the process we would have to be careful not to dominate them too much or we would destroy their individual differences and the integrity of their reality. But we also understood that they would have to grow into a certain type of person if they were going to be able to understand what we had to show them and give to them. And of course we realised that they would begin their growth as our children, but that what we really longed for was not that they should be our children, but that they should slowly mature and become our companions and friends.

For our longing was to share this undemanding gladness in other centres of being who were in harmony with us but who were truly independent individuals to us. We understood this relationship to be the most delightful, and one which was open to endless variations, and these variations seemed to us of the greatest value since they had an absolute creative context between them. I mean that when we had companions who had matured to this position, and had decided to accept your mother and myself as their friends, and one another as friends, then there would be an endless variety of possibilities for future projects of creation in which we could all share and which would give us tremendous enjoyment in the doing of them together. For we are not limited in any way that matters and there is nothing that we could not try out as an experiment so long as it seemed to us to have in it that integrity and affection which is the very basis of our nature.

In order that your being should mature slowly and fully, we had to think of a way to bring experience to you which would awaken you without overwhelming you, and in the process of awakening you enable you all to become different in your individual ways. As you already know, the quality of wholehearted affection and the quality of integrity or stability were two of the qualities most important to understand. Knowledge, both factual and of qualities, was also a part of this.

I want you to understand just how subtle this process of growth and development had to be in order to retain the fundamental factors which carried the real value of your very being and which would give you absolute value of being which would, to you yourself and to your friends, be recognised as a gift of the very best of our ability. For it is only the very best thing that your mother and I will allow ourselves to give to you, and over this we have to take the responsibility and over this our decision is unshakeable. So we had to design a school with classrooms and playgrounds, and invent a curriculum which would not only cover all the qualities we wished to talk to you about, but also would allow you plenty of time to assimilate these qualities, each in your own way. You see how the individuality of your own being was of the essence of the matter from the very beginning. You were the one who was eventually to become aware of your own uniqueness and individual value, and you were to learn to carry the responsibility that goes with this gift.

We, most of all, felt as our deepest and dearest wish, when the time came that you understood what it was that we had undertaken on your behalf, that you would be glad, and choose to take up this option we have offered to you as our most loving gift, and live together with us as your friends and helpers. But, as you know, in the case of friendship, the relationship between the two sides must be one of perfect balance and understanding and has to be freely and spontaneously taken up and maintained. Therefore our purpose was to bring you to a stage in your experience when you could understand what we were offering as friends, but we had to arrange for you to have an alternative open to you, for friendship and love cannot be thrust upon people or they cease to be real.

Now, if you will follow me carefully I will try to explain what the alternative was. If you have understood that our personal love and friendship was one way for you to take, then our impersonal eternal being was another way for you to take if you so chose. In both cases you would come to eternal life, as this was the basis of our gift, but if you did not notice or did not respond to our personal nature, then you must be in a position where you could respond to all the qualities that we hold to be valuable but which do not involve our own personal love or friendship, thus uniting with our impersonal aura or being, which is itself bathed in love. If this seems to you to be too involved, then let it go for now, since it does not matter until it feels to you that it matters. Already we have laid the ground for the great problem which faces you in the world today and, so far as you know, has always faced your lives on earth.

I have always heard you ask why I allow the terrible things to go on in the world between man and man and between man and nature. You not only wonder why hatred and anger and fear should lead people to do unspeakable things to one another, but you have wondered why the universe seems to be indifferent to your very existence and to be unconcerned which way you act. Indifference is one of the worst responses to feel coming to us; we would quite rightly prefer praise or blame to this cold and empty feeling.

The value of my answer to you will only increase as your understanding increases, so you must try very hard to see the problem from my end or you will never understand it at all. I hope that all of you, when you were children, remember a time when your parents acted for you in such a way that it infuriated you, when they acted as though you were not there, or as though you were only an extension of themselves. Perhaps they apologised to someone on your behalf instead of letting you do it yourself, or they got you out of some trouble by using influence which you knew was unfair and left you, as a person, out of the reckoning. You knew that, when you were not allowed to carry the consequences of your own actions, you lost some vital essence in your own being.

These consequences may be good or bad, but carry them you must, or you cease to get the feeling that you matter, or really exist at all. And this is the truth of it, and you were quite right to consider it to be a devaluation of your nature. Now, I have to see to it that this does not occur at the level of your true being, your soul, as you feel you must not let it happen at the level of your personality or outer self. So I have made your school in such a way that it becomes real to you and does not remain a game.

I and your mother have hidden ourselves away amongst you in order that you should not escape too easily your lesson in responsibility. This lesson in responsibility must not be in half measures for it is just as important to your understanding of our highest qualities as the lessons in sympathy, affection and beauty. Responsibility and integrity are your strength to appreciate the significance of loving kindness and beauty. For kindness and beauty are nothing if they are not wedded to strength, and strength is nothing if it is not wedded to kindness and beauty. Such is the beginning of my answer. However, another big hurdle will be facing you and that is how you are going to find enough time to do what, you now know, you have to do.

In order to help you to understand my attitude towards time I must explain what time is as a part of the carrying out of my undertaking for you. If you can imagine that what I have to say to you and teach you were written down in a book, then time is that interval of consciousness which is necessary for the contents of the book to be read and understood by you. Since you realise that each one of you is a little different to the other, you will also realise that some read quickly and others slowly, but also some assimilate what they have read quickly and others more slowly.

You see here an infinite number of requirements, and you also see that to read quickly is one thing, but to fully understand the significance of what you have read is quite another. To put you all together in the same situation, and expect you all to respond in the same way and in the same time, would be completely contrary to my hopes and expectations for you. So what I have done is to design a curriculum which allows each of you to grow and respond in your own time, and in your own way, and thus the complexity of time is as the complexity of this condition of our collective engagement in the use of consciousness. Or shall we say it is in fact a meal that we all eat but which we all differ in the way we eat and digest it. So time is not what it appears to be, it is only what you require it to be to receive into yourselves its content.

Now you ask me how you can do this in one lifetime, and you also show me the unfair positions that some of you start from, and you doubt if I can possibly say anything that can help you on this score. Well, I can help you, but only if you will pay very close attention to me, and do not let the essence of what I am saying pass you by.

You must realise that you see my creation from one end of it only. You discover yourselves to be born of a mother into the physical body of a baby, and you grow in body and understanding from the position of that young child, but you know nothing about the work that went into my creation before this birth of yours occurred. While understandably you take the world and the universe for granted, the familiarity of your surroundings causes you to forget that they are neither fully perceived nor fully understood by you. You become involved in trying to survive as a personality, and you forget that the stage on which you are acting is not only made by me but also has to be continually maintained by me and my helpers.

This stage on which you act is a schoolroom in my university, and as you would not expect one of your children to learn all that the university had to teach in one day of attending class, so I also never expected you to spend but one day in the classroom. From where I now speak to you, one lifetime on earth is but one day in your classroom in my university, and, when the evening comes, I look for you to come home, where you will be nearer to me and where I can give you rest and refreshment to make you ready for the next day at school.

Now you understand how I see you and how I created you. You realise that I am asking you to think of yourselves as essentially fragments of my own being. But the nature of your being is given to you as a growing potentiality, and not as a ready-formed thing, so that you can weave and wander a pattern of your very own through the classrooms of the universe, and in doing so weave a pattern of your very own into that being which I have given to you as your own.

Thus is your value to yourself and to all other selves built up, but, while you weave an individual pattern into your own essential nature, there is much that we will find that we have in common with one another. For my responsibility was that you should grow into the sort of person who could appreciate the very things that I hold most dear, and wish most deeply to give to you, so I could not let you grow into just any sort of person; I could not allow you to develop your nature in such a way that you would become alien to the basic qualities that I know to be good; I could not give you total freedom, and you would not thank me if I had, for you are beginning to realise that such a freedom is not freedom at all but is licence, and can lead to degeneration and self-destruction. For you can destroy yourselves if you persist too long in attitudes that neither your being nor your outer nature were designed to withstand.

Our alikeness to one another comes from the fact that, although we are all weaving different patterns into our nature, the warp and woof of that nature is already given, and the wools and cottons you weave your designs with are provided by me, and are of my nature. So, whether we arrive at a personal or impersonal relationship eventually, we will always be able to rest in this perfect harmony which is already present in our separate individual beings.

If you do not accept that you are a piece of my living being, temporarily inhabiting a physical body, then I will not be able to take you much further in understanding your position in the universe, but if you begin to perceive that you are essentially an inhabiter of a body, as a diver inhabits a diving suit, then you and I will be able to make headway together, and I will be able to draw you closer into the beauty and aptness of the scheme I have chosen for you. For you will also accept that, when the diving suit is worn out, you leave it behind, together with the element it has been operating in, and you will return to the surface of the ocean where the air exists that has been pumped to you down the life lines of your diving suit. This is a cumbersome and heavy thing, but necessary if you are to start by exploring the lowest levels of creation before climbing to the mountain tops.

The diving suit is helping you in ways that I have not yet explained. It is restricting your activity and behaviour while you are still learning to do it for yourself and by yourself. This heavy restriction and resistance of the diving suit, and the weight of the water of the oceans, is slowing you down so that you can witness and observe in slow motion the meaning and value of what you are doing. If you were suddenly to be transported to a free and more responsive condition, you would be unable to maintain your balance or self-control. You would miss the slow but most important introduction to all your classes in my school, and you would not be able to follow through the meaning and significance of the lessons that are being taught in higher classes.

For you are learning the lessons of integrity, affection, kindness, beauty and honesty. You are learning to differentiate between the outer nature, that you experience the world with, and the inner nature that considers what it has experienced and which makes a structure of values out of this experience, and you are then learning to try and live by the best of the values that you have discovered against the resistance of their opposites. Thus you are becoming strong, but strong in what you deem to be good. When you have become strong enough in this way, then the heavy opposition you feel will no longer be necessary for you, and you will be able to move on to less restrictive and less basic lessons.

This separating out of the inner attitude of your being from the outer attitudes of your personality can be quite dramatic, and is spoken of in your religious language as being saved or 'seeing the light' or 'finding oneself'. When we behave badly, we say we forget ourselves and this is a good analogy of the deeper condition that exists all the time.

When the inner nature is perceived, and believed in, it immediately brings us close to the essential nature of my being where we find all those pleasing things that have the most fulfilling effect upon our nature, and help us to feel that we are being more fully ourselves. I know you think you are searching for happiness. But really you will find that this is not so. What you search for is fulfilment, or the exercise of your whole being nature; this produces the condition of happiness but you will then be too busy to notice. If you try to capture happiness for its own sake you will find it illusive, for it only exists as a by-product of your success in living most fully and truly the values and responsibilities of your own individual nature.

If you identify yourself with your outer personality only, then the fulfilment of these outer needs and ambitions will not satisfy you, but if you link the outer with the inner, so that you work hard in the world to fulfil in the best way you can the ideals of your inner nature, then you will not only make great progress in understanding, but you will also know that you are doing so. This certainty is most helpful in building up your confidence in the delicate and more ethereal side of life which you find is hard to hold your faith in.

This faith in what you know to be good, in the face of harsh opposition, is the only way I can strengthen the roots and foundations of your being, and it is only upon this strengthening that you and I can build together something that will last, and which will be your own unique self, but do not think that I am asking you to feel that the physical world experience is in any way unfortunate or lacking in importance towards the total aim of my endeavour. If you will bear with me further, I will try to explain to you why the contrary is the truth of the situation.

I would like you to consider that, in your own experience, if you intend to manufacture something which has not been done before, you do many calculations and drawings on paper, and you have many consultations with your helpers before you consider starting work on the material object itself, and you know that, however careful and accurate you have been in your planning stage, that the problems of putting the ideas into actual physical working condition are always great and always contain some unpredictable elements. You know well that to carry an idea about in your head is one thing, but to make that idea an actual physical reality requires the effort and focus of your whole attention, craftsmanship and art.

How many of you can picture a beautiful work of art in your imagination, often in great detail, but you do not begin to put it into painting or musical form because you know you lack the ability, and you feel that you would destroy the very beauty of the thing if you tried, and that would be hurtful to you. You know that you can live and be creative in your imagination, but that you only really get to grips with such a creation when you try to put it into its most objective and concrete condition, namely in that slow, resistant and demanding world outside you, the physical world.

Now the same situation applies to your mother and me and our sincere and affectionate undertakings on your behalf. We have planned and calculated in the freedom and responsive condition of our imagination, and then we have gradually and carefully transferred the results of our least restricted imaginative consciousness down through more and more solid and resistant forms, and conditions of manifestation or manufacture, until we reached your physical condition, which was the most demanding and most difficult that we could achieve. For we could not go beyond that which we could safely manage, but we had to go to the very limits of our ability in order to draw out the greatest benefit and treasure from our endeavour. Your individual reality is the benefit, and your eventual gladness in it is our treasure, so you see that the very difficulty and opposition of the physical universe that you are in is also the very measure of your value to us.

If we had not cared so much about the reality of our gift to you we would have spared you and ourselves the pain and difficulty of this extreme form of concrete and differentiated experience. As it is, we very often stand outside the railings of your playground and weep over the bullying that goes on amongst you, and we are tempted to interfere when we know that we must not do so. For, if we did interfere at the wrong time, we would immediately detract from the essential condition of individual responsibility which you must be taught to take up for yourselves and know to be an essential part of your reality. For, if you do not accept this responsibility, then you cannot accept or receive the gift of your own individuality.

This is our gift to you, and understandably you feel more inclined to hate us for it than thank us, for its birth in you must be painful as well as joyful. This you will shortly understand. The fact that you would have to experience pain and joy in order to know good and bad, and better and worse, was known to us from the beginning, but many of the details and consequences of this remained for us to resolve as they occurred.

You can be sure that the physical universe is my greatest handiwork, and in it I achieve my most valuable and creative work, and, if this physical condition is where I do most of my work, you can be sure that it is here that I am giving you my very closest attention, even if, as I have said, I hide myself from you and do not interfere with you.

At this point of my effort, every aspect of my nature comes together in its most concentrated and differentiated condition. To put it another way, my more adaptable and responsive stages of creation, which you call heaven and paradise, do not contain the earthly condition, but the earthly condition does contain the other conditions of my manufacturing process, from the most heavenly and tenuous, down through the intermediate stages of formation, to this, my most highly defined and slowed-down condition. Although you only gradually become aware of the presence of these more delicate stages of my work, they are nevertheless all around you, so it is here that you can get the greatest understanding of my nature in its detailed significance, and it is here that I continually learn things about you and about myself.

Only here are you in the best position as spectator to judge and value the qualities of being and consciousness as they work out amongst themselves in practical situations, so here also is the best position to learn wisdom, but I do not wish to make your work and my work sound easy. The situation is such that it can demand and absorb our very best efforts all the time. This means that, if you or I do not respond to our position as teacher or learner sufficiently well, then troubles and difficulties set in which demand special remedies.

For instance, I know you wish to ask me why there should be so much illness and disease in your world. One answer is that the collective feelings and thoughts, as well as actions of the people of earth, have for so long been contrary to those of kindness, affection and sympathy that the physical and psychological atmosphere has been contaminated by them, and weakened from my true intent by them, but, as I have told you, even if it takes a long time you must as far as possible live out the consequences of your activities.

Now, if the atmosphere of your world contains the energies of your wrong thoughts and feelings, these energies, as any scientist will explain to you, will have to go somewhere and cannot be immediately dissipated or neutralised. Their effect is therefore to cause pockets of inharmonious imbalance in that delicate scheme which we call the balance inherent in all creation. Without this balance there would be no stability, and without this balance the inter-related and complex activities of living cells and organs become disorganised, and produce contrary results to those that they should produce, but I want you to understand that disease and suffering is not a thing that I would wish on you, and, if you will believe me, I suffer these pains with you and for you although I cannot just take them away from you since they are part of that context of responsibility that is your essential burden.

There are so many other things I wish to say to you that I must allow you to carry this argument into all the practical situations for yourself, for the effects of this sternness on my part, and the painful savouring of them on your part, are unlimited and form the strong and unflinching basis of my work with you on your own reality. If such disease and pain, malformation and destitution were the end of things for each of you, then it would be different, but, as I have tried to explain, you do not know it but I keep you and cherish you in ways that would amaze you, and I am not averse to repeating lessons and situations in your schoolroom on earth until you understand what I have to say. And if those 'days' be very many, and each day a lifetime in your sight, then try and understand my purpose all over again from the very beginning, and realise that time and the world are at my service and were formed by me to teach you the one thing that seems to you beyond the bounds of your wildest dreams, which is my divine affection and the qualities that go along with it.

Whether this divine quality of consciousness be taken up on a more or on a less personal basis, the same loving concern is shed from me and from your mother upon each one of you, and the personal relationship we take upon us is between you and us individually, and no other person has any say in what it is or how we make it, for there lies one of the endless mysteries of our love.

One of the most important ways I have chosen for you to learn what is vital for your understanding is to find yourself a part of a family situation on earth, for here you are able to go though the experience in one single lifetime, and with unbroken continuity, the experience of being a child, a mature individual and a parent. In this situation, if you will only learn to pay close attention to it, are all the mysteries of the universe that matter to you. If you take the trouble to stand apart and observe closely all the relationships that exist in your family situations, you will be able to observe as completely as you will how the problems of life arise, why they arise and how they are solved. The family situation is a very special gift to you and one day you will be surprised that you took it so for granted.

I have not yet explained to you that you are not my only children, and that I have not brought you all up in the same way. I explained that I have gradually brought the physical universe into being by planning it and organising it at more ethereal levels of manifestation where the stuff of manifestation is more responsive and mobile. These levels are called by you more heavenly levels of being, for in them everything is more in harmony and more expressive of the intense beauty which to me is so valuable.

As these ethereal forms of manifestation were brought into existence, so did I cause other of my children to be born into them. They grew up and matured in these conditions where their attention was filled with the direct and indirect presence of your mother and myself. We wished them to become familiar with us in this way because we were going to need them as helpers while our plan of creation grew outwards from us to more remote and unconditioned levels where our personality also became less dominant, and where other personalities, your own, would in future time be able to grow up in a slower and more difficult environment but a more independent one.

You understand that, at this very point in my description, you are face-to-face with one of the great secrets of my work, which, until now, has been kept hidden from you for the children of heaven have never had that independence that you have had. They have been through happier times, but they have had greater need of me and my strength, for they were not weaned at the beginning on the strength and independence which you have been weaned on. On the other hand, without their loving help which they have given to me, I could not have undertaken this difficult outer classroom work where I need them to guide and instruct, to maintain and repair the classes, classrooms and playgrounds on which you thrive and on which your reality and future depend.

Slowly you will come to understand that the standing alone and apart in my universe, without being able to detect me directly, is a gift to your development which my other children have not had. This gift is a painful gift for much of the time, but the depth of the understanding it produces is far greater than the understanding produced in the happy states of heaven where the qualities of my being are dominant. For joy and delight fill the days of these heavenly children, but such lessons are one-sided and do not teach them the intrinsic values of such delights because they are not valued against the experience of their opposites. You, on the other hand, value all these opposites from the very beginning and in so doing gain an insight which is beyond my ability to explain to you at this stage, but I can say that your more detached and objective judgements will one day put you in a position where the added depth of your understanding will show you the merit of my endeavour.

My heavenly children help me to guide and teach you, and some of them come to earth and join you in your present situation as ordinary human beings; thus they come partly to give you a little of heaven, and partly so that they can experience a little of this earthly situation themselves, and so gain in wisdom and knowledge of me from another direction, so be quite clear about the fact that, although they help you now to overcome many of your problems, one day you will be able to give to them the fruits of your experience, and you can be sure that when that time comes you will do it very gladly.

Try to become clear in your own understanding how you feel towards your own children of earth. When you feel clearly the real depth of the attitudes you should properly find within yourselves towards them, then nearly all of the questions you have about my attitudes towards you will be answered. For, if you have not yet learned to love your own children properly, then you are not yet ready to learn how I feel towards you. If you are not aware that your responsibilities towards your loved ones are an exact analogy of my responsibilities towards you then you have not begun to understand why I have put you on earth.

I know, and you know, that the world has produced some strange and unpleasant ways of picturing me and doing me service. There are religions in the world of all sorts and the confusion in your minds about your own reality, the reality of the universe and about the nature of my being is a terrible tangle of fear, doubt and human shortcomings. I would like you to try and raise your eyes above all this towards the one simple and salient fact that my nature is made of a degree of love which will go far beyond any longing you have ever carried in your heart as yet, and, if such was my nature from the beginning, then such will always be the starting point for any understanding that you have of me. If your understanding tries to start from a lesser position, then it will produce for you a lesser vision and one which may well hinder and hurt you if you try to live by it or serve it in ways which would be foreign to my ways.

You often picture me in your hearts as something less than a kind and strong human being, but, if you look at all the fine qualities that the world has witnessed, and then think of me as having them even more abundantly, then you will come closer to my bigness of heart and bigness of mind. Remember, I do not look for reward or praise for my gift to you; I give it with gladness and without thought of you being in any debt to me, but you must realise clearly that the very nature of my gift requires that you must value it and love it as I do, for I too love the qualities that I value, but I do not worship them. I adore what I aspire to.

I am living, which means I have ideal objectives for which I work and to which I aspire. These objectives I love. If I worshipped them I would feel that I had an exaggerated and unbalanced attitude towards them. To love something is one thing, but to worship it is another. Worship creates a gap in our understanding and valuation and into this gap creeps fear and self-deprecation. Neither of these qualities are good in my sight, and I do not desire that you should worship me for it produces servility and fear where I should prefer friendship and affection.

Adoration is an extreme form of affection, and, as such, it is a wholesome thing for it does not destroy the adorer in any way. Hard though some of these words will be to you, it is better that you try to understand them and in so doing understand the one who draws you by the affection he has for all good and beautiful things. Love expresses itself in action and you call this loving service, but, in this context, I do not like the word 'service' for it hides the true meaning of love in action.

Love in action does not consider itself to be service or anything measured in terms of merit, but there is such a thing as service which is not love in action and is performed to make the performers feel good, or admired, or to obtain hope of a reward from some source of power they think of as their god. While you will understand that the intrinsic degree of love in service is a graded proportion, you will understand that, where there is little real love, the things that take the place of love are sometimes harmful to those involved. So you see how it hurts me to feel that you are serving me or worshipping me if the motive of love is lost or forgotten.

You will tell by my letter that my considerations are such that, in your eyes, I would appear to be what you might call humble and approachable, and quite simple where my affections are concerned. Now you examine in your own imagination the deepest and most perfect form of affection which is my love, and you will realise for yourself that there is no motivation to be above you in the sense of being superior to you.

My responsibility to you is such that I remain your keeper in the overall sense, but if you knew with what degree of sweet care that keeping is carried out, you would no longer wonder at my 'coming down to your level' as you put it. In the past I have come to you through the kindly help of my most understanding and developed children, and one of these especially fulfilled the task of presenting you with a picture of my nature which you could witness directly. To this day there is hardly one of you on Earth who yet understands that which he tried hard to teach you. The one thing you find so difficult to bear is this very simple and wholehearted affection which I have for you and which he showed you. You would rather have me in any dress but this one.

I know you feel I should be treated with great importance and reverence, but in so doing you make me untouchable and unapproachable, thus you destroy the vision that was given to you with so much love and courage. The one who gave it, and the one he gave it on behalf of, is with you still. There is no reason why you should not gather up the threads again with more understanding and with our help, but you must get rid of your own hard hearts and small-minded attitudes.

My dear son who came to you in this loving way is called by the personal name of Jesus, but with him was my firstborn son, the image of my aspiration for you, who, as my eldest son-daughter, I have given the special task of taking charge of the middle and outer portions of my creation, so that he will keep that aspiration alive in those regions, and in order to give him that experience of such great responsibility and the wisdom that is learned through such responsibility. So my first-born son-daughter is for you all, in this special way, both father and mother to you. He will bear you up as his child until he knows you are ready to become more directly, as he is, my child. For his part of the school of the universe is the lower school, and there he works, and I along with him as any of you might need us. For, in my school, the higher and the lower continually overlap because the highest is always trying to penetrate to the lowest and most outward forms of my creation to make them more and more perfect.

I am afraid that to those of my children who still think that the universe is some accident, and that they are in the position of being some strange growth out of this accident, my words will sound foolish, and they will be repelled by them, but they are in my school nevertheless, and, as they study the world itself more closely, so will this vision of the truth become clearer to them.

Soon now, I hope that this, my beloved eldest son-daughter, who was created and nurtured of me to be a special expression of my highest aspirations for my great family, will come among you to give you greater help and guidance. If and when he does so, I would like to find some of you prepared for what he will wish to say to you.

You must take well to heart all those deeper and simpler considerations that bear upon the matter of my everlasting and undemanding love and affection for each individual one of my children. It will not be for him to describe the especial value of his nature. He will not wish to have to claim his authority and more developed vision in the face of hostility from you. You must realise that it will be for you to recognise him and welcome him with this sweet and gentle gladness that I have tried to prepare for you.

You must try to open your hearts and minds to the great timeless sweep of the picture of my purpose that I have begun to put before you. If you would prepare yourselves, then pay attention to the basis of the affections you can find within yourself. Free yourselves of mechanistic and power interests. Realise that, although I accept all your actions towards me in the best spirit that I can, there comes a time when you must understand that the only aspect of them that I am concerned with is the integrity of the affection which they contain. This affection may be for me as a person, for beauty, kindness, love, or any ideal quality, but it must be truly meant.

Repetitive exercises which treat me as though I were some huge and insensitive robot, to be humoured and tricked into supplying what you need, are far from complimentary and what is worse is that they prevent the proper growth of your own vision of yourself and the worth of the gift I long to give you.

You will notice that I have been talking to you as a person, and using the word person, when I describe our relation to one another. Now you know as well as I do that this can be a misleading term to use for the reason that it can refer to a 'diver's suit' with little or no 'diver' left in it. By this I mean that the outer physical personality can lose touch with the child of my being who should inhabit and control it. In fact, the child can find itself as the diver being controlled by the diving suit, and it may become identified with the wishes and desires of the strong and heavy diving suit which is a living thing and not a manufactured garment.

Thus our analogy is not a complete one for it only describes half the situation. When you use a man-made diving suit, it is an inert thing that you have to contend with, but when you inhabit a physical body it is a heavy and cumbersome garment, yet far from inert. As a living thing in its own right, your physical body can use and dominate your real identity for the sake of satisfying its own needs and pleasures, and to reduce its fears and anxieties.

You were right to think that I was making too simple a case for the situation you find yourself in, for, while you are an individual portion of my being, you are also likely to be less aware of this reality, and more conscious that you are driven from one thing to another by the needs of your physical nature which can seem to be your whole nature. Part of the work of my school is therefore to show you slowly but surely that the situation is not a correct one when you feel you are identical with your physical personality. The development and strengthening of your real identity needs this opposition, and the stronger the physical characteristics of the body it is associated with, the stronger the nature of your real self will have to be if it is to determine and guide the expression of the outer physical nature.

If you find it hard to control this lower nature you will feel it to be better to inhibit this outer self as much as you can because nearly all its actions make you feel ashamed of it, but, if you succeed in being able to control the lower nature, you will wish to express yourself through it as fully as possible, and will feel that this is doing your best in living a life which you are not ashamed of but rather fulfilled through.

You are in a situation where your own private world which you live in will be what you make it. If you allow it to be dominated by the wishes of your physical nature, you will feel alien to it even if you are carried along by it. If you feel like a stranger to yourself it will make you unhappy, and you will doubt your own true identity, and you will lose faith in all the higher values in life. You may disguise the situation to the people around you but inside yourself you will feel lost and helpless and degraded.

My work is to increase your sense of reality to yourself, and make it feel of great value to you, without it spilling over into pride and selfishness. The balance between the over-subdued nature and the over-inflated nature is not easy to keep, and is a necessary balance to be achieved before other values can be built in. The foundation lessons to be taught are thus integrity and responsibility, combined with affection and sympathy, but added to an ability to feel a balanced importance in the scheme of things.

It is not an easy thing to believe you have great value and ability, and at the same time maintain a temperament which does not try to show off and impress people, and perhaps even dominate them. Every new gift I give you with trepidation because I know you are more likely to misuse it before you learn to handle it correctly; so, to me, a gift can appear like an ordeal and a temptation, and I am worried when I see some of you working to achieve special powers which may well be your downfall so far as the graceful balance of your temperament is concerned. On the other hand, I am glad when I see you developing gifts as a result of loving aspiration and wise discrimination, for such gifts I know will surely benefit you and all those associated with you.

I am aware of the great problem and pain that confronts those of you who are trying to live a life which is aimed at expressing those qualities that would please me. I know that the piercing point of such pain is just this very matter that concerns your own intrinsic and individual value and responsibility. It is here that faith is not enough to uphold you in the face of your own self-criticism and feelings of inadequacy.

You can visualise the task to equate the condition of your own nature, and the world around you, with the qualities you sense in my seemingly perfect nature, but when you fall or stumble you easily become submerged in hopelessness and an inner sense of guilt, and self-loathing creeps up inside you, and you are then as a person divided against himself. For one part of you has its face turned towards my sun, and the other part observes your inability and unworthiness to act with love or beauty or grace.

Such is the battlefield, and if you attempt not only to love me but also to understand me, this can make matters worse when life conditions are set against you, for then you wonder if such knowledge is not itself a form of arrogance for which you should rightly be punished and feel remorse. My answer can only be of comfort, it cannot be comfortable.

My dear child, I have placed you in a hard school for I am endeavouring to give you an outright gift of your own being, and the intelligent and loving understanding to go with it. If I give you the power of intelligence, without the love and wisdom to go with it, the result you know can be horrible, and can only bring misery upon you, so it is my duty to allow you to experience all the forms of pain in order to save you from the extreme mistakes which would lead to the breakdown of your nature and exclude you from that eternal reality to which I would lead you. So, while I have tried to make light of your shortcomings in my sight, and while I have tried to make you feel why I forgive you all your mistakes, and why you should forgive yourself your mistakes, there must be a recognition in you of the factors involved, and that is why, at this time, that I am trying to show you more of myself and more of what it is that I am educating you towards. For if you begin to understand these biggest factors in creation then you will find it easier to orientate yourselves around them and find that you can avoid many of the problems and pains that at present seem to be unavoidable.

If I can make the vision and motive of 'my sun' clearer to you, then, when you turn to it, it will supply you with strength and understanding which, added to your faith, will uphold you more firmly in times and conditions of adversity. The sun is held for you within the innermost heart of my nature, and it was from this heart that my aspiration was personified for you in the nature and being of my eldest child who loves you as I do. For, in personifying him, I have clarified my aspirations to myself, and at the same time created a living guide, helper and friend for your benefit, to ease the difficulties of your growth and comfort you by his presence. But you say to me, 'Please comfort me and ease my pain all the time,' and I say to you that many of those pains you must bear yourself until you realise that you are the cause of them. You see, it is nearly true that, if I would really punish you, I would give you what you ask for in your prayers to me.

I am sorry to have to place this predicament so squarely before you. However, you can take comfort from the fact that I would not be writing to you in this way if I did not consider that a great many of you were ready to move on with me to this higher and more complete form of understanding. The uncompromising nature of my position towards you would be a terrible thing if I were not able to make you understand the affectionate regard for your own being which I hold as my most sacred trust. I bind up your wounds with tears in my eyes, and these tears are neither of joy nor sorrow but of some unfathomable mixture which stems from my innermost love to give, and to share, and to participate in experience with friends.

Slowly and gently, I must allow my gift to dawn upon you, for too much at once would shock and frighten you. You need time to constantly adjust towards it if you are to retain your identity in the process. If you should lose or give up your own individual identity then I have lost the essential part of my gift, which is to have someone to give it to. You will have lost not only the understanding of the completeness of my endeavour, but you will also have given up that separateness of identity from which you could have loved and enjoyed my friendship.

To some, my words will seem like heresy, but I do not want merely to love myself through you as mirrors. If you are afraid to be yourself for my sake, with all your faults, then you have taken yourself out of the very soil in which I could have nourished you. Remember that it is the identity of your own children that you love, and, when you bid them to be unselfish, you do not intend them to either give up or devalue their identity.

You do not wish to have perfect children any more than I do; we both want to have real children, so if I give you the gift of being a real individual it would be an unworthy thing if I were to take it back from you again. On the other hand, like all gifts, I cannot force you to take it.

So there are some of my problems: I can hold out my loving aspiration for you, but I cannot force the matter to a conclusion for that would be to destroy the nature of the gift. What I can do is to continually meet you halfway, and draw you carefully into a fuller understanding of my purpose, and, in so doing, put you closer to a position where you can say to me, 'Yes, I understand what it is that you are trying to give me, and why it is such a difficult thing to do, and I am amazed and overwhelmed at the degree of care you have for me, and the gift you would enable me to take up.'

But we have a long way to go, for some of you consider that the universe is but a mirror for me to view and adore myself in. If that were the case, can there be any merit in such an objective? A human being who did such a thing would be considered to be vain and foolish. How much more should I deserve these terms? Some say that I am like a man who wakes up in bed, goes over to a mirror, stares at his beauty for a time, and then gets back into bed and goes to sleep, to wake again another day in order to repeat the same action. That action is not worthy of any of us.

It is true to say that I love those qualities that I hold most dear in my nature, knowledge and experience, but is it more likely that I should play a game with myself in manifesting myself as many people if I could bring to birth real individuals to share my treasures with? Those who think so do not believe that I am the 'worthy one' they say I am. They secretly believe I am a pretender and a taker-back of gifts and insincere in my play, so I am sad when such half-love is imputed to me; I am sad when my gift is feared and thrown back in my face. But, while my gift demands much of me, I know it also demands much of you.

Because I know what I have put into you, I know that I am not expecting too much of you. However, I realise that I may reach a point in our development and relationship with one another where you are not able to take up more than a part of my gift, so I have allowed for you to come back into my house and be with me until I can arrange some other classrooms in some other playground where I can again send you to school and show the subtlety of the situation to you in some way that will enable you to be glad of it with your whole heart.

Such time as this would seem a long time to you, but remember that time to me is a very different thing. To me it is the correct intensity of expression of the things that I wish to talk to you about and to show you. It is exactly a measure of the proper growing pressure that I consider appropriate in any situation to make the best use of that situation. Too much intensity and hurry would burn your nature, and too little would leave you fast asleep and untouched.

Another question you would like to ask me is why I should need so many children around about me in this scheme of mine. Why would not twenty or fifty be enough? To begin with you do not yet know the depth of my nature. You do not yet know just how much I have to give. If what I had to give were just a simple thing it would not require an elaborate situation to give it in, but what I have to give is most elaborate, and so, to create the necessary width of understanding, I need to find expression for all my qualities, and lay them all out for you to see. As many of these qualities have to be lived, so I need many different children to live amongst one another.

My plan was vast in your sight because my being is vast also, but do not let that be a cause to think that any of you do not matter to me; you matter to me all as individual children and also as players in my play. If you do not play your part, who is to do it for you? No one can, and it thus leaves a gap in my book. As my book is a long one it needs many words and you are both my children and my words to one another. You are all players in my orchestra, and I cannot make the sounds I had hoped for if any of you are unable to play the individual parts that make up the whole piece of music. My orchestra is not like yours. In my orchestra no two parts are the same but they are all needed to make up the true beauty of the sound I have visioned.

When you take notice of the complexity of the atomic and sub-atomic world I have made, you will more easily appreciate that the content of my book may well need you all to say fully and completely my message, while at the same time be able to contain you with the same measure of my attention between its covers. I need a large family because I need to express a large number of characters, so do not think only of rushing to my heaven, for it is not necessarily in heaven that you will be able to learn the part you have to play.

Remember that where character is concerned it is the hardest experiences that stamp the deepest patterns, and, when you think of my music, try to remember that it is a continuous creation and not a single piece that is to be repeated. I have no desire to repeat my music, rather do I spin it newly all the while, so what you add to it now, and at any other time, is continually affecting the performance.

You and I are making this music now, and each of your sounds is valuable to the effect, and I am the one who all the time gathers them in and weaves them together into a whole of constantly changing music. Thus I even make use of the discordant sounds since they all express in some way the reality of the complete situation. Not that I would have you think that I sit back and coldly conduct this music, or feel any pleasure from discordant notes. I am doing many things at the same time in ways that you would not yet understand, and each discordant note pulls at my heart and my sympathy.

My music is not made to entertain, it is the expression of our endeavour, and effort, and suffering, woven together with the beauty of the beginning and the end. It is the sound of the whole book as it is being read by you all. It is this very music that I use to order and adapt my school to the needs that I sense in it. It reports to my sensitive ear the exact condition of my whole work and my nature responds to its beauty and its needs.

So you begin to realise that I am both he who stands apart from my whole work to view it objectively, and also he who can be within you, or at your very elbow as another physical person. There is no position that I cannot take up in my work if it so pleases me. Those of my children who were born into heaven, and who later came to work with me in this outermost earthly condition—in order to bring you, their other brothers and sisters, to life—have acquired much of the experience of this testing condition, which they have added to their experience of heaven, and the blending of the two has given them much wisdom and understanding. These are therefore working among you already as my mature friends and companions, although they may well not care to make their activities known in any obvious way. These are neither angels nor men of earth, but they are the staff of my educational faculty.

You yourselves will have to decide if anyone you meet as a teacher is teaching my book properly or not. You will have to find one who teaches in a way that suits your particular temperament, but they are all helping to lead you from class to class of understanding and experience, even if, at times, they cause you to feel they must be at cross purposes. But to those who teach my heart of hearts, the misunderstandings can be seen as a necessary preparation in the need to use your discerning powers and widen the basis of your valuations.

I would like you now to be able to view the world in the perspective that I have given you so that you can feel that no great calamity has occurred, and that I have not made some serious error. I would like you to be able to understand that what you refer to as 'the fall' was indeed a falling away from the conditions of heaven, but not a falling away by accident.

You will now be able to realise that heaven is still about you, but that you have arrived in a condition of greater differentiation and testing than heaven could ever have. This very differentiation and opposition is absolutely necessary to the longing I have for you to develop strong and different characters within the context of loving kindness. So it was necessary that you should know hate and cruelty if you were ever to know the real meaning of love and kindness and the significance of your own ability to view all things objectively as I can. So I had to stand by, and let you make mistakes, and let you think you knew best about everything, just as you do with your own children.

Life was not meant to be comfortable for those to whom I would give my gift of individuality. How could it be? You now understand that I could have taken many other easier ways out in your education, but I chose the hardest one for your sake because it was the only thorough one.

I know that when you understand all this you will forgive me for being so stern towards you when I could have relented, and you will understand that this very unrelenting attitude was founded on the absolute rock of my integrity which is as valuable as my affections both to myself and to you. What would my loving affection have been worth if it were lacking in this unmoveable strength and integrity? It would one day appear as a terrible disappointment, and all the more terrible because of its seeming beauty which was unfounded.

Your loving father.

Also available from

Letters From A Father: Selected Writings by William Arkle

Toward Awakening: An Approach to the Teaching Left by Gurdjieff by Jean Vaysse. Foreword by Lord John Pentland.

Venture With Ideas: Meetings with Gurdjieff and Ouspensky by Kenneth Walker.

The Doctrine of the Buddha: The Religion of Reason by George Grimm.

sunwisebooks.com

Printed in Great Britain
by Amazon

40842447R20142